P9-ANZ-900

King Lear: The SPACE OF TRAGEDY

GRIGORI KOZINTSEV

King Lear: The Space of Tragedy

THE DIARY OF A
FILM DIRECTOR

translated by
MARY MACKINTOSH

with a foreword by
PETER BROOK

UNIVERSITY OF CALIFORNIA PRESS
Berkeley and Los Angeles

University of California Press
Berkeley and Los Angeles, California

ISBN 0-520-03392-2
Library of Congress Catalogue Card Number: 76-50248

First published by Izdatelstvo Iskusstvo 1973

First published 1977

Printed in Great Britain

FOREWORD BY PETER BROOK

Dear Grigori,

To close our correspondence, alas, just one more letter . . .

I remember with gratitude your joy and excitement and your deep seriousness. I remember, in your *Hamlet* and in your *Lear*, your searching for truths about man's condition and your wish to speak through your art about one subject only: about humanity – no more, no less.

The last shot in my memory's film of you is of our last meeting in the hall of UNESCO in Paris. You told me you had had warm invitations from an official to come to this conference. Time passed, his letters had got more and more pressing until you convinced yourself of his personal feeling for you. When you arrived at the airport you'd expected to find him there. All through the conference you expected him to come and take you in his arms. And of course he never appeared, because the illusion of a relationship was in your heart, not his . . .

You told me this story with delight and sadness and made a little ironic movement of the mouth.

Humanity was your theme and through your book you can still pass it on to others.

Goodbye,

With love,

Peter

September 1976

CONTENTS

LIST OF PLATES

TRANSLATOR'S INTRODUCTION

GRIGORI KOZINTSEV'S *King Lear* was first shown in London in the summer of 1972. Those who have seen the film will agree that it is impossible to regard Shakespeare's play in the same light after the experience (at times deeply moving, and at times harrowing) of seeing the Russian film. Russians have never been known to use half measures in artistic expression. Kozintsev's *Lear* is no exception. He sees the play as symbolizing the apocalyptic encroachment of the Last Day of Judgement, the end of the world. Lear, a blind despot, renounces his power, and in so doing becomes human, but a human caught up in an inevitable path leading towards disaster and destruction. It is the ultimate irony that Lear finally discovers happiness in his reconciliation with Cordelia, only to lose her again and to die himself.

Lear has no unifying theme, no ultimate 'interpretation', so Kozintsev believes. It is a vastly complex play in which the general mingles with the particular, the supernatural with the earthly, in which prose alternates with poetry, the pace constantly changing. There is no perfect way of producing it. A director can only project his own personal interpretation on to the tragedy. And so we have a deeply moving, deeply Russian view of the play, which, being Russian, throws a completely new and startlingly fresh light on many parts with which English audiences have become over familiar.

Tragically, Kozintsev died in May 1973, less than a year after his last visit to England when he introduced the film. It was then that he brought over the diary that he kept while making the film. The diary unfolds as a day-to-day meditation on the play. Problems of interpretation are discussed as the need arises (often in the order in which the various scenes were shot).

Interwoven with the discussion of the play are two constantly recurring strands: the influence of other forms of theatre, particularly Meyerhold's, of nineteenth-century Russian literature, of the early revolutionary cinema with Eisenstein as leader; and in lighter vein, the story of how the film was made, how the actor for the title role was found after long despairing months of unsuccessful screen tests with unsuitable candidates, how the locations were chosen, and how the shooting very nearly collapsed in total disaster at the end through lack of time.

The book retains its diary form with spaces between the entries. In his last letter after he had finished revising the first version of the diary, published in monthly instalments in the Russian periodical *Iskusstvo Kino*, Kozintsev wrote: 'I have tried to keep down the number of short excerpts and to collect them into chapters. There are only four chapters which somehow stand out from the rest.' (Chapters 9 – Russian Tragedy, 11 – Pregnant Ophelia, 14 – The Turns of the Spiral, and 22 – The Muse, the Angel and the Devil.) In addition, the first chapter, Notes from Japan, describes how the idea for the film first began and how Kozintsev was influenced by the Noh Theatre and the cinema of contemporary Japan.

In translating the diary I have tried to make the book read more easily for the non-Russian speaker by using surnames rather than patronymics. Names and titles are footnoted where it would seem to illuminate the text, but the sources of the many random quotations from Russian and Soviet literature are in most cases not given, since they are quoted in passing just as an English writer might quote Shakespeare, almost unconsciously. Since the structure of the book is a continuous narrative, the past tense (rather than the Russian 'historic present') is used where actual events are being related, as being more natural to the English ear.

I am deeply indebted to Mrs Kozintsev for her help and encouragement, to Edward Thompson, whose enthusiasm was responsible for this English translation, to Peter and Natasha Norman for their help over obscure passages, to Ivor Montagu for his most valuable detailed reading of the manuscript with his many suggestions for clarification and improvement, and to John Krish for his advice on technical cinematic terms. I am also grateful to Edward Craig for his advice on the extracts from Edward Gordon Craig's letters, to Alexander Anikst for supplying some last-minute references, and to Jay Leyda and Ernest Callenbach for their helpful criticisms and corrections to the page proofs. Finally to my husband whose patience carried me through the last stages and for the four valiant secretaries at the Department of Geology, Oxford University, who typed the manuscript in record time.

M. A. M.

AUTHOR'S PREFACE

I NEVER REGARDED a new production as purely professional work. It was not just a question of applying my specialized knowledge or experience to the project. It meant somehow beginning to live all over again. Events and destinies, sometimes created centuries ago, would burst in on my life and occupy an increasingly large part of it. This would continue until the imaginary began to seem real: every day I would discover more and more completely realistic characteristics in this particular world, and in the people who lived in it.

Some alien person's life would merge with my own. This is how the flesh of the cinematographic forms would begin to take shape, and the words would become visible.

And then this most naturalistic art of photography would capture movements of life in full flight; they would be transferred from the pages of a book on to the screen.

And heaven knows what did not happen during this transition and what did not get involved. I searched my memory: the books I had read, the countries I had visited, my childhood, arguments with friends or with myself; all these played some part.

I always had to find fault with past films or to argue with people who were no longer living. Professional practices and experience not only did not help, they hindered: I had to step beyond the bounds of the profession, to turn my experience upside down. I had to go back to school – indeed I was reduced to studying every day, taking lessons from experts who seemed to have no direct connection with my work – they taught me more than anything else. I had to do my homework and to swallow my disappointment when I got a bad mark for it: during this time I would give myself a bad mark for the same essay for which ten years ago I would have got the highest mark – or so it seemed.

A multitude of the most contradictory thoughts and feelings welled up inside me. But I – the person 'hereinafter named the director' (as contracts put it), and the organization 'hereinafter named the film studio' had entrusted a production to me. From a certain day onwards my thoughts and feelings were accounted for and programmed. The meter had begun to tick, the production had begun. However my thoughts and feelings did not want to be subjected to a schedule and a lot remained outside the boundaries of the everyday work of the department, named the 'filmstudio'.

Then to the notes – sketches for the script and sets – were added other notes; sometimes they referred to the day's filming sometimes to the day's experiences. The notes grew, some congregated together, others remained separate – the pages of a diary. I kept it up during the making of the film of *King Lear*. The first version of this work was the theatre production (Gorky Theatre 1941), the second – a chapter of the book, *Shakespeare: Time and Conscience* (1962), the third – the film (1967–70).

G. K.

Chapter One

THE MORE I work on films which are called historical, the less I understand the meaning of the term. I have tried for a long time to neutralize everything which has anything to do with ancient settings, to tone them down and make them less obtrusive. The boundaries which divide the centuries can be accentuated, but they can also be smoothed over. (What should one look at: the cut of a dress or the faces of people?) The boundaries of time are particularly vague in Shakespeare's plays, the action of which takes place supposedly in historical times.

As the future grows into the past
So the past fades into the future

Anna Akhmatova's lines illustrate this confused process.

Let us turn to the matter in hand. The play is *King Lear*, place of action: a King's palace, a Duke's palace, a hovel, the road to Dover, the universe; costumes: the height of extravagance and the filthiest of rags; props: a crown, a map of the kingdom, a hangman's rope.

The time of the action? According to the author, it was a time when they swore by Apollo and Juno, christened their children, and had the rank of captain in the army. Apart from this, the author considered that the action took place in pre-history.

How is one to solve the problem? At least find some precise dates. For instance the events took place not later than the author's death. All right, and not earlier than what? Not earlier than the appearance of governments and the concept of the idolization of the monarchy.

THE PROBLEM IS to ensure that the inner action, the intense exploration of life, should not explode at the end of the film but should continue on in the spiritual world of the audience. One should not demonstrate, but provoke.

I HAD ALREADY become a friend of the artist Virsaladze with the making of *Hamlet*. I was relieved at the thought that we would again be working together.

'The most important thing is that altogether there should not be very much', said Virsaladze at our first meeting.

All right, so there would not be very much. I tried to understand what these words meant. Perhaps it would come to me.

Chapter Two

NOTES FROM JAPAN

A SMALL COURTYARD, enclosed by low mud walls with little tile roofs. On the ground, which was covered with a light-coloured gravel, there were some stones of varying shapes, each quite far apart. Some people were sitting on a wooden ledge round the edge of the courtyard. They had taken their shoes off at the entrance according to the Japanese custom and sat in silence, their legs dangling, keeping absolutely still, staring at the ground.

The place was one of the most famous in Japan. It is included in every tourist excursion.

Still not understanding what there was to look at, I took off my shoes and sat down in an empty space. The influence of the stone garden began to make its presence felt by a feeling of light emptiness, a scarcity of precise form. There were significantly few elements in this picture, locked within its frame of clay walls, but each of the elements was different, had its own character, its particular interdependence on the other elements. The gravel was arranged in straight parallel lines; concentric circles radiated outwards from the stones (another arrangement of the gravel); the circles cut across the straight lines. A stone, empty space, two squat stones against each other, as if they had grown into a sharp-cornered fragment, more empty space, another dimension. Some of the stones had a smooth surface, polished by time, others were rough.

The consecutive sequence of empty space and individual shapes concealed within itself some deep significance which was hard to grasp. The stone garden had to be studied like music. The harmony of the space took hold of one, the natural law of its construction began to unfold, and one began to live in the rhythm which the artist had given it.

They were no longer stones and little paths hollowed out in the gravel; the first and simplest associations had given a realistic content to the abstract form: the sea, the incessant movement of currents of water, the succession of the outgoing and incoming tide. The stones of differing shapes appeared to be cliffs, towering over the abyss. The rhythms changed and stone islands appeared in all their variations, oases in the monotony of the watery desert. I was overcome by a feeling of peace, of the significant movement of life. It was the ocean, Japan seen from the height of a bird's flight.

Then something happened. The light changed or perhaps my eyes picked up something new. The currents had changed direction, the point of focus had shifted. It took on a different meaning: whole continents, worlds had risen up out of the ocean, had spread over the ocean, over the clouds. The universe, planets in space . . .

Our patient and good-natured guide tentatively tapped my shoulder: time was unfortunately running out, we had stayed there too long, our programme would not be fulfilled.

I did not want to leave – after all I had seen so little. My eyes had only just begun to open, I had only touched upon the substance of this creation and it was impossible to unearth it, to grasp it in words. The only things that came to mind were simple associations. The point was not in the garden itself and what it contained but in me, and in what had been aroused in me at the encounter with art. With gravel and a few stones.

There are some ancient philosophers' sayings about the everlasting revelations and developments of nature, similar to the eternal ebb and flow of the ocean.

THE STONE GARDEN is in the town of Kyoto, the ancient capital of Japan; it is 30 metres from east to west and ten metres from north to south. It was created from fifteen stones by the artist and horticulturalist, Soami, who died in 1525. The stone garden is part of the shrine of Ryoan-ji.

Close by is the extravagant grandeur of the palaces, tombs, villas, gardens, an elegance of form overloaded with detail, the tiers of the pagodas, little hump-backed bridges over green water with golden fish (little bridges and fish, not bridges and little fish!), gnome-like gardens and toy orangeries, where everything is contrived, every flower artificial, every living movement measured, enclosed in its preordained dimension, every detail patiently raised up in an effort against the natural. There is even a moon reflected in the pond; at the appointed time it becomes a detail of the scenery for the 'ceremony of tea' presentation on the terrace.

The time was the day of the première: the evening of 15 August at full moon.

HOW COMPLICATED simple things can be sometimes and how completely simple, complicated things. I am referring to the song of the nightingale. Is it true that after hearing a poet describe it, one can discover something new, hitherto unknown? I was lucky enough to hear its trills and warbles in peculiar circumstances which gave new shades of meaning to the magical song.

Here in this seventeenth-century courtyard everything was elegant: the priceless wall fresco – depicting seas, mountains, flowers – the mannequins arrayed in their ancient dress. The refined ceremonial brought life to these figures: the officials waited for signs from the ministers, the Emperor and his consort sat on their mats like gods.

The strip of corridor leading to the bedroom had a special mechanism. You only had to put one foot on the floorboards to set a cunning mechanism in motion: the boards gurgled, squeaked and whistled, and the nightingale's song rang out through the palace.

Art surrounded tyranny and bureaucracy, it caressed its eyes and ears. From time to time it even fulfilled a practical function: following the nightingale's aria ran the guard with drawn sword. The trills of the songster of love became related to the bark of the watchdog.

IN AUGUST 1928 the Kabuki Theatre visited Russia on tour. I did not miss a single production. Eisenstein and I often went together. To the generation of young artists in the twenties, brought up to hate naturalism, the Japanese artists' productions were a festive occasion. Here before us was an art form which had influenced European directors' boldest experiments in the twentieth century. We greeted the hanamitshi (the flower troupe), the kuroko (servants in black who shifted the scenery in front of the audience) like old friends. But seeing the real thing turned out to be twice as interesting.

Eisenstein discovered the structure of cinematography in Kabuki aesthetics: reality was taken apart and then put together again according to a different code, in which each component became only one unit of influence, an equal irritant in the order of editing, in the montage of attractions.

Synthetic art, which was so much talked about in the first years of the revolution, was before our very eyes. The cascades of movements executed by Sadanji Ichikawa were broken by static poses, gesture was followed by sound, sound turned into colour, song into dance. Everything was metaphorical and had a particular significance which was far removed from its apparent likeness.

I was struck by the force of passion, the completeness of form. And, indeed, by something else: the magnificence of the 'elegant show' about which Meyerhold wrote so much.

Kimonos made out of brightly coloured and embroidered material (treasures handed down from generation to generation); the fantastic spectres of the masks, the furious triumph of the ritual of the fighters, the lightning of the Samurais' swords; the doll-like grace of the actors playing women (the height of virtuosity); the unity of the drama, acrobatics, song, dance – to see all this face to face seemed a miracle.

I considered that I had discovered genuine Japanese art. As it happened, I had discovered significantly little.

THE AUDIENCE SAT waiting for the beginning of the performance; many had books – the text of the play which we were going to see that day. On the stage were some mats and a low, light-coloured wooden screen. I waited for the opening of the Noh Theatre's production. Memories of the Kabuki Theatre's opulence of colour and movement were awakened.

But there was no question of anything even faintly resembling the Kabuki Theatre.

There was a soft, dry sound, a clap. The musicians in black kimonos walked unhurriedly on and squatted in front of the walls of the house; there were flutes, small drums, and the drummers wore wooden thimbles on their fingers. More figures in grey-black appeared just as calmly: the chorus took up their position on the mats.

There was another clap and the flutes and drums began to play.

An elderly Japanese man without a mask, modestly dressed in the same dark colours, took his place beside the musicians. This was the second actor. I had failed to notice the entrance of the first. The audience's heads turned to the left – I followed their gaze. A man in dark blue was walking slowly and silently; the first actor was wearing a white mask, framed with locks of hair; in his hand he held a slender stick.

The chorus sang. The audience followed in their books. My neighbour whispered the translation to me. At first it was difficult to understand the essence of what had taken place. The words of the chorus and actors did not seem like dialogue. This was not a play but a philosophical poem with lyrical digressions, commentary on the action, and monologues by the author.

The leader of the chorus addressed the actor in the white mask, however none of the chorus looked towards him and he, gently tapping his stick on the ground, sang softly, without taking any notice of anyone else; the voice of an elderly man could be heard, and then the orchestra were playing alone.

Now before my very eyes I had seen and at last understood the art of classical drama. I had been shown the true presentation of tragedy, the dialogue between the chorus and the protagonist, the addressing of the audience, the entrance into the action of the deuteragonist (the second actor).

The story reminded me of the counter plot in *Lear* – the story of the Earl of Gloucester and his heir, Edgar. Once upon a time an important nobleman cursed his beloved son and drove him from the house: the son had been unjustly slandered. The son experienced all the grief that can fall to the lot of one man. He became a miserable beggar – this was the title of the play, *The Miserable Beggar*. The exile wandered through distant and alien lands, begging for alms, and went blind with grief (in contrast to Shakespeare's story, here it was the son who lost his sight). Many years later he wandered home without realizing where he was.

The Kabuki Theatre surprised and deafened the audience; their art was founded on the frenzy of the heroic epos and comic buffoonery brought to extremes which would be impossible in European theatre. In the Noh Theatre, peace, extreme restraint and complete clarity reigned supreme. The décor and costumes were very modest. Here philosophy was at one with the emotions, poetry with music; the power of lyrical concentration was the greatest influence.

The audience understood this perfectly: they had not come here to identify with the heroes, to get excited about what was going to happen next or to wonder how the play would end. While following the text, they were enjoying the poetry, assimilating the verse at the same time as the music and the singing. In the same way musicians sometimes listen to a concert while following the score which they have brought with them.

Here there was no question of any special effects or diversions. It was not even that the dramatic and emotional was not accentuated, it somehow just slipped by. There was practically no action. The masked actor and the elderly Japanese man – father and son in the play – did not talk to each other, they did not even look at each other. The protagonist did not act like a blind man: he did not grope his way, his walk was not laboured. The monotony of the soft taps, the continuous rhythm of the tapping stick created the feeling of blindness. The epic grew as if of its own accord, by sounds and poetic images, by the interrelationship of story and thought.

You could hear the stick lightly tapping, the rap of the wooden thimbles on the drum. The leader of the chorus asked:

'Why have you altered your pace? What has surprised you?'

'I hear the smell of the fields, covered in flowers,' the masked actor replied. 'I recognize their smell.' The drum was beating. The old man sat motionless, looking at no one. The stick went on tapping. The white mask took a step forward.

'I remember the smell of these flowers from my childhood.'

'Which flowers do you remember?' asked the old man.

'Chrysanthemums, peonies, tulips . . .' replied the mask, looking straight ahead. 'They grew in the garden by the house where I was born.'

I did not manage to get a copy of the text. I quote only the general drift of the conversation.

The audience turned the pages of their books.

The father recognized his son. Or rather the chorus sang to us of how he recognized him. Then a miracle happened: the mask became the face of a blind man. One could distinctly see the deathly pale face, distorted with grief, of a man, who had dark cavities instead of eyes.

Evidently the actor turned his head, and changed the fix of the mask, but the movement was almost imperceptible.

NOW A SIMILAR mask hangs on my wall at home facing my desk. My whole family greeted its appearance with disapproval. They wanted to remove it and take it away as far as possible. The mask is so flexible that it can change its expression even when it is motionless. The artist breathed life into a piece of wood; the slightest change of light, or change in the direction of one's glance makes one look again at the slanting eyes with holes instead of eyes. It is as if the mask follows you, spies on you, enters into a wordless conversation with you. There is something sad and tragic about its expression.

Its shape is simple, the colour is an even white.

The mask is a special theme in the art of our times. I shall probably have to come back to it more than once.

WHEN I SAW the Kabuki Theatre again, it seemed to be over-decorative, over-exotic, and moreover a calculated export product. The decorations forcibly reminded me of souvenir stalls; outward refinement cannot conceal inner insignificance.

THE WEATHER WAS warm and humid throughout my stay. The town was masked by a fine network of rain; everything looked grey, the colour of asphalt, and a steady stream of wet umbrellas moved slowly along the streets.

Japanese art, which I have now fallen in love with, was a hazy dark-brown, grey-black; its shapes were peaceful, its voices soft. I was struck most of all by the depth of concentrated lyricism.

Of course these were only a few aspects of Japanese art, aspects whose existence I had not even suspected before: Japanese touring companies and reproductions of painting had accustomed me to another sort of expression.

In 1929 Eisenstein wrote that the paradox of Japanese art lies in the fact that although many aspects of its structure are cinematographic, it has no cinema. Japanese films did not rouse interest in those days. Many years have elapsed since the writing of that article. Japanese cinema has not only made its appearance but has shown itself to be a significant influence on European cinema.

Akira Kurosawa is not interested in the Kabuki Theatre, but, as he has said many times, he has been influenced by the tradition of the Noh Theatre. When I heard this, some time before my trip to Japan, I was amazed: what connection could there be between ancient conventionality (the Noh Theatre has retained much of its thirteenth-century traditions) and cinematic expression which is apparently always life-like?

'Likeness to life', 'cinematographicality' – do such terms exist in a single, frozen state?

KUROSAWA'S *Idiot*, I thought, was a miraculous transformation of a classic on to the screen. Dostoyevsky's pages came to life, words – the subtlest definitions – took shape. I saw Rogozhin's eyes on the screen, wild, flaming, burning coals of fire – exactly the eyes that Dostoyevsky described.

But Toshiro Mifune (the actor who played Rogozhin) had slanting eyes. And the action of the film takes place in contemporary Japan. Everything is different. A steamer instead of a train, a buddha instead of a cross, every custom is typical of another people, bearing no resemblance to Russia.

And indeed at first, when the first shots appeared, I was half amazed, half embarrassed: how unfamiliar it all was. Whatever anyone says, we all watch foreign productions of Russian classics with suspicion. Or at least we watch them with suspicion to start with. But I soon forgot about the way of life; the facial characteristics of another race became normal. Snow was falling on the screen, the shop windows were frozen over, but you could see a photograph, a woman's face through the frosted glass. I recognized Nastasia Filipovna instantly, her tragic beauty. But – the Japanese eyes? I didn't see them any more. I found myself in Dostoyevsky's world, among his heroes; this was the complex and fantastic collection of his characters – their strange encounters and partings; it was all outwardly different and yet completely the same in its inner action, the same world that the author created.

Then I distinctly saw people walking along my familiar Sennaya Market. But there was no question of St Petersburg on the screen. There was only one detail which was close to Russia, which ran throughout the film as a linking motif: it was snowing. The white flakes accumulated, the snow drifts piled up, people slipped on the ice, the streets disappeared, and everything became white.

A white face. White snow. Two apparently dissimilar images: the Japanese mask and Blok's 'Snow Mask'.

ANY FOREIGNER WHO opens a film with the reproduction of everyday details which are alien to him is destined to failure. An American film director began *Anna Karenina* in this way: caviar was spooned on to plates with soup spoons.

What did Kurosawa manage to grasp which was fundamental, much more important than the external objects, and why was it he and he alone who succeeded in overcoming this difficult problem? He was able to express on screen the 'fantastic reality' about which the author wrote so persistently.

Here all the external details were different and yet they reminded one of the core of the work, the link between one thing and another. The life of the film contained at the same time a contemporary reality, and a kind of ancient religious element, the strange peace of Prince Myshkin's spiritual world, and Rogozhin's inflamed conscience.

Kurosawa wrote:

> (Dostoyevsky) is still my favourite author. He is the one who writes most honestly about human existence . . . He seems terribly subjective, but then you come to the resolution and there is no more objective author writing . . . Making the film was very hard work – it was difficult to make. At times I felt as though I wanted to die. Dostoyevsky is heavy enough, and now I was under him . . .
>
> People have said the film is a failure. I don't think so . . . Of all my films, people wrote me most about this one. If it had been as bad as all that, they wouldn't have written. I trust my audience . . . If a director does not make a habit of lying to his audience, he can trust them. (*Sight and Sound*, 1964, No. 3, pp. 112–13)

The Russian classics have influenced much of Kurosawa's work. do not just mean the production of *The Idiot*, *The Lower Depths*, but other films as well. In *Ikiru,*[1] a film of the Japanese book, it is not difficult to find a similarity between the mummy-like official and Gogol's Bashmachkin, traits from *The Death of Ivan Ilych.*

Kurosawa is perhaps one of the most daring innovators. He has not been afraid to refute everything that was considered to be the basis of cinematographic art. In *The Throne of Blood* (the Japanese name for *The Castle of Intrigue*[2]) taken from the story of *Macbeth,* he refused to have any close-ups. The most tragic scenes were taken in long shots; the actors sat for a long time in silence on mats. The décor was sometimes no more than a patch of mould on a paper wall. The Noh Theatre had migrated to the screen: Lady Macbeth was made up like a mask; the actors' walk made one think of the ritual step; the movement of fingers like a dance; the asymmetrical arrangement of figures on the bare stage – the style itself belonged to ancient times.

But when the samurais' horses burst out of the mist and one saw the ferocious eyes and black threatening weapons – the signs of death and the signs of greatness, and the fighters circled round the same place eight times, powerless to break out of the mist – one caught one's breath at the greatness of Shakespeare and at the same time the greatness of the cinema.

Toshiro Mifune could turn himself not only into a Russian merchant, but a Lord of Glamis. Nevertheless he always remained a Japanese artist.

The complete authenticity of the strength of feeling and conventionality of form suddenly merged into a living whole.

What hunts and pursuits could compare with the inner dynamism of this almost motionless film?

AT A RECEPTION for the Japanese delegation during the Moscow Film Festival I was introduced to a Japanese man of medium height who was wearing a dinner jacket. He smiled in welcome and we exchanged pleasantries. When we said goodbye and he had walked away, I asked someone who he was. Great goodness, I had not recognized my favourite actor. How could I have failed to recognize him?

At the final ceremony the film *Red Beard* was awarded first prize. The chairman of the jury read out a name. The crowd aahed and froze. A man of astonishing masculine beauty wearing a grey-black belted

[1] Called *To Live* in U.S., *Living* in U.K. [trans.].

[2] As it was called in Russian [trans.].

Kimono and carrying a fan walked on to the stage of the Palace of Congresses; his very bearing, his walk, every movement was full of strength and dignity. His face seemed like a dark sculpture with black slanting eyes. World-famous 'stars' suddenly seemed insignificant in comparison. Six thousand Muscovites applauded Toshiro Mifune.

Of course only years of training and schooling (as for classical ballet where they start in early childhood) can develop such a great artistic technique.

I VISITED Toshiro Mifune in Tokyo and questioned him about the beginnings of his career. I wanted to find out the details of his training.

While we talked I watched Mifune's eyes: their expression was constantly changing, the depth of concentration, the fullness of emotion was amazing; an ordinary conversation was no different from a scene on film – he did not substitute replicas of himself, he lived.

Now he was smiling: he was refused entry into drama school because he lacked talent, he failed the exam. And he had never acted in the theatre. His drama school was Akira Kurosawa. And Kurosawa's school was the tradition of the Noh Theatre.

I WAS LUCKY: I talked about these traditions to Kurosawa. The Japanese director can talk for hours on end about the Noh Theatre. I began to understand that 'putting on a mask' was just as complicated a process as 'getting inside a part'. Before the opening of a production the actor stands for a long time in front of a mirror. A boy hands him the mask. The actor takes it carefully and silently studies its features. The expression of his eyes alters imperceptibly, his face changes. It is as if the mask enters the man. And then slowly and triumphantly he puts on the mask and turns towards the mirror. They are no longer two separate entities, man and mask, but a single whole.

Much depends on the actor, but no less on the mask. On festivals the museums lend out masks dating from the fourteenth and fifteenth centuries – national heirlooms. The honour of wearing them falls to great actors.

It is not only Kurosawa's words which are important but also his gestures. Standing before me now was not only an unusually tall (for a Japanese) thin man wearing dark glasses, but a whole invisible theatre which he was masterfully directing.

He would use sharp, authoritative movements, instantaneous changes of rhythms. The soft voice, alternating with throaty cries, accentuated sibilants, made one feel as if one was listening to a bird call. The heroes of well-known films came to life in his movements and in the rise and fall of his voice: I recognized them all – the wild samurai, the little girl, the hysterical train guard who prays, no, calls out to God.

How can the feeble world of the studio microphone stand such force of passion?

'Zen?' asked Kurosawa. 'Europeans cannot understand it. A teacher asks, "What were you before you became a man? Find the answer within yourself but do not speak." Then he raps the pupil's back with his stick and tells him he is wrong.'

It is like Stanislavsky's famous and much described cry 'I don't believe it'.

A piece was chiselled from the wood. A sculptor was making a mask. This face was chiselled from humanity, a part of an unknown continent called 'man'. In every one of them – masks polished by centuries – there was hidden a sign of character or spiritual state. In order to act with the mask one has to find the sign, unleash the movements, give it the fullness of life.

AN EMPTY STAGE, completely bare walls, the succession of immobility and dynamism, everyday movements and the rhythms of ritual – all this could apparently create another meaning to life, a contemporary significance. The white mask could be brought to life both by the complexity of Dostoyevsky's spiritual world and by the political passions of Shakespeare's heroes.

Kurosawa loves very hot weather, fierce frosts, downpours of rain, snow. As he says, extreme manifestations contain all that is most true to life.

His favourite artists are Van Gogh, Toulouse-Lautrec, and Rouault.

The Noh Theatre, Dostoyevsky, Rouault . . . a strange combination of names. And what unity of feeling for life is contained in the work of this film director!

NO, THE COMBINATION is not as strange as all that. Snow falls over Japan as well as over Russia.

In *The Throne of Blood*, instead of the Shakespearean witches concocting spells over the cauldron, an old man with grey eyebrows and a beard (another mask from the Noh Theatre) watches a never-ending thread. Perhaps this is the ancient yarn, 'the unifying thread', for which, as Dostoyevsky said, mankind has to search in order to be able to withstand all the epidemics and wars, the tortures that fall to his lot.

INFLUENCE IN ART is not only the result of one artist learning from another, it is the threads of the twisting spiral of history, the continuity of life where old contradictions develop new forms and new generations ask once again the age-old and very simple question: 'What does man live for?'

KUROSAWA HAS long since joined the classics.

The young Japanese man with a handsome swarthy face and short-cropped, prematurely grey hair did not want to be a follower of Kurosawa. He treated him with respect but thought that the time had come for a new art.

I was watching a film by Hiroshi Teshigahara. His films are well-known in Europe but I had not seen one before. *Woman of the Dunes* after the novel by Kobo Abe is perhaps one of the barest of films in actual resources. Most of the scenes consist of two persons and sand. The sand is at once the plot, the atmosphere of the action, and a philosophical commentary on what takes place. The world is hemmed in by ridges of sand dunes, the sand moves, slithers, smothers the village built deep in a well in the sand. Here there is no escape; the people live by digging sand.

It is requiem for the sand.

Drops of water, sand on the skin, blinding sunlight, heat and thirst are translated on to the screen with a physiological sensitivity. This is an example of purely visual art – or so one could describe it if one had not read Kobo Abe's novel. However Teshigahara reproduced with complete accuracy not only the scene and the characters in the book, but also the shades of meaning, the style: the philosophical proverb, the allegory.

'With the twentieth century we have entered the world of the short story,' wrote Abe, 'which one can call either a story or an essay.' I copied this down from a dialogue between the writers Kobo Abe and Kenzaburo Oe, which was published in *Foreign Literature*.[1] Oe expands the idea:

[1] A Soviet periodical [trans.].

> You can compare the stories of the nineteenth century to a cock with a flowing comb. The stories of the twentieth century are like a plucked hen. No feathers, no brilliance – they bear no resemblance to a hen. But all the same, a hen it is. Yes, you may think this a strange, clumsy and ragged creation – but nevertheless it is still a hen, a most genuine hen. To show this is the aim of story writers of the twentieth century.

Kobo Abe wrote a novel, not a short story, but the life which he portrays in it is just such a 'plucked hen': anything which could possibly conceal the bare essentials of his portrayal of life is excluded. But this is the life of mankind, its meaning lies in the increasing effort, the continuous labour, the digging of the sand: tomorrow the sand will slide back again and threaten to bury mankind.

It reminds one of Camus' *La Peste*; or hell in the form of an ordinary room which has no exit, as in Sartre.

KOBO ABE REFERS also to Gogol: 'The inner tension, the white heat of passion in his stories which make up their perfect form were always combined with a profound and active interest in his own times.'

Inner tension, the white heat of passion – this is what links Shakespeare, Dostoyevsky, Gogol and Japanese artists.

Teshigahara invited me to see his father's work. Sofu Teshigahara was the founder of the school of Sogetsu, linked with the Ikebana (literally translated as 'a flower arrangement').

From the building where the school is, a choice selection of styles is sent out into the world, combinations of flowers and leaf arrangements on pieces of china which match the selection. The school produces textbooks which show both an aesthetic form and technological expertise. These guides are readily available.

Enough has been said already about the Japanese flower cult, their innate feeling for beauty. This is probably true, but does it mean very much?

I will begin with the 'feeling for beauty'. I put the textbooks aside and read the book written by the head of the school.

Sofu Teshigahara writes:

> Ikebana is not just a matter of beauty, but of character. Although it may seem strange when put down in cold print, I regard Ikebana as people . . . The beauty and dignity which one can see in a face lined with age and a body bent with years of hard work are also present in a withered flower, and it is for this reason that such a bloom may be represented in Ikebana.

However, just as a face which is bloated and coarsened with dissipation is ugly, so is a flower which is beginning to droop, since it calls to mind a picture of gradual decay. (*Sofu: His Boundless World of Flowers and Form* by Sofu Teshigahara, Tokyo 1966, p. 104.)

The master is familiar not only with natural combinations, but also with the unnatural and the supernatural: Ikebana does not copy, it creates nature. There are only three elements: line, colour and the abstract spirit – the last being the most important. 'Do not try to produce a facsimile of something in the material world, but rather give shape to those thoughts and feelings which exist within you.'

The beginning of beginnings, the first and foremost is the art of cutting. Eisenstein would have gone into ecstasies on reading these words. He would undoubtedly have quoted them, adding that the English word 'to cut' means, in addition to its literal sense, 'to edit a film'.

A gardener's scissors would seem to be nothing more than part of his professional equipment. What is so mysterious about them? However in the hands of Sofu Teshigahara they look more like ancient knives. The love of flowers leads to their annihilation, the cult is born of destruction. The point is not in the charming allegories which have long been associated with each of the flowers – mad Ophelia remembered them when she was gathering her last bouquet – but in symbols which lie much deeper. There is something powerful and cruel in the work of the artist of Ikebana: he destroys flowers in order to give them new life, breathing his own life into them; he kills in order to prolong the life of his own soul.

Of course the creator of the Sogetsu School's persistent teaching that one must cut, cut and cut again, is a beautiful example of the economy of resources in art, the accuracy of form and restriction to the barest essentials. This can be compared with a writer's ability to erase, which both Chekhov and Hemingway wrote about.

This is all very well but there is another deeper meaning in all this. In explaining the significance of cutting, Sofu Teshigahara uses (not in the textbooks but in his own book!) the word 'sacrifice'. And the definition which appears as a result of this makes one think hard about the essence of certain features of Japanese art: 'Ikebana is a pre-ordained drama played out between man and flowers.'

Now, one sees everywhere bunches of flowers arranged in the Ikebana fashion and the little plastic vases with holes for the stalks. They remind one of Japanese art in the same way as the fan and the kimono, which are sold on the exotic souvenir stalls.

IN PICASSO'S SERIES of drawings of a bullfight the bull is gradually transformed, from drawing to drawing, into a sacrificial victim; the heathen symbol takes on a Christian form: the bull is crucified.

In Spanish cathedrals you can see statues of the Virgin Mary which have figures of tiny golden bulls pinned to the velvet hem; before the fight the toreador prays to her and brings as a present a symbol of the animal which he has to kill.

IN JAPAN ABSTRACT art looks different from European or American abstract art: Sofu Teshigahara's sculptures look natural beside the hieroglyphics on the walls, but the pen and ink sketches are like the silhouettes of trees on the road to Kyoto. The hieroglyphics – the stroke of a brush on a white square, black spots and lines – remind one of the tapping and clapping of the Noh orchestra.

TALKING TO Hiroshi Teshigahara was very interesting. He was full of idiosyncratic ideas; he was about to start filming a comedy, and said, 'Humour lies somewhere in between the boundaries of fear and laughter. I want to portray an everyday story in which domestic happenings and discord waver between comedy and fear'.

In his room he had some optician's eye models; he is a surrealist artist turned director.

IN THE HIROSHIMA museum I watched the behaviour of some school children. The boys were falling about laughing in the hall where the horrifying exhibits are displayed, the very few remains of human life from the area which was destroyed by the bomb; the children were playing some sort of game and their teacher could not get them together and quieten them down.

The exhibition begins with a hall of paintings whose general theme acts as an introduction to the subject. Where are the sources, the prime causes of one of the greatest tragedies of our time? They have been lost in the darkness of man's pre-history. The creators of the exhibition talk of them with the greatest calm. Man invented fire in order to make life easier. There was a picture of our ancestors, primitive man, gathered round their first fire. From then on it would be easier for them, warmer and lighter. This place, which has become one of the most famous in the world, is hard to find. The entrance leads from behind a small fence on the street. What is there to fence off? There is nothing to look at, only a modest inscription, 'When the heat reached 5000 degrees man disappeared'.

Now, as I looked, I could distinctly see a shadow on the stones, the silhouette of a man quietly sitting there.

In Chamisso[1] the devil took away man's shadow; he bought it at the going price, wrapped it up in a bundle and walked off with it. Here man was destroyed; he was neither struck down, nor cut to pieces, nor were his tortured bones and flesh thrown away, nor was he burnt. He simply disappeared. His shadow was left behind.

It is a new manifestation of the sculptor's art carried out by the most advanced technology.

THE SCHOOL CHILDREN were somehow gathered together in the last hall. A final inscription appeared over the door leading to the exit: 'Men and women, young and old, let us pray for the souls of the dead. May they rest in peace.'

There was laughter, shuffling of feet: the boys went on with their game. Evidently both the traces of suffering and words describing the suffering had become unreal to the younger generation, referring not to the comparatively recent past but to pre-history or ancient legend, a fiction which could not possibly happen in real life.

I WORKED ON *King Lear* and pondered over all this.

THE STONE GARDEN in Kyoto is a monument to Zen art. Zen teaches that language is a coarse and often treacherous instrument; neither letters nor words are capable of grasping the truth of nature. Years of obedience bring man to a freedom from external influences and false thoughts. The highest form of intuition, of spiritual strength capable of direct communication with reality is awakened. Truth is revealed in all its simplicity without any instructions as to how to find it, or how to define it. Man is freed from worry, care, anxiety; and he is prepared for death at any time.

Ivan Kireyevsky[2] wrote:

> A logical awareness translates deed into word, life into a formula, and fully grasps an object, destroying its influence on the spirit. When living

[1] Adelbert von Chamisso (1781–1838), famous for his melancholic/ironical ballads and romances [trans.].

[2] Slavophile philosopher (1806–1856) [trans.].

> by this way of reasoning, we are living by a plan rather than living in a house. If a thought is clear in one's mind or is accessible in words, it is powerless over one's spirit and one's will. When it develops so that it cannot be expressed then only has it matured. This inexpressible quality, which is reflected in expression, gives strength to poetry and music.

Pasternak considered that the merit of poetry was that there was more left unsaid than there was said.

THE CHIEF PRIEST of Rioan-ji's tomb (the stone garden was in his grounds) writes that the depth of significance of Soami's work is so great that it should have been called not Seki-Tei (garden of stones) but Mu-Tei (garden of oblivion), or Ku-Tei (garden of emptiness).

What the artist left unsaid is communicated to all who come into contact with his work. I tried to name the images which came to me while I was looking at the gravel and stones. Of course they are unsatisfactory and dull. But still there remains the feeling of looking down from a much greater height than existed in reality. I seemed to have seen the world from the height of a bird's flight while sitting on that small ledge.

Again an approximate definition. Even now we often look down from such a height or even higher. We have grown accustomed to looking from this altitude.

I HAD ALREADY been living there, or rather living in the same surroundings, for several days, had grown accustomed to it and felt at home. My things had found their place and I could reach any object without looking: the pocket edition of *King Lear*, notebook, oranges, cushion. I already knew my neighbours, their habits, tastes, and degree of sociability. We swapped jokes and smiled at one another. It was warm and comfortable.

The grey-haired man with glasses was reading a detective novel. The young woman had put her baby to bed and he had just gone to sleep in his cot. The man with a towel over his shoulder was waiting for the lavatory to be free. The student in the sweater raised his glass to his lips: judging by the way he was sprawled in his seat and by the colour of his face, it wasn't the first time that he had made the movement. We had all got to know each other. A little girl ran around the area playing with a number of people; her mother pretended to scold her: 'you must not behave so badly'.

They were communal quarters. But beneath us, 50° centigrade below zero, the elements howled and raged in a hole ten thousand metres deep. The communal quarters were flying over the ocean. The flight from Moscow to Tokyo (via Tehran, Rangoon, Bangkok, Manila) took almost five days.

Chapter Three

LONDON. Day after day I would go to the British Museum and find myself unable to get down to work. My work was the glass cases of early medieval exhibits, but I kept on looking at other things which had nothing to do with my main concern. I spent hours hanging around the Egyptian and African halls.

The lesson of history is clear. At the thresholds of the centuries you meet new ideas, situations, climaxes and finales. The centuries are gathered together in the halls in order to act out a parable, the simplest of parables. But what a conglomeration there is! The enormous sculptured and fantastically painted pharaohs; sarcophaguses of mummies; little prostitutes with gold faces and bare gold breasts. Then a small swathed body, a shrivelled corpse, bones in a pit. How many ampules are there in a corpse? Not very many.

Encrusted skulls (the nose of each corpse has been preserved) from Borneo; the god of war 'Kukailimocu' from the islands of Hawaii; the painting on the shields designed to terrify.

Here is early man, shown in all his simplicity. The force of artistic expression is not weakened by a need to qualify.

IT IS WELL KNOWN that Picasso was influenced by the idols of south-eastern Polynesia. This is of course true, he was indeed influenced by them.

But what influenced Ilse Koch's collection of lampshades made from human skin at Buchenwald?

KIND AND WELCOMING English people took me to Lear's 'places'. Newcastle-upon-Tyne, a ninth-century cathedral, castles, Anglo-Saxon monuments . . .

I did not yet know what surroundings *Lear* was to have. Only not these; the action could not take place here.

THE PARABLE ABOUT the overlords of history and the bones in the pit is not a simple one. The answer to the question, 'How much land does a man need?' – 'four arshins' (the length of a coffin) –

aroused Chekhov's indignation. He replied, 'A corpse needs four arshins but a man needs the whole world.'

Regan, the Duchess of Cornwall, explains to her father, who has given away all his power to his heirs, that now he is away from home she has not enough provisions to feed a hundred knights – his train, or his personnel as we would call them today. According to his daughter, the father is thus receiving all that he needs.

The door slams shut. Lear is left alone (this is how I would shoot this scene), an argument begins, but not with his over-calculating daughter, but with some other force, another idea.

'O, reason not the need,' says Lear, 'Allow not nature more than nature needs,/Man's life is as cheap as beast's.'

This is no longer a contrast between the poles of extravagance and death. The quarrel is between freedom of thought, the breadth of desire on the one hand, and calculation, restriction and hard-heartedness on the other.

'Not very much' is a difficult demand for a Shakespeare production. He is the least ascetic of authors. The poetic philosophy in his works does not come through on the screen as a result of an absence of living circumstances.

PETER BROOK'S BOOK which came out in 1968 is called *The Empty Space*. Looking at the title I did not think that this English director had Japanese art in mind. After reading it I was convinced to the contrary: he mentions Zen more than once.

I first talked to Peter Brook about *King Lear* in 1967. It turned out that we were both about to make a film of Shakespeare's tragedy. He had just finished filming his production of *Marat/Sade* which gave him a new cinematic form ('half way between theatre and cinema', he explained), in seventeen sequences.

I like Brook very much; I find his work in the theatre, cinema, his articles, and conversations with him extremely interesting. I am attracted by the artist's personality which shows in everything he does: his breadth of interests, restlessness of thought and strength of feeling.

I SAW BROOK'S production of *King Lear* for the National Theatre during the company's tour of Russia.

The bareness of the evenly lit stage, plain sackcloth, a few pieces of iron, the leather costumes (reminding one of decayed sheepskins dug up by archaeologists from an ancient burial ground) enclosed the action of the tragedy in a cold and timeless emptiness. It was as if all the clocks in the world had stopped. Only one rusty repetitive mechanism, sometimes buzzing with the vibration of metal (the sound used in the storm scene), drove men along their eternal path of misfortune.

Brook evidently gave the greatest significance to Kent's last speech, words which I had not paid much attention to before: Kent interrupts Edgar with these words as Edgar is trying to bring the dying Lear back to consciousness. In Peter Brook's production Kent did not speak quietly (as would have been natural in the presence of a dying man), but shouted them furiously at the top of his voice, rudely demanding the right of happiness for his beloved master. The greatest happiness for Lear, for mankind, was death:

> Vex not his ghost: O, let him pass! he hates him
> That would upon the rack of this tough world
> Stretch him out longer.

One of Søren Kierkegaard's books opens with a description of a tombstone somewhere in England upon which is written the laconic inscription, 'The most unfortunate'. The author suggests that there ought to be a pilgrimage to this place, 'Not to the holy tomb in the happy East, but to the mournful tomb in the unhappy West'.

'All that I see' wrote Kierkegaard, 'is empty, everything I live by is empty, everything in which I move is empty.'

In an emptiness where there is iron, rotting leather, corpses – Peter Brook wanted to create an image of the 'rack of this tough world' in all the magnificence of scenic desolation, in the greatness of the span of centuries (millennia?).

BUT WHAT ABOUT Cordelia? What was the meeting like between the father and his youngest daughter? In Brook's production the old king's madness was replaced by a sort of blessed numbness. Paul Scofield was carried on to the stage in a chair; his figure had taken on the stylized pose of a medieval statue. There was little joy and even less that was touching. Brook had pared away all sentimentality from his production just as people kill bedbugs before moving into a new flat which was previously occupied by people with dirty habits.

It would not be hard to define the interpretation of this production: the tragedy of the meaninglessness of man's existence, the absurdity of history; it is no coincidence that Brook himself and all those who write about him frequently and readily mention the name of Samuel Beckett.

Be that as it may, however, I did not feel at all oppressed as I left the theatre. On the contrary it had awakened another feeling in me: in a production which emphasized hopelessness, hope triumphed. There was nothing heroic about Scofield's Lear, but another hero existed on the stage. Its presence completely altered the essence of what is conventionally called the 'interpretation'.

This hero was related to the only positive hero in *The Government Inspector*. It is well-known that in reply to the criticism of having concentrated entirely on the negative side of life, Gogol replied that there was one positive hero – laughter.

Art won a triumphant victory in *Lear*; it was the main hero. As far as I was concerned Peter Brook and Paul Scofield were talking not so much about the powerlessness of man, but about the power of art. But this art was created by man. The complete harmony of production – its rhythm and the music of Shakespeare's poetry – was too powerful to appear as a last prayer for mankind.

And even the emptiness of the cold iron surfaces reminded one of the warmth of life, of the continuing movement of art: I recognized them, I saw them at the beginning of the revolution in the Counter-Reliefs of Tatlin; now they had come to life in England and had taken over the stage. The wooden wheels of Meyerhold's *Magnanimous Cuckold* turned once again but this time in a different way and I distinctly heard the voice of Gordon Craig, when he came to the Moscow Art Theatre for the production of *Hamlet*.

Nothing had vanished or disappeared without leaving its effect behind.

THE MOTIONLESS FIGURES of the soldiers in the background, the depth of the brown colours and the music of the speech were particularly beautiful.

One could feel marvellous theatrical magic in the production. The scene opened, people came together and heaven knows how, the stage suddenly, by some means or other, turned into a palace: the characters were sitting on rough wooden benches but I distinctly saw a hall with a throne and a palace ceremony.

In one of Samuel Beckett's plays the traditional good-natured humour of the hangmen is mixed with the absurd ravings of a hospital where H-bomb victims await their last days. Indeed Brook was trying to find the characteristics of two such comedians in the mutterings of the two old men, mad Lear and blind Gloucester.

Scholars have already written about the strange mixture of horror and circus comedy in *Lear* and not only in the character of the Fool but in the scenes with the hero himself. Wilson Knight's research in his book, *The Wheel of Fire*, is devoted to this subject.

PETER BROOK AND I agreed to describe our plans to each other. What interested Brook most of all was the delocalization of space. He wanted to film *Lear* without any traces of history showing on the screen.

Brook introduced me to Alain Resnais, a French film director who tried to overcome not only reality of space on the screen but also the reality of time.

WHEN I HAD returned to Leningrad I received a letter from Brook. He wrote amusingly that directors who produce Shakespeare with realistic scenery, faithfully reproducing historical details, are behaving dishonestly and cheating their audience until they begin to believe that in 'historical' times people did not talk naturally to each other but in this strange way (as in Shakespeare's poetry).

He sees the main part of filming a Shakespeare play in close-ups. Here are the most important ideas in his letter:

> When I write an idea on to a screen with a camera, I have a piece of celluloid of a certain length. What gives the natural length to this piece of celluloid? The material inscribed on the celluloid dictates its length. So if I have a close-up of a man, the length of the close-up is in proportion to its interest, in its context, in relation to what the face expresses – and says.
>
> What happens when the close-up, in Shakespeare, carries material through another vehicle? As the speech ceases to be dialogue and becomes the vehicle of inner meanings, I then recognize that in Shakespeare speech is a carrier. Speech in constant glow is the vehicle . . . then (if) you destroy the speech rhythm and follow the image rhythm, the power of the Shakespearean text is destroyed.
>
> Is the best we can achieve a safe compromise in which our close-up is longer than 'normal' film, but short of 'boredom length'? I say close-up – but what is the relation of close-up to fullshot – when the fullshot always reveals background? Can we make a Shakespeare film closer to the manner of Dreyer's *Jeanne d'Arc*. I want to avoid background. How? To what degree? And you?

From a letter to Peter Brook

Dear Brook,

Thank you for your interesting letter. Like you I have been thinking about the power of delocalized space on the screen. But close-ups as the foundation for the action are often less effective in sound films than they were in the silents. Dreyer's marvellous *Jeanne d'Arc* would have lost its strength if we had been able to listen to dialogue.

A close-up is essential when there is a need to look deep into a character's eyes, into the man's spiritual world.

I see Shakespeare's text not only as a dialogue but as a landscape, notes from the author's diary, lines of verse, quotations. This was beautifully expressed in your theatrical productions: the rhythm of the speech is the greatest influence, not always realistic but like the movement of waves of sound. In the audible sounds – the voices of your actors – one could hear palaces, horses, battles and the storm. But how can the cinema help such expressiveness? Here the strength of the visual outweighs the audible.

I am trying to find a visual *Lear*. Nature in this context would have to become something like the chorus of Greek tragedy.

Chapter Four

EISENSTEIN'S SEVENTIETH BIRTHDAY was being celebrated in style. True, the man himself was not present; he had been dead a long time (or so it seemed). On the other hand a great many of his books and books on him have been published in a great many languages. Learned committees have awarded many masterships and doctorates for research into his work.

I had to chair one of the meetings at this jubilee conference. There were an enormous number of Eisensteiniens (to use the term from *Cahiers du Cinéma*) gathered here. We had two meetings a day and clearly not enough time to hear all the speeches. That day the speakers were an Algerian biographer of Eisenstein, cinematographers from socialist countries, a researcher from West Berlin, and some structuralists and moralists.

In the morning we had a talk from a man who had taken part in Eisenstein's early productions. He explained that the lanterns which the actress (or rather the actor) wore on her breasts in *Enough Simplicity in Every Wise Man* did not shine constantly as has been described in articles, but lit up only in moments of passion.

The audience in the hall grabbed for their notebooks and it was evident that new works on him were already in preparation.

One of the speakers had written a book called *The Return to Eisenstein*.

In the twenties Lunacharsky published an article called 'Back to Ostrovsky', and how many puns were composed around the word 'back'!

If you look carefully the two already seem to be side by side, the author of *The Wise Man* and the director of the montage of attractions in the production of Ostrovsky's play. Perhaps, joking apart, if the playwright had lived to see the première of the Proletkult[1] production he would have come to like its interpretation, and if the film director's heart had been a little stronger he would have assimilated the traditions of the Maly Theatre.

There was an excursion to Pera Attasheva's[2] flat (where Eisenstein's books and a collection of his possessions were), and a visit to

[1] Proletarian Culture Theatre [trans.].

[2] Eisenstein's widow [trans.].

the Novodyevichi Cemetery where he lies or rather what used to be he.

His manuscripts are in the Central Archives of Literature and Art. The speakers talked about the condition of each sheet of paper on which he wrote. Minutely accurate instruments had measured the temperature and the degree of humidity. Everything was preserved untouched, the lines running away with the impetuosity of thought, the galloping words and the sloping parallels.

And his films have been preserved. In Belyi Stolbi[1], the archives near Moscow, in the Cinémathèque Française, in the Museum of Modern Art in New York, the Cinémathèque de Belge, the film archive of Argentina . . . skilled hands have restored each frame with the greatest care. And strange and eccentric directors will tentatively question each other when they meet, jealously enquiring whose copy is the best.

And even non-existent film appears to be realized. The negatives for *Bezhin Meadow* were destroyed during the war but frames were kept from each shot. Yutkevich and Kleiman arranged them in their correct sequence and set them to some music by Prokofiev. Prokofiev, it is true, did not compose the music for this film but he did write the music for *Alexander Nevsky*, *Ivan the Terrible* and, what was most important, was near at hand, living in the same block of flats in the Pantheon.

The critics in foreign cinema magazines considered *Bezhin Meadow* to be among the best of the month's new films; they awarded it three stars, but gave it four (the highest mark) for the editing of the frames.

It was good to read this. The main body of the conference was also pleased about the exhibition which had opened in the House of Cinema[2].

Was there any particular intention behind the photographs exhibited on the stands? I do not know. But the result was that it seemed as if not only the auditorium but also Eisenstein himself were listening to the speakers. His young, cheerful face looked down from all four walls.

Looking at photographs of a man is often no less interesting than hearing about him. As I looked at the smiling Eisenstein I uncon-

[1] The Russian Film Library, literally translated: White Columns [trans.].

[2] I would like to mention the names of Naum Kleiman and Leonid Kozlov. I met them a long time ago when they were collecting material for the archives in Pera Attasheva's tiny flat; in those days there could be no question of a book on Eisenstein. Their work was responsible for a significant part of the six-volume edition, the exhibition of his sketches, and the conference.

sciously began to link the expression on his face with whomever was speaking and it seemed as if while he was listening to what was being said about him he would sometimes give a knowing smile.

I tried to tear myself away from the 'vertical montage' (his phrase) but just at that moment the speaker said, '*Bezhin Meadow* revealed the greatness of the still on the screen, the beauty of motionless nature, the impassivity of the faces of the ploughmen; in this film it is only the music that reminds one about time; does not this hold the key to future cinema?'

I grew very angry. For heavens sake, I thought, there was no question of stills in the film and the church was destroyed not to the accompaniment of symphonic music but to the singing of 'The days of Volochayevsk' – a not unimportant stylistic detail.

The man whose birthday we were celebrating bore no resemblance to an Olympian god, the creator of eternal harmony. He was a man who belonged to a difficult age. He not only lived in his times but lived by his times. Was it necessary to freeze his spiritual world with compliments just as they freeze a heart before an operation? Why transplant an alien heart into his body?

It is true that now he has to hear more than straight compliments. To the stars awarded to him by foreign cinema journals have been added black single large spots (the lowest meaning 'evokes antipathy'): so much the better. It means that even frames from his shots are capable of evoking someone's fury.

This is less shameful for him than the realization of Blok's bitter prophesy:

> It is a sad fate: how complex
> How difficult and useless it is to live,
> And to become the property of the professor
> And to give birth to new critics.

His plans, which often went far beyond the bounds of what we know about cinema – frequently unfinished and even more often torn up – have become a part not only of the history of cinema (is that much for him?) but of the living flesh of the age, of the moving and changing times.

This is why it is impossible to step backwards with Eisenstein, even to his own works. He is no companion for such a journey.

IN *Ivan the Terrible* Eisenstein used the force of plastic art to turn theatrical and even operatic qualities into tragedy. The face of the

Tsar lingers long in the memory: it was not for nothing that Eisenstein thought out long beforehand and made a quantity of sketches of every aspect of the Tsar's figure, the backward slanting beard, the accentuated sharpness of the top of his wig. The stark contrasts, the clashing of opposites (of the plastic elements) were realized with astonishing consistency. His sketches came to life on the screen.

The spiritual life of Ivan the Terrible (his fits of cruelty and repentance) seemed normal for the portrayal of this character; the only addition (which played a significantly large part) was the 'progressiveness'.

The book by the academician S. B. Veselovsky, *The Oprichnina*, published after Eisenstein's death, has shattered the legend of these characteristics. The work of another scholar with a different specialization has recreated a picture of the Tsar. There were no fewer contrasts in this picture than in the film: 'The skeleton has signs which at first glance would seem to be mutually exclusive; on the one hand the massiveness of the skeleton speaks of a man of immense power and fitness, who evidently possessed legendary physical strength; and at the same time there exists the formation of osteophytes, the growths of an old man's sclerosis on the bones . . .'

This is the result of research into the remains of Ivan the Terrible (disinterred in 1963 from the tomb in the Archangelsky Cathedral in the Kremlin), by the anthropologist M. M. Gerasimov. What would seem to be the connection between the medical terminology and the art of tragedy. What connection does it have with 'osteophytes'?

Apparently there is a connection. 'His whole torso was chained as if in a corset,' writes Gerasimov. 'It is said that he prayed fervently. I do not believe this. He could not have knelt down without help and certainly could not have got up again on his own. I do not believe that he fasted either.'

Pictures of the Tsar dressed in a monk's habit fervently bowing to the ground before an ikon have vanished into the realms of legend; a new portrait has appeared in the vast expanse of history: 'a cruel, fastidious face, protruding lips, a heavy, sharply asymmetrical nose, eyes of unequal size – the right eye was smaller than the left because the right eye socket is much smaller than the left.

A small forehead, a highly developed cranium and asymmetrical eyebrows. A small head, a very strong neck, powerful shoulders and a wide chest.'

Every deduction from a study of his bone structure refutes the usual portrait: he weighed not less than 95 kilograms; he lost his milk teeth only after the age of fifty and new incisors were growing two years before his death; the cause of death was lack of mobility, overeating and alcoholism.

Is there much left of kingliness and 'demonic tragedy'?

Eisenstein and the excellent make-up artist, V. Goryunov, transformed the face of Cherkasov but history itself worked on the real figure. The second part of *Ivan the Terrible* made a great impression on me but now that I have read the conclusions of this anthropologist I think that the unadorned face – with its bearlike strength and immobility, the surly dullness and cruelty – would have been just as impressive.

One cannot imagine anything more interesting than the real figure.

EISENSTEIN'S ATTITUDE towards Shakespeare was cool; of the Elizabethans he was more interested in John Webster and the mannered theatre of horror.

HOW IS ONE to portray history on the screen while avoiding the genre of the historical film with its elegant external features, its pomp and its battle scenes? How is one to find the mean of greatness about which Yuri Tynyanov[1] wrote:

> History contracts in its number of characters; it reaches a single man and then suddenly expands beyond all boundaries.

AFTER ONE OF the sessions of filming *Ivan the Terrible* Eisenstein came straight round to me (in Alma-Ata we lived in the same building) and said: 'You must work with Buchma. During today's filming I accidentally noticed his eyes: their tremendous depth and fulness of emotion.'

He smiled slyly and added, 'You understand, I cannot do anything with him.'

Of course the 'accidentally' was said on purpose. It was good advice; unfortunately I could not make use of it. Ambrose Buchma died in 1957.

[1] Writer and scenarist (1894–1942).

Chapter Five

I WOULD LIKE Lear to be short and the people surrounding him, the mainstay of his kingdom, enormously tall. Folds of heavy cloth, square figures with heads like bulls. They enter the action in clans, families and whole companies. While the kingdom is divided they stand in strict order of rank: the head of the family, the eldest son, the councillors, the guard. They stand with their feet planted firmly on the ground; to them it does not seem to move.

The eldest daughters, the heirs to the throne, are tall, fat and big-boned. They are not princesses but old women.

The guards' horses are covered with heavy dark-coloured cloths with slits for their eyes.

It would seem like the world of a solid, everlastingly unshakable ruler. And suddenly it all totters, collapses, falls apart and is destroyed.

IT HAS BECOME an accepted fact that in contemporary drama, drama in the old sense of the word is no longer possible. Everything that is solidly built, tightly bound and firmly tied up is not allowed to be shown on stage; nowadays one is not even allowed to talk about the 'drama' in the best circles. Art as we all know is a reflection of life. Is it really possible for any self-respecting mirror to reflect something which has no connection with real life, and in which relationships are inconstant, feelings changeable and the contours of characters unstable?

If you look into the depth of the action in *Lear*, far from the external events, the rational seems absurd, the fixed turns to chaos; it would not be easy to answer questions about it. So Shakespeare himself has not fallen behind the times.

However the events in the tragedy are still loud, the action is swift and whatever anyone says, there is a plot and it is conventional into the bargain: the unfolding of the plot is naive, the dénouements rely on chance, and the characters have a certain stereotyping of role.

All this has been discussed before and in order not to cast a shadow on the classic, art has been separated from craft: it is well known that Shakespeare wrote versions of existing plays; the stories belong to former variants but the poetry and philosophy (which transcend time) belong to him. It is a just division of rights.

And so I thought too until comparatively recently. But time goes by and it is worth juxtaposing the drama of the 'plot' not with new aesthetics, but with our own contemporary life, and then the situation loses its clarity. The bloody melodrama which has long seemed alien to reality has died on the stage and come to life (and with what force!) in everyday affairs: political treachery, heads of state overturned, documents forged, secret assassinations, a career forged out of the blood of those nearest – is this really only a theatrical fantasy?

While art was searching for a means of expressing the slow flow of everyday life, bloody melodrama has entered our lives and has become a daily event which seems no more extraordinary than Chekhov's tea-drinking or a game of whist.

And this is how it must be shot – as the everyday events of *coups d'états*, changes of power, and of political crimes.

I AM NOT a reader of fantasy novels. It is difficult to fantasize in our world today. Indeed a good subject for fantasy would seem to me to be the most improbable: man peacefully and unhurriedly living his life with his family in one place, nothing particular happening to him. One could only dream such a story.

THE REFLECTION OF life in art is of course not brought about by a mirror. But how then?

Only a worthless object, cheap glass with a coat of amalgam simply reflects. One can reflect suffering in art only with sympathy and with hatred for the cause of grief.

The evil doings of the Duke of Cornwall, Edmund, Regan are caused not by the pathological make-up of their characters but by the circumstances of political activity. They have to get results as quickly as possible. It is necessary for their affairs. There is no time for subtleties.

The problem is not to link Shakespeare with art, even the most contemporary art, but with life.

THE SHAPE OF the film forms of its own accord when one begins to understand the everyday course of events as opposed to the theatrical events. Then the action breaks through its theatrical wrapping; realistic situations intensify until they are clearly visible:

far distant horizons begin to appear, and thousands of people can be seen behind the mere handful.

There is no need to invent, it is all in the poetry. The difficulty is to overcome the stereotyped effect of reading: *Lear* should be read not like a play but like a novel where far from hiding behind his characters the author often follows historical reality in all its breadth and depth and in all directions. Here we have customs, landscapes, the daily life of the palaces and the villages, the highways and byways.

We have grown accustomed to feeling this intangible reality only in the speeches of the main characters who exist within a defined space.

Kafka wrote in his diary, 'Sometimes it is as if the play has gone to rest up in the flies; the actors have torn strips off it, the ends of which for the sake of the drama they hold or wind round their bodies, and only here and there a strip badly torn off drags an actor aloft to the terror of the audience.'

'In the flies' rests the history of 'the naked, homeless beggars'. They must come to the fore, enter the action, not only because Edgar assumes the form of one of them, Poor Tom, when he is escaping pursuit, but because one cannot portray the life of a king without portraying the life of his subjects.

The rhetoric falls silent and the hoarse horn-call of the beggars is heard as they gather alms. Lear in rags becomes indistinguishable from the other beggars. It is an endless, well-trodden road – no longer the boards of a stage, but earth, the 'life of a cur'.

SHAKESPEARE'S SOLILOQUIES are often not only speeches spoken by the main characters, but whole scenes in code: they contain their own characters, landscape, objects, their own peculiar interpretation and a wealth of life-like details. All you have to do is to break the code in which it is written, rather like in a detective novel: to compare the past with the present, single out the people who could have been involved, establish an entrance into the action.

You have to try out a multitude of hypotheses until the main clue has been found: the way to the interior, to the essence of the action, to the unfolding of the thought behind the whole tragedy.

CONTRASTS IN *Lear* are not so much between good and evil but between human and inhuman. But human does not by any means mean humane. Lear is a person even at the beginning of the action, in spite of his tantrums and capriciousness. The violence of his impromptu actions belongs to the realm of what we call human which is not at all a synonym of humaneness, but which can often describe a completely different and contrasting side of human nature. But underneath the mask of power there is a live personality which will reveal itself in time.

Edmund, Lear's eldest daughters and the Duke of Cornwall are heartless individuals. For them Lear, Cordelia, Kent and Gloucester are die-hards from the chronicles of ancient time. The new age has reared new citizens: they are distinguishable by an excessive will, an absence of prejudice, and a cold sense of purpose. In essence they are programmed calculating machines of power.

These robots come to life only when certain reflexes and instincts give the necessary signal – instincts of sex and fear.

SHAKESPEARE DEVOTES particular attention to the one hundred knights – the King's train which he cannot do without even after he has abdicated his throne.

What sort of people are they? The very word 'knight' is completely meaningless: knightly valour or, the opposite, 'the knight's curs'? Their master is insulted in the most alarming way but not one of them says a word in his defence. What does this old man need with these hundred men? They do not look after him, neither do they carry out his orders. Not once are their swords unsheathed. They are not people, but a way of life.

It is evident that they are not a hundred swords, but a hundred flattering tongues: a hundred backs ready to bow down before whoever is in power and to turn away from whoever is in disgrace. There is no need to look at historical textbooks in order to imagine them.

What does Lear's palace, its atmosphere remind one of? Perhaps the description which I read today in *Pravda*: 'The chief engineer of the automated stations says, "space is an aggressive substance, so far as man is concerned, harmful to life. Everything is against us – the enormous vacuum, unimaginable temperatures, cosmic radiation, interminable space . . ."' How do people feel in the presence of the King? I turn to the same article: 'One side of the station is lit by the sun, and figuratively speaking, is like being in the Sahara Desert but twice as hot, the other side which is in shade is twice as cold as the Antarctic. But when the station turns, the whole system is reversed.'

This is how the banishing of Cordelia and Kent happens; and the quarrel with the King of France.

THE FIRST SCENE (the division of the kingdom) bears no resemblance to palace ceremonials, it is more like a gambling house, only everyone's eyes are fixed not on cards, but on a geographical map. None of the characters moves an inch, it is almost as if nobody breathes. Only one tiny movement is perceptible in the enormous hall: the King's finger traces lines on the parchment, outlining the new boundaries of the kingdom. They will be announced any moment.

The question the King asks his heirs – 'Which of you shall we say doth love us most' – is a kind of invitation: 'faites vos jeux.'

A strange miniature ballet begins: an almost imperceptible movement from a courtier (his nerves couldn't stand it any longer) alternates with a similar almost unnoticeable gesture from someone else: someone catches his breath and in reply, someone else makes a small step forward.

A more noticeable movement comes from the flames flickering in the candlesticks. Drops of sweat break out on the foreheads of those standing in front. In the background behind those gathered round the throne stand the courtiers who are not taking part in the game but only betting on the players – thus binding their own fate with the others. In the darkness of distant halls stand the phalanxes of the guards, forming the boundary which separates those who hold power from those who hold no rights at all.

The people without rights, the crowds in their thousands, await their fate outside the confines of the castle, outside the confines of the second line formed by the cavalry. In their ignorance they mistake the game for divine providence. The old man, who is no different from them, seems to them like a god as he now bends over the map. The game comes to an end, the lights go out – the lights on the battlements of the towers; soon another fire will flare up, the time of ruin, destruction and war will begin.

THE WORK OF a director lies in selection and restriction. Directors of epics seek out from ancient customs and mores (or rather from books which describe them) all that is most effective, that will be interesting for its own sake on the screen: beautiful to look at and unusual. The producers spare no expense in the preparation of what is 'effective', money is its own justification: apart from the story of the film, the audience is interested in seeing with their own eyes how people lived in ancient times – the magnificence of the dress, the pageantry of the ceremonies. They pay in order to be distracted from life. I wanted to bring *Lear* as close as possible to life. This is why I was not interested in the unusual or the beautiful, but on the contrary, in everything which had been completely deprived of interest for its own sake. We needed a style of costume which would not attract attention, customs which were not remarkable in any way. There should be nothing to admire.

I did not want to shoot the film in colour for this very reason. I do not know what colour grief is, or what shades suffering has. I wanted to trust Shakespeare and the audience: it is shameful to sugar *Lear* with beautiful effects.

Of course the life (or rather the superficialities of life) shown on the screen should not resemble our contemporary existence; a minimum of historical detail is essential. It was most important to decide what one was looking for among the available material: 'unlike' or 'like'? There was an abundance of both to choose from.

I was looking for the 'like' only.

A mother breastfeeds her baby: a beggar wraps himself in rags to protect his body from the cold – what century do such details belong to?

One can show how beautiful ancient palaces were and one can also show the unpleasant business which was usually carried on inside them. There is an arithmetic of life and an algebra of existence. I wanted to deduce the formula of history on the screen; the natural law of build-up followed by explosion. This was the formula deduced by Shakespeare's poetry.

It was not just a question of keeping a modest amount of historical detail but also of exercising modesty in the method of shooting in portraying them. The visual angle and light had to help to create Shakespeare's world, in which what had come down through the centuries with all its life-like qualities was clearly visible and in which everything which belonged to a specific age was only dimly discernible, with only the general outlines showing. The figures of people had to stand out; the utensils and walls had to be less clearly visible.

Only real materials should be used: wood, wool, iron, leather, fur.

One had first to clarify everything (for one's own benefit) as far as possible down to the last concrete detail, and then take away the archaeological and ethnographical, leaving only the most general features, making them into visual tokens.

THE ABSTRACT AND apparently meaningless titles of the Dukes of Cornwall and Albany are definitions of a type of character, of the behaviour of both the dukes and their entourage.

They are a peculiar type of administrator living apart from

other people according to their own standards and in their own surroundings. Their nature is as like to each other as Georgians to Lithuanians.

Lear's train differs from Goneril's servants; Cornwall's young thugs look like a band of robbers when they are in the courtyard of Gloucester's castle – something like General Shkuro's Savage Division.[1]

THE POVERTY OF epic films with lavish costumes is due to the fact that men are divided into three categories: courtiers, knights and citizens.

Once one succeeds in tearing oneself away from these empty and meaningless ranks of people the life-like qualities of the characters immediately become evident.

The make-up artists would have little to do. Real faces would create not only the peculiar qualities of Shakespeare's world (not people one would meet on the underground), but also a natural-seeming course of events. Perhaps Baltic faces would be the most suitable; the people who are least like the main characters in *Lear* are the contemporary English.

ONLY A TIGHTLY-WOVEN cloth of film – unity of method in shooting and editing – would create a realistic (without existing in reality) scenery, a historical world but at the same time devoid of historical definition.

Conventional décor and costumes have not yet succeeded in creating anything convincing. The camera has filmed the play, but the editing loses impetus and turns into a gluey mess. Perhaps this part of the text would be boring if taken from the same angle? Perhaps it should be filmed closer? Or perhaps with a tracking shot?

The tragedy has no main scenes, no places which are more important than others. The falsely conceived significance of separate 'famous' soliloquies hinders the scope of the whole. It should be a life-like unity of continuous action, taking place on all planes at once; there should be no moving out into the foreground of 'the most important'.

This is how the travelling companies once used to play Shakespeare:

[1] General Shkuro (1887–1947), who fought on the side of the Whites in the Civil War, was renowned for his cruelty [trans.].

the soliloquies were spoken at the footlights in the centre of the stage; the speeches of the other players were cut as much as possible. Was there much of Shakespeare left?

To give an example, my own experience taught me that Hamlet's first soliloquy succeeded because it was spoken (like an interior monologue) among crowds of people hurrying to the carnival against a background of noise and music and of faces flitting past.

Everything lies in living movement, which must be taken from an objective standpoint, not with a specific focus.

From the first screen tests one had straight away to shoot not simply an actor, but his whole living environment, a single cell in the world of tragedy. I wanted to see Lear in the midst of the fear, flattery, and lies of the sleek figures of the officials, with their imaginary importance and their false values – the world of politics.

The brazen, tough faces of Cornwall's band are like members of the Ku-Klux Klan with their nooses of rope and cans of petrol.

Can you understand the Duke of Albany without seeing him in a library surrounded by books? Of course he is a book-lover.

Gloucester's dying, decrepit little world: wrinkled, grey-headed old men shivering over the fire; the tapping of sticks along empty corridors, coughing and muttering.

Tramps, beggars, newly released convicts – the many faces of Poor Tom; in their midst Edgar and later Lear are homeless among the homeless, on the 'rock bottom' of the kingdom.

THE TRAGEDY OF *Lear* is created not only by madmen (this is well known), but by collective madness arising on the crest of events. It is related both to the deification of the King and to the epidemic of suspicion and fear which catches hold of the elder sisters and their subjects.

If all this was shown, then the soft voice of Cordelia, the genuineness of the Duke of Albany and the honesty of Kent would become all the more powerful.

I HAD TO look at war documentaries. The shots taken by our newsreel men seemed to me to be perfect in their portrayal of real tragedy. Burned houses, scorched ovens in a landscape covered in snow, bodies of the executed dug out of pits; the inhabitants had returned to their village (or what used to be a village) which had been laid waste by our army (a large number of old people were with them); they wandered among the bodies lying in the snow, recognized members of their families, wept, and could not tear themselves away from the bodies of the dead.

Their grief, immortalized by the camera, had to be stored in the memory. In comparison with them, conventional theatricality and pictorial tragedy seemed shameful. Pictorial means cardboard.

So should one imitate the style of the documentary? Of course not. This was not the point at all. The main point was the depth of human suffering, and of the people's grief, not the style.

HOW IN A word was one to define the development of the image of Lear? As a thawing. At the beginning of the play all life in him is frozen by the habit (or the necessity) of ruling.

Grief warms him. Disaster melts the ice; his heart quickens and begins to beat. In the first scene with Cordelia and Kent he is not bad, but inhuman and soulless.

Shakespeare performed with this image what Bunin considered to be the basis of Tolstoy's art: 'His most cherished artistic idea was I think this: to take a man at the highest point of his career (or to raise him up to this point) and then to confront him with death or some tremendous disaster, in order to show him the insignificance of the worldly, to uncover his own imaginary importance, his pride and his self-confidence.'

BORIS EICHENBAUM SAID with a knowing smile that the relationship between Tolstoy and Shakespeare was not simple. Tolstoy vigorously condemned *Lear* for its unnatural situations which would be impossible in real life, and then found himself in a very similar position.

One can say that in comparison to the manner in which Lear abandoned the house of Gloucester, reduced to despair by his elder daughters, the way in which Tolstoy left Yasnaya Polyana is even closer to theatrical howling and the sound and fury of show-business.

The coachmen led out and harnessed the horses. Everyone on the estate ran for shelter from the storm: washing was taken down from the line, the cattle were herded into the barns. The watchmen opened the creaking gates; the wind swirled up the dust on the road.

Chapter Six

I HAVE LITTLE faith in the term 'professional' when applied to a director's work with his actor. In struggling with figures such as Lear one lives the same life, and becomes so close that one even shares the same objects of love and hate.

AT THE AUDITIONS, each actor who came in declared before even shaking hands: 'One can't act a king. The people who surround the king must act him.'

I pretended that I had not heard this before. The second thought followed: 'The most important thing is not to act.' I agreed readily. Then they continued: 'And he must not wear a crown.' But of course he mustn't. But what should he be? Who is Lear?

PETER BROOK WRITES that the relationship between a director and actor is like a dance. 'A dance is an accurate metaphor, a waltz between director, player and text.'[1]

Besides a waltz there is a similarity to the beginning of a Russian dance: the actor is like the beautiful girl who is standing in her place gently waving her handkerchief; the director coaxes her, inviting her to dance. It often happens that the dance finishes at this point.

The most difficult task in working with an actor is to persuade him first of all to 'close shop for stocktaking'.[2] Whatever role is offered him he begins with his last one. He tries to adapt all his past successes to the new role. Sometimes this process is unconscious.

These sorts of goods are no good for Shakespeare.

It is particularly difficult with film actors. They are usually invited to play a role which they have already performed several times before. They are moved on to the screen like a ready-made piece of décor.

'IN THE MIDST of grunting and roaring, whining and shouting, her voice, like the voice of Blok, gained in strength and power,' wrote

[1] *The Empty Space*, MacGibbon & Kee 1968, p. 124.

[2] This expression has a particularly ironic and humorous flavour since Russians know only too well how often shops display this sign [trans.].

Osip Mandelstam of Vera Komisarzhevskaya. 'The theatre lived and will go on living by the human voice.' (*The Egyptian Stamp.*)

Emphasizing the same point, the power of natural speech, the poet exclaimed, 'It is better to have Petrushka than Carmen and Aida, than the ugly mug of declamation.'

Film directors who are fighting for the natural, contrast declamation and pathos with everyday speech. Their actors mumble into the microphone and the words seem to evaporate, making the Russian language sound like Esperanto.

People certainly do sometimes talk like this in real life. But there is a different voice sound in Russian Shakespeare (in Pasternak's translation): the natural prosaic quality, the even deliberately unpoetic quality of certain parts is all the voice of a great poet, and the rhythm of his breathing is always audible.

SOUND IS A very complex conception. A certain tone. Are we really only concerned with what is heard?

> What was sobbing within her? What was fighting?
> What did she want from us?

wrote Blok about Komisarzhevskaya.

Gogol heard the strange sound of a string ringing through the mist and his *Diary of a Madman* finishes on this note.

Blok repeated the image but strengthened it, changing the quality of the sound:

> So ring out like an arrow in the mist
> Angry mood and angry sigh!

Lear can (and evidently must) speak quietly and of course completely naturally, but his thoughts and feelings must sound like an arrow in the mist. Quite a lot happens before Lear finds himself alone. At the beginning, the crowds of well-fed and sleek cringers surround the King. Then Lear's heiresses reduce his staff; then it reduces itself: who is going to serve a man who has lost his power? . . .

Kent and the Fool remain. Then Lear is alone, a mad old man.

There are a lot of *volte faces* in the play but the duration of time is not long. Simultaneously with losing power man ceases almost instantly to be a man.

THERE MUST NOT be anything wild, primitive or prehistoric about the beginning of the play. It should be as similar as possible to contemporary diplomatic receptions: polite inscrutable faces; the savage animal beings are hidden behind a civilized exterior.

EDMUND BECOMES A general. He is not only a brave fighter but, more important, is making a political career for himself. He has come a long way even in outward appearance from the layabout in his father's house who has no legal rights. When at war he is surrounded by guards who carry out his orders.

The Nazi leaders waged war in a similar way: the general's car was guarded by ranks of armoured cars and motor cycles. In our case – horses covered with armour, enormous shields with the Gloucester coat of arms on them.

If the story of Lear has the main features of the medieval parable about the humbling of the proud king (where Pride, Poverty and Nakedness are the main actors), here we have the parable of the Fearless Warrior. The bravest, the most valiant, he has conquered everyone and has fought them all. And then he will writhe in the dust, forsaken by everyone, gasping for breath, conscious of the approach of something he is powerless to forestall either with his mind, his will or his sword.

Lear is the oldest of them all: he is a living anachronism, a man belonging to the past century. This is how he is at the beginning of the play. Later he is a different man, nearer to our times.

He belongs both to the ancient past and to the present. His inner life is characterized by burning obsessions: he has both the complete blindness of tyranny and then an agonizing enlightenment, a total rejection of everything he believed in, everything on which his life was founded.

Enlightenment comes to him not only through suffering but also through irony; irony sweeps away the empty notions about the greatness of power.

DOSTOYEVSKY WROTE OF Raskolnikov, 'Now all his thoughts were centred on one point which seemed to be the main one, and he felt that this main point did indeed exist and that now, even now, he was alone with it, face to face.'

What is the main point for Lear? There are perhaps two: 'Off, off, you lendings' (what exactly is a real 'unaccommodated' man in this society?) and 'None does offend, none, – I say, none'. In the extremity of the situation in which he poses the questions, they are fearless thoughts.

He does not only ask questions but demands an answer. 'Is man no more than this?' ('. . . unaccommodated man is no more but such a poor, bare forked animal as thou art.') It is as if he puts a knife to the throat of his interlocutor and cries out for an answer: 'Why should a dog, a horse, a rat have life, and thou no breath at all?'

He no longer believes in words. Instead of an answer, let anatomy open up Regan's bosom (or any other person living in those times): 'Is there any cause in nature that makes these hard hearts?'

He talks to the skies as an equal: the clouds are as white as he is; the character of the storm is like a king's.

And who is he addressing? Who is he questioning?

Both himself and us.

Lear addresses man in general not because everyone has to grow old and will perhaps know the ingratitude of their own children, but because there will come a time when everyone will discover (alas often very late) what is truly precious in life and what is no more than gilded tin.

THE MOST IMPORTANT punctuation mark in Lear's speeches is evidently the question mark. But how is one to fit the questions to the character of his temperament?

Mikhail Svetlov once said jokingly that the question mark is an outdated form of exclamation mark.

If there are no answers to the questions Lear asks 'then it follows that our whole planet is a lie and is founded on lies and mockery. It follows that the laws themselves are a lie and a vaudeville of the Devil.' (Dostoyevsky.)

The definition of the genre 'Devil's vaudeville' is precise and expressive enough. Lear himself was thinking of something comparable:

> When we are born, we cry that we are come
> To this great stage of fools.

YURI TYNYANOV SAID that while working on a film, a great deal is formulated while going for a walk or in conversation.

I conceive Shakespeare's tragedies while I am walking; I hold imaginary conversations with friends who are no longer living and with favourite authors. I argue with them and learn from them.

PUSHKIN CONSIDERED THAT Gogol's best quality was his portrayal of vulgarity. Dostoyevsky manoeuvred the trivial and vulgar, brought to fantastic proportions, into tragedy. The heroes of tragedy and the vulgar man existed side by side. But they were no ordinary vulgar men: they were fantasmagoric; life-like and illusory at the same time – as Smerdyakov, and Marmeladov.

Isn't there something vulgar and trivial in Gloucester's superstition, Oswald's subservience, Cornwall's business, Regan's meanness and Goneril's lack of shame?

Bunin could not stand Dostoyevsky. In *The Whorled Ears* he called him 'a nasty malicious writer who shoved Christ into all his cheap novels'.

Shakespeare is doing something of this sort in *Lear*: shoving mystery into an adventure novel (or to put it more properly 'a drama based on reversals of fortune').

One can quote as examples an endless number of paradoxical juxtapositions. The play has them all from domestic squabbles to scenes from horror films.

DOSTOYEVSKY IS FULL of melodrama – unashamed and intense emotion. Not one of his novels is without it.

There is nothing wrong with intense emotion; it is the absence of thought which is bad. This is what distinguishes theatrical melodrama from tragedy.

Dostoyevsky is also full of what is called 'sentimentality'. Geniuses do not have to think twice about the concept of 'good taste'. They know the taste of wormwood, of life.

The action must take place not against a background of scenery – whether realistic or conventional but in the midst of the people's grief. This is the justification for filming the tragedy, the point of transferring it on to the screen.

THE TRADITION OF acting the role of king exists in all aspects of the theatre.

A sad figure comes to mind: a tall man in a tattered old-fashioned overcoat was walking with squelching galoshes through the puddles. It was the autumn mud in Leningrad. There was something downcast and ordinary about his whole figure. 'For decades he danced the same role in ballets', said my companion, 'the king'. She told me his name and I immediately remembered seeing him on stage. He had only two movements: a circular movement of the right arm as it unfolded – the king invited someone to dance – and a circular movement of the arm lowering, pointing the index finger to the ground – the king was angry.

HOW DIFFICULT IT is to take the starch out of these figures. They stick in one's memory – straight, rigid, and speaking in beautiful, contrived voices.

One must get Goneril moving and ruffle her hair. She slops about the house in a rumpled evil-smelling gown. In an odious and imperious voice she sets Oswald at her father.

Her entrance into supper does not look like a duchess's in any way. She rebukes a servant on the way, takes a spoonful of soup, blows on it, and frowns.

At home she is slovenly and sullen. She carves fatty meat.

When *Hamlet* was being discussed at the Leningrad Institute of Theatre and Music I came under a lot of fire for the hens which cackled around the courtyard at Elsinore. In the opinion of the drama experts hens lowered the tone of the tragedy. Alas, I did not admit my mistake. Let hens have their cackle during famous soliloquies.

Long live hens and down with pathos!

BOTH DIRECTOR AND actor derive a lot of help from the method of the physical action. You cannot act anything before you have imagined the action in all its concrete details, in its abundance of precisely presented problems.

You have to tread carefully on floorboards in order not to wake up people sleeping in the next door rooms; open the door without it squeaking; button up your coat when you get outside – it's cold at night; look to see whether the carriage is waiting.

Every movement must be thought out and directed towards the main purpose.

On the other hand, however correctly these actions are performed, the result is still not Leo Tolstoy's exit from Yasnaya Polyana. So how do you succeed in getting the little gimlet-like eyes to light up with their peculiar colour under the bushy eyebrows?

I WORKED WITH yet another actor who had come for an audition. He used the term 'sketches'; this is what roughly knocked together outlines of décor are called in the theatre.

We tried 'sketches' of make-up; a beard, eyebrows, tightening the face with a special sort of paper to make wrinkles so that you get an old man. You can even get a very old man.

We got an old man. But Lear? . . .

I needed another sort of 'sketch' – the oppression of distracted ideas, the black chaos of tyranny.

And more than that: suffering turning to sympathy for the next man, and then to sympathy for the most distant men.

And yet more sketches: the healing of a wound; the thawing of spiritual life; the contempt for power. And so on.

I WAS LOOKING for a Lear who would be a kindred spirit, an actor with imagination, a lover of strange decisions. The four arithmetical rules are little help here.

Today it is the fashion to talk about a contemporary style of acting which is based on restraint and laconism. Of course these are admirable qualities. But did they determine even to the tiniest degree the art of Mikhail Chekhov, Charlie Chaplin, Tarkhanov and Ernst Busch? Of course not. Their acting was distinguished not by their method of performance but by the strength of their personality. They were first and foremost 'exceptional', unlike anyone else.

Evidently serious talk would begin with the first actor who did not tell me that 'You can't act a king; the actors who surround him must act him'.

IN THE FIRST scene Lear's face must not be visible; only the mask of power. The change in his position is illogical. He is completely uninterested in all details of human life. He is blind and deaf to everything that is natural.

There is no hint of the real suffering and then the thoughtful eyes which appear later, when the mask has disappeared.

I repeat: at first it is a mask of power rather than regal serenity.

THE FILM HAD come to an end. We had been watching one of our best historical films.

'I don't understand,' I overheard one of the audience say, 'None of the characters were like people and they did not walk and talk like humans at all ...'

'You ignoramus,' retorted his friend. 'It was a stylized production!'

ARTICLES ABOUT THE Dark Ages, paintings by Holbein, Goya and Picasso do not help.

My task was to relate the screen not to painting, even the greatest painting, but to reality, to convince the audience of the actual existence of a world such as Lear's, which is not like prehistoric

Britain (although who knows what that was like?), nor Shakespearean England, nor our century.

It is like all times.

How was one to achieve this? So that each member of the audience recognized that there was a similar situation in his time, that such a thing happened to him, a similarity recognizable not by the costumes or the way of life, but by the essence of the action, by the thoughts which tormented him and by the emotions which he himself had experienced.

It is the system of living links which must be similar, not the outward appearances taken one by one. Sometimes the links are very complex, sometimes extremely simple. Here is an example of a simple situation: someone calls and someone else answers. This is also *Lear*.

THE PLAY ITSELF is disorderly with an ill-assorted collection of material, a dissimilarity of styles, an abruptness in the frequent changes of scene. This is all the unity – not of unartistic style – but of life, of history.

Marx wrote that history repeats itself, first as tragedy and then as farce. In *Lear* there are a large number of such repetitions. Tragedy and farce are so entangled at the dusk of civilization that they are almost indistinguishable.

Lear has no end – at least there is no finale in the play: none of the usual solemn trumpets of tragedy, or magnificent burials. The bodies, even of kings, are carried out under conditions of war; nobody even says a few elevated words. The time for words is over.

The people that remain are scorched and tempered by fire. They watch the dawn of a new, inhumanly difficult epoch, life struggling to rise up again from the ruins.

Making a film does not mean arriving at a specific time in a specific place (a rehearsal room, studio) and working with a team of people with various specializations who have been gathered together specially for this work. It means living for several years under the persistent influence of Shakespeare's picture of life, which you see as yet only dimly, one feature at a time, but the main point is the 'all-embracing thought' (Dostoyevsky) – which you take as the most important. And every day, everything you see, hear, read and learn convinces you of the burning necessity of displaying this thought, making a picture of a life which really exists.

Otherwise professional work becomes drudgery.

EVENTS ARE SET in motion not by heroes but by groups of men. They are fused together like blocks of human relationships, like structures of life.

And so before they are separated out as characters, the dukes of Cornwall and Albany enter with their wives, children and followers; then the courtiers and the soldiers follow.

It is a block of ice with twenty officials frozen inside it. They are all the same, with a single official's face. The cut of their clothes and caste of their chains of office round their necks are identical. The expression of terror before the King is also identically moulded.

In the same way in lessons during national service the conventional marks of the army fuse into the conventional background; generals are only mentioned in passing, their personalities are not yet taken into account.

Let us imagine a lesson in world history where conventional marks of state, and of power – both military and diplomatic – are moved across the map of time.

I WAS TRYING to grasp the outlines of the shots and to fix them with these notes. I condensed associations of thought until they were visible – the thought had to be materialized; once it was transformed on to a piece of film it ceased to exist as so many words. Otherwise it was nothing more than a piece of pavement art.

Working on a Shakespearean tragedy reminds one of archaeology; the search is always going deeper, beneath the limits of the top layers; the whole is usually reconstructed from fragments. But the strange thing is that the deeper you dig, the more contemporary everything that comes to the surface seems as it reveals its significance.

The fragment relates to the past but it is as if the plate was broken today; it is possible that just such a plate will be broken tomorrow.

One must show not some single unifying theme in the work (there isn't one), but the path of exploration into human nature and the process of history – man making history and history making man.

WHAT LOOKS AT first glance as if it is going to come out best on the screen is invariably the worst. It is not difficult to shoot a storm for an effective scene on film but there is a catch here straightaway: the realistic portrayal of very bad weather (even the worst possible weather!) is far removed from Shakespeare's poetry. No quantity of fire brigades and wind machines will 'ensure', as film administrators will say, the image.

The visual construction of a scene must not be on one level alone; the metaphorical significance here is more important than the literal. This applies also to the sound: it is not so much the noise of the wind and thunder that one must be able to hear, but the voice of evil celebrating a victory.

According to the text the act opens with wild animals: they hide in the swamps, sniffing the approaching storm and the evil deeds which people will commit during that night: the predators are more merciful than Goneril and Regan.

Sometimes the landscape is clearly visible, at other times it completely loses all definition: Lear and the Fool wander about both in a definite region (if one wants to one can find it on an old map – somewhere in southern Britain, between Gloucester's house and the road to Dover) and at the same time in the chaos of the battling elements at the hour of judgement.

However even with apocalyptic hyperboles there are enough life-like details. One must begin with them: reality is the best guide. I would like to draw attention to one of these details which I see as very important, carrying a great deal of weight.

According to Cordelia, her father spent the night on straw, among swine and beggars. The lonely hovel out in the open is not a decoration, an insignificant bit of knocked together scenery, but a symbol of the last open hearth in life, a fading remnant of animal warmth, a minute haven amidst eternal darkness, cold and fierce cruelty.

The storm has thrown one who stood on the highest rung of the social ladder to this place, to the lowest point of existence. Here in the thick of this miserable life where dirt, straw, beggars and swine are all muddled together, Lear asks the question:

> Is man no more than this?
> – Thou art the thing itself – unaccommodated man is no more but such a poor, bare, forked animal as thou art.

In *Hamlet* the words about not being a pipe on which the king's men can play whenever they like seemed to be more significant (though of course such comparisons are relative) than the famous 'To be or not to be! The most important part of the storm scene seems to me to be the speech about 'unaccommodated' man rather than the rhetorical 'Blow, winds'.

The background against which these words are spoken (and against which such thoughts could arise) are just as substantial as the fact that when Rodion Raskolnikov (*Crime and Punishment*) was making his plans it was a very hot summer, unbearably stuffy, the staircase in his house was crooked and covered in cats' droppings, and the room in which he lived looked like a coffin.

If it were possible to achieve unity of spiritual and material life on the screen by a literal reproduction of such descriptions, the solution of the problem would not be too difficult.

'BLOW WIND! Blow until your cheeks crack!/Pour rain in buckets'[1] – even if spoken with all possible feeling and at the top of one's voice it does not convey the impact of the original. The Russian translation (in all versions) is not comparable to the triumphal 'Blow, winds, and crack your cheeks! rage! blow!' . . .

I have seen great actors play Lear but I have never yet been lucky enough to hear the magnificence of this alliteration. But I have heard something similar and of equal weight in the tragic *forte* passages in Shostakovich's symphonies.

In this scene the voice should belong to music. Music is nearer to the original. What sort of music should it be? . . . The rumbling of darkness moving over the earth. Music from the past, man's pre-history? . . . Or a foreboding of the future, of what might happen if the powers of evil are not held in check?

PASTERNAK CONSIDERED that Shakespeare's genius was most evident in his prose, that his verse was often overloaded with metaphors, and too complex. He thought that the flow of unrhymed blank verse was no more than a method of speed writing: the poet was forced to hurry and this was the most convenient shorthand for his thoughts and feelings.

Pasternak approached each of his translations with a different attitude. He wrote in one of his letters to me,

> In a work such as *Faust* which is directed at me, whether from the pages of a book or from the stage, it is enough that it should be clear to me, that I should understand it whether I am reading or in the audience. But for the objective, realistically performed Shakespeare play on stage you need a completely different sort of understanding, a different viewpoint and a different degree of intelligibility. Here the actors are not addressing me, but are throwing sentences out to each other. It means little if I understand them; I must be convinced by the obvious visual evidence that they understand each other to the last word.

[1] This is a literal translation of Pasternak's verse since Kozintsev is concerned here with the Russian translation [trans.].

I always considered that it was essential for me to capture this lightness, smoothness and fluency of the text; and I strived to achieve a visual comprehensibility which was neither literal, nor off the point, but directly related to the area of the stage. And I was always upset and annoyed when producers diminished, suppressed and broke up this essential fluency and involuntary quality of the language, which my translations have by no means captured, for the sake of unrelated and ephemeral ideas, for the sake of the acceptability of these works within the changing concepts of contemporary society.

Pasternak had in mind the editors' requirements: 'They forced me to make these translations so close to the original that the two coincided literally, but not out of respect for the original but in order to have something to refer to and someone to blame in case of argument'.

Obvious visual evidence; action within a real area, not within a literary and confined text; fluency and smoothness – this is what I want to achieve on the screen.

From a letter to L. E. Pinsky *August 1968*

Dear Leonid Yephimovich!

I was very interested to read the manuscript which you were kind enough to send me. The chapter on *Lear* is excellent. It deals with an enormous amount of research material with complete freedom; everything is related; the theme and situation, the heroes and the events, the history of the subject matter and our contemporary art. You develop your main theme with confidence and frequently divert from it to new subjects in order to come back to it again, having strengthened your idea with generalizations. It all seems to be firmly linked together, showing in conclusion a universal picture of the tragic.

The flow of thought reminds one of Hegel's constructional architecture.

The completeness of the conception makes me reluctant to pick holes in it, to make any critical comments. This is an original work with a lot that is accomplished; the chapter on *Lear* helped me to discover more not only about the subject of research but more especially about the researcher. However, while following the thread of your thought I began to think about Shakespeare in my own way. This seems to me the merit of the book.

I do not believe that there is one single correct interpretation of Lear. The more deeply you study the text the less clear the essence of the tragic, the secret of its influence becomes.

My work has begun to torment me. The difficulty of my position is that thinking like you about the nature of heroic identity I do not want to show anything visual which is connected with the idea of poetic heroism;

1a. Act I sc. i: Yuri Yarvet as Lear.

2. [*overleaf*] Act III sc. iv: the hovel – 'Is man no more than this?'

1b. Act I sc. i: Goneril (Elsa Radzin), Regan (Galina Volchek) and Cordelia (Valentina Shendrikova).

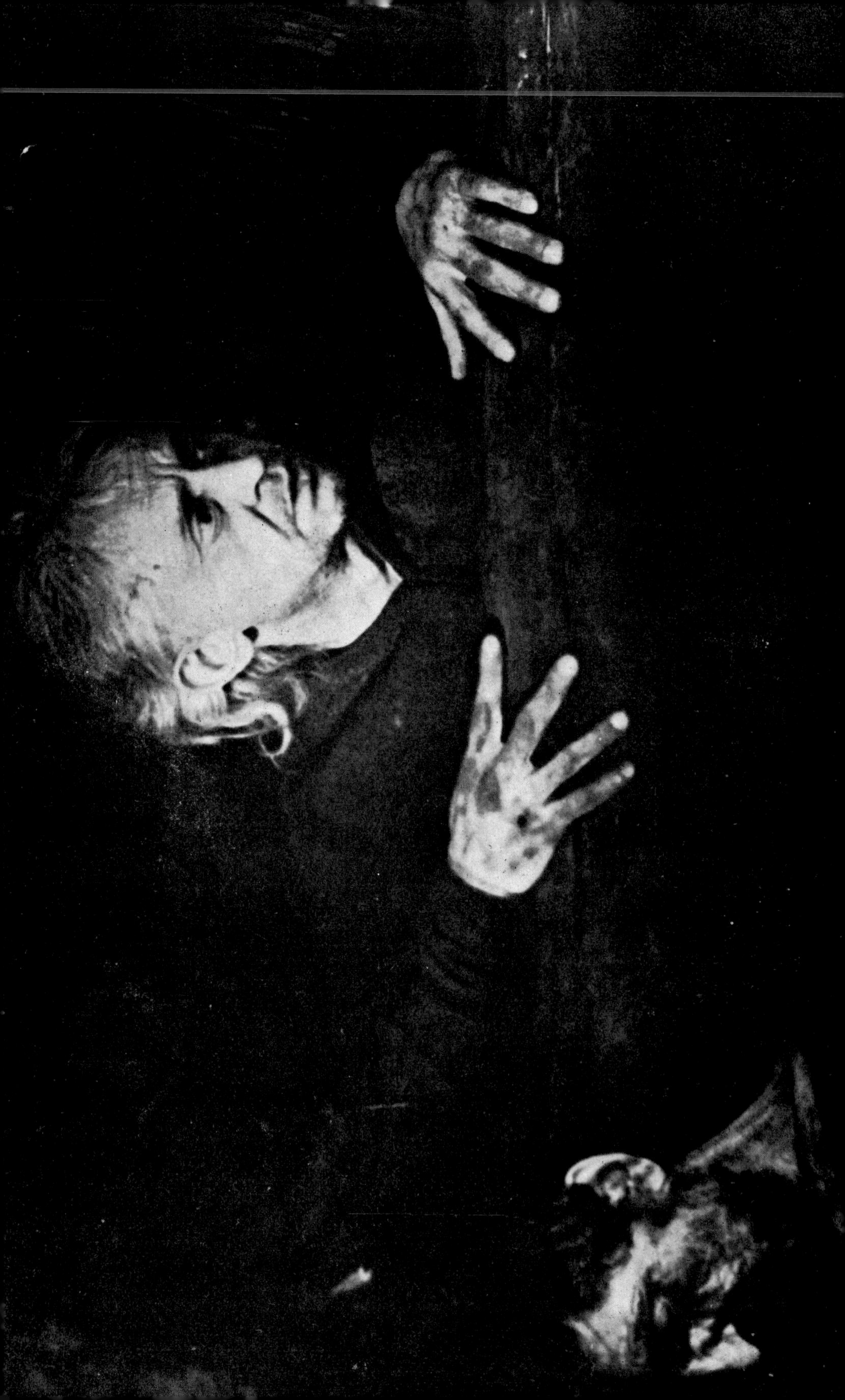

I do not want to allow anything at all 'titanic', 'mighty' or even 'elevated' (in appearance) on the screen. I am also against showing scenes from the heroes' everyday lives – turning Shakespeare into Walter Scott.

I have nothing to show for it as yet. A large quantity of thoughts and methods but all, alas, only in my head; in art it is a well-known fact that intentions mean nothing.

In conclusion I will allow myself one criticism. Do you not dispute the idea of power a little too decisively? It always seemed to me very important especially before a war. In the heat of my first experiment with the theatre production of *Lear*, I stormed the romantic treatment, and without qualifications or subtleties I showed power and despotism as the basis of the tragic dénouement. I made stupid mistakes and now I see a lot of it differently but the idea has remained.

Without the theme of power Lear's mad speeches about the functions of a king become abstract. Shakespeare's generalizations are always related to the particular.

From a letter to L. E. Pinsky *September 1968*

I understand this idea as a network of certain defined relationships, a network which was both created by Lear and which created him. These relationships have arisen from the dishonest and inhuman elements in man but Lear has ceased to see this – he has been blinded by kingly power; the people who have accepted this power as just are also blind. The picture (in the portrayal of the literal as opposed to metaphorical figure of blind Gloucester) is universal:

> ''Tis the time's plague, when madmen
> lead the blind.'

As far as 'edification' is concerned, alas, the whole of *Lear* is edifying, and to what a degree! I do not think one should worry about this.

INVENTED ELABORATIONS do not make up for cuts – this is a thought to which I constantly returned; the solution seemed to be easy: one should keep as much of the text as possible. However it was not at all easy. Experience dictated otherwise. It seemed that there had not been one occasion when the filming of a scene from a Shakespeare play based on the text had been more effective than exactly the same scene in the theatre. The best parts of Orson Welles' films seemed to me those which had no mention in the play: Iago in the iron cage hoisted up in the air (the prologue to *Othello*); the coffin of enormous proportions which is dragged along the ramparts (Falstaff's funeral).

Akira Kurosawa completely re-wrote all the dialogues in *Macbeth* (*The Throne of Blood*).

If the poetic structure of the words in a particular place remains intangible and this place has to be 'set up for the cinema' (broken down into long-shots and close-ups and positioned in front of the lens, etc.), I feel that it is awkward and unnecessary to turn the play into a film script.

But when you discover, in the very poetry, seedlings of what can be developed into dynamic visual reality, the whole business begins to have a point and one's work succeeds. There is no need to invent anything, all one has to do is to show what is there. Inventions ('on the same theme', or 'for the occasion') are easy to discard; belief in the necessity of such contrivances soon wanes.

The greater the detail and exactitude of life-like action with which you show what is contained within the text – and only in the text! – the less important the words themselves become. The reason for this paradoxical situation is that part of the text does not consist of conversational remarks and dialogue although it is spoken aloud in conversation by the characters. Tolstoy's criticism of Shakespeare's language (that his characters speak with the voice of the author) is true to a certain extent. However it is just such speeches, which do not have characteristics peculiar to a particular role that open up the picture of the world, the atmosphere of the age and the tide of events. These words illiminate themselves as they become the reality of life and of nature.

ONE MUST FIND one's material in the book itself, rather than invent it. However this is only the ultimate aim. 'To find' is no easy task. You read the play until it falls into holes, reading until the familiar places seem to have lost their meaning. It is not easy to read into it what is relevant to life and of everyday importance. Every director has his own method of approach. As far as I am concerned experience has taught me that in order to overcome the desire to invent I have to start by doing a great deal of inventing.

And so I usually start by 'having a good inventing session' and dream up heaven knows what. Evidently the sins of my youth as 'the gadget co-ordinator' (this is what they called the director in the Manifesto of the Eccentric Theatre in 1922), as one of the founders of FEKS,[1] have not yet exhausted themselves. The 'beautiful inventions' then fall away from the play like a husk and I grow ashamed when I remember what I had thought up. But all the same they serve their purpose. Something in the play begins to look different – where once I only heard rhetoric now action and reality

[1] The Factory of the Eccentric Actor, a group set up in Leningrad by Yutkevich, Kozintsev and Trauberg in the early twenties [trans.].

has appeared. In order to see this, I had to change my angle of vision, to forget for a while what I considered to be of fundamental importance and to move the less important to the fore.

It is just what looks just like being easy to dispense with from a cinematic point of view that one cannot cut – the heroes thinking aloud. The personalities of the main characters seem to be quite well enough defined without these passages, the characters' actions speak for themselves, and soliloquies are a theatrical form.

But, nevertheless it is these very 'superfluous passages' which are most important, representing the intellectual atmosphere of the action, their individual outlook on life; Lear quarrels not only with the other characters but with the very laws of creation, with history; without these passages Edmund becomes a common villain, Edgar a conventional figure; if Cordelia is deprived of her rhymed aphorisms (is this an ancient convention?) she loses part of her poetry, her innocent charm.

The characters have not only their own trains of thought but also their own kind of fundamental theme; they are obsessed by it, with all the force of passion. Dostoyevsky called this situation 'being obsessed with an idea'. They are all obsessed with their idea – Lear, Cordelia, Edgar, Edmund, and blind Gloucester.

In Lear it is shown as a never-ending road traversing whole layers of thought. 'Cut to the brains', he forces his way through to the very depths, to the central all-embracing paradox.

The 'superfluous' passages are the main characters in close-up.

The advantage of the cinema over the theatre is not that you can even have horses, but that you can stare closer into a man's eyes; otherwise it is pointless to set up a cine camera for Shakespeare.

One must construct the script from whole blocks of action rather than from isolated little scenes. The outlines of the blocks become visible, representing strata of life: echoing steps in empty stone courtyards, the ceremonial parade of corpse-like courtiers, taking up their positions according to rank; backs turned as one man on him who has fallen out of favour; wide expanses laid waste by servility and fear. The government cabinet of wax figures.

This is the world of the King. Without such an atmosphere Lear's whole behaviour at the beginning of the play is unjustified.

One cannot 'justify' the King's actions in psychological terms (Tolstoy was right) but seen across the expanse of time they are natural.

How is one to define the diminutive world of Gloucester? Perhaps a kind of fifteenth-century *Nest of Gentlefolk*.[1] Walls overgrown with

[1] A novel by Turgenev [trans.].

ivy, a pond with stagnant, weed-covered water, an old servant knitting a woollen stocking, a gardener pottering about in the unkempt park, logs crackling in the fire-place, and the lord of the manor dabbling in astrology in his old age . . .

It is a pity that one can't have a cuckoo cuckooing in the old wooden clock or the far-away sound of a grand piano floating through from distant rooms.

It is in these comfortable patriarchal surroundings that the lord of the manor has his eyes gouged out.

Beyond the halls of the palace and the rooms of the estates, beyond the fortifications and fences are the villages of the poor, the fields and peasants' vegetable strips, the well-trodden paths; beggars wandering about in search of food.

Beggars, roads, vegetable strips and fields are inscribed on the universe. Clouds rage over the world, a scourge of fire thrashes the earth.

Black, charred logs, metal fragments and ash are the end of the story. The survivors return to the ashy ruins and life goes on.

ALEXANDER BLOK WROTE that verse is a covering stretched between the spikes of several rhymes. I can begin to write a script when these spikes – the points of visual images – are clearly visible.

The rest is easy: to throw a covering over them 4500 metres long.

IS IT POSSIBLE to compare the summits of visual images with the endings of lines of poetry? Perhaps not. In *Lear* there are no keys to close scenes with but rather the alternation of opposites, the overturning of what has been before by what follows. If you have this and rhyme then you have 'probably a deeper meaning in the pauses' (Marina Tsvetayeva).

A FEW YEARS ago I spent a whole evening trying to convince the critic and theatre expert, I. G. Mochalova to give up the idiotic idea of becoming an assistant film director.

'You will lose all concept of day and night, you will be snowed under with work; every day there will be a panic, an emergency,' I told her. 'Look at the telegrams which are sent to the film studio and from the studio; there are only two versions: 'We are threatened with total breakdown' and 'We are on the verge of catastrophe'.

I could not convince her. Mochalova worked with me on *Hamlet* and was now gathering the team together for *Lear*.

The first conversation I had with Donatas Banionis convinced me that we had a Duke of Albany; with Elsa Radzin as Goneril and Galina Volchek as Regan we could set sail with a light heart. I do not like screen tests; the more candidates there are the less clear it becomes which is most suitable. The first (and most valuable) impression of an image completely fades.

Screen tests remind me of Arkady Averchenko's story of how a drunk got home: putting the key against his stomach he rushed at the front door hoping that the key would fall into the keyhole.

Mochalova brought an excellent Cornwall from Kalinin, A. A. Vokach; Oswald was also quickly found – A. V. Petrenko; his profile alone was worth a lot. These parts were all instantly settled.

– But what about Lear?

Mochalova had already scoured several towns, we had looked at hundreds of photographs and done a large number of tests. But we still did not have a Lear.

Of course I understood that no artist would be capable of immediately creating such a figure; but I understood equally well that if he had already played this part on the stage, this would only confuse the issue. So we had to do serious tests. And this is what we did: we rehearsed with each actor for two or three weeks; we started shooting only after serious preparation.

From a letter to one of the cast *March 1968*

. . . the team have started work; as always there are a great many complications: the cameraman, Gritsus, is in Vilna, the designer, Virsaladze, is in Moscow; each have a trail of past uncompleted work behind them, something that needs finishing off, but meanwhile our time for preparation is already running out.

I agree with you that the beginning of the film has enormous significance. One wants to introduce the world of tragedy with great force, with the din of the alarum bell. In other words, before Lear's entrance to create that very atmosphere of tyranny and madness (of course not in the pathological sense) in the context of which the behaviour of the ruler of this particular world seems in its own way quite natural. The King must be raised to an unattainable height and then cast down so that he can count with his bones the steps of the whole staircase which he himself constructed. He must fall from the heavens to the very depths not even of human but of animal existence.

There should be no idealization of his image in the first scene. All the rest of the play is retribution. The punishment is inhumanly cruel, but the man condemned to torment is by no means innocent.

From a letter to Dmitri Shostakovich *May 1968*

Dear Dmitri Dmitriyevich,

It seems that the usual period has elapsed (somewhere between five and seven years) before I ask you once again for a favour, to compose the music for a film. The film in question this time is *King Lear*.

We will begin filming at the end of the year. You will be required to take part towards the end of the following year, i.e. 1969.

Naturally I hope very much that you will say yes. To name a few mitigating circumstances: there will be less music in this film than there was in *Hamlet* and there won't be any noise of horses' hooves.[1]

[1] On the rough tape-recordings of the sound track of *Hamlet* it turned out that there were a lot of sound effects and that they were too loud. 'If it is a question of choosing between music and the text,' Dmitri Shostakovich said, 'I agree that Shakespeare's words should drown the music. But I am not prepared to agree to horses' hooves drowning the music.'

Chapter Seven

THE TRANSITION FROM working on a script to starting production is terrible. Nothing is ever ready. The first costumes (prepared without Virsaladze), the sketches for the make-up (the Lenfilm Studios had a crisis: they had run out of hair for wigs) were a series of blows, shocks, attacks of despair. Whenever the door of the make-up room opened I was ready to die of shame: would an outsider see this mess?

'It is never any different,' said the producer, Shapiro, in an attempt to soothe me (we also worked together on *Hamlet*), 'Every film (particularly historical ones) begins like this – with false beards, fancy dress, and a feeling of shame. After a while it all falls into place.

But what if it did not fall into place?

We had the first finished costume. I collected it and took it to Moscow. The dressing rooms of the Bolshoi Theatre were in a state of chaos: the première of *Spartacus*[1] was approaching. I met a tormented Virsaladze – yesterday they had got the colours of the material wrong, tonight he had to copy them out all over again (it never rains but it pours). While the concubines of the patricians and the slave girls were changing, our costume was pinned up on a dummy. Virsaladze looked at it for exactly one minute.

'There is no point in discussing it,' he said.

The slave girls and the concubines were now ready; they filed out, wrapped in tunics, walked up to the mirror and took up ballet positions.

We continued our conversation. Our only finished costume turned out to be no good. We both agreed. This one circumstance, a mutuality of conception, made me feel happier. The most important thing is that with Virsaladze, almost without mentioning work, but talking about it all the same, one can sit down in a corner and chat about anything, and criticize what we both do not like. So, between one thing and another, in the course of an hour we advanced the outlines of the costumes forward by four centuries – from the eleventh to the fifteenth (that is in the most general outlines).

I have a clear picture of the filthy back street where Lenfilm's costume workshop is. It is a heap of disordered piles of material, thick

[1] The ballet with music by Khatchaturian [trans.].

felts, evil-smelling leather, fur. It is so full of smoke that you can't breathe. Virsaladze with a papirosa[1] between his teeth ripped a finished costume apart at the seams although it had already been fitted and, without listening to the cutter's explanations, pinned the material together himself; perching on the edge of a box of plywood he picked a newspaper up off the floor and sketched the pattern with a stub end of pencil.

I began to feel better.

LEAR WILL OF course have a costume. But will anyone be found who will fit it?

Another actor arrived, summoned by us for a screen test. He was a talented and very experienced man. And once again, as he walked through the door he said 'One can't act a king . . .'

How much harm has this saying done. All right, the surrounding actors would play the king. They would play him to the best of their ability, with all their might throughout the play. So much the better. But the king also plays those that surround him, even when he does not notice them and does not pay them the slightest bit of attention.

Who said that you can't judge by appearances? You can. Is it really true that the appearance of poets does not resemble their poetry. Look at Anna Akhmatova, Mayakovsky, Yesenin.

In Shakespeare's plays – *Lear*, *Hamlet*, *Othello* – they are all not only kings, princes, warriors, but also poets. Poetry is in their blood. Here it seems was the difficulty.

The film had undoubtedly to be life-like. I was convinced of this. But between the life-like and the trivia of everyday life there is a great gulf fixed. Would I be able to keep from falling over the edge?

A DIRECTOR CAN (and must) help the interpreter of a role a great deal. But there is one thing which he is powerless to do – to substitute his own personality for the actor's. The actor's personality is by no means the same as it is in real life. It can happen that these two natures are almost contradictory.

In order not to repeat the same word over and over again in these diaries, I sometimes write 'actor' and sometimes 'interpreter' – it is clear what I am talking about. But the fundamental meanings of these two words define two different kinds of gift, two dissimilar qualities. An interpreter could not become Lear.

[1] A popular type of Russian cigarette with a built-in cardboard mouthpiece (now rather old-fashioned) [trans.].

The relationship between director and actor is very delicate in this situation. You cannot cut out an image; you can only develop it, or rather, achieve it through suffering – suffering together.

WE HAD ALREADY shot several thousand metres of screen tests for the title role. Almost a whole film. Some excellent actors had taken part in it.

'Why don't you make up your mind and settle for one of them?' all my colleagues tried to persuade me. 'You can't go wrong. They are great artists, they have yet to show themselves. It is time a decision was made. We need to make his actual costume, to perfect his make-up and to start lengthy and serious rehearsals – the end result will be Lear.'

No it wouldn't be Lear. None of them looked like him.

What rubbish! How could you define such a likeness. Had I ever seen a photograph of him or met him? Could one talk about a likeness such as this?

But all the same not one of the shots contained the least hint of a resemblance. The ability to become Lear depends not on a similarity of outward appearance but on a kinship of spiritual substance, the constitution of the actor's inner world.

The others shrugged their shoulders. When I was young this kind of talk was called bloody-mindedness (and I called it this myself).

Only one person, Mochalova, fully understood. We both heard 'we are threatened with total breakdown', 'we are on the verge of catastrophe'.

Someone told us there was a Lear in Vladivostok. We summoned him and he bore no resemblance to Lear.

There are some productions which are prepared for very gradually – you make other films but the unfinished work lies in note form; extracts of documents, thoughts, shots. The files grow and the notes continue. This is how I conceived *The Way Out*, a film about Tolstoy's last days. It had already been scheduled by Lenfilm for 1966 but *Lear* seemed more ready. However it turned out that the work on the two films seemed unconsciously linked. I recognized certains aspects of Lear in the man who did not like Shakespeare, particularly in his personal tragedy.

I do not mean of course a resemblance – whether outward or inward – but the calibre of the man, the force of personality; a kinship of living substance.

How is one to define his age? An elderly man? He should not be prosperous or well-padded. A wizened old man? Even worse – there is no question of that. A bowed old man?[1] No, he does not bow before anyone or anything. Nothing could bow him.

He should be very old but at the same time not at all decrepit: all his spiritual powers are there, and to what an extent!

Tolstoy galloped straight through the wood, avoiding the road, on his white arab mare, Delira. He was over eighty. He spurred on his horse, through a clearing, jumped a small hurdle which turned out to be a ravine. He soon decided that he had no right to own a horse any more. After all he was the same as everyone else, no different from his fellow men.

And so he made his decision; he, whom all could distinguish from other men, except as far as his height was concerned.

Meyerhold described how on arriving at Yasnaya Polyana, he waited for Tolstoy to come out with bated breath and nearly missed him. He had fixed his eyes on the top of the doorway, convinced that a giant would appear, but out came an old man of medium height.

LEAR SAYS THAT he is recognizable as a king at first sight, that he is 'every inch a king'. Illustrators have taken this phrase literally; they have produced an enormously tall old man, one of the race of titans.

The phrase is ironical. The force of irony is one of the qualities his mind has. The greatness of his personality lies not in his appearance but in his boldness of thought, his power of spiritual response.

What does his thought concentrate on? At first on what he considered to be the basis of the universe – the uniqueness of his own personality as the symbol of power. He is heroic, if one is going to use the word here, in that having once been the overlord, he recognizes and lays completely bare the absurdity of power, the worthlessness of its actions and the falsehood of words.

Is he a heroic personality from the beginning? No, *Lear* is rather the tragedy of a personality who flattered himself into thinking he was heroic. He becomes great only when he understands that he is like any other man. Have there ever been despots who were capable of recognizing this at the end of their lives?

At the beginning of the action one cannot yet recognize Lear: one can see a mask of power in an abstract and illusory form. It is as if his words and actions were near to the divine, beyond the comprehension of the ordinary man. Divinity is suddenly transformed into

[1] Literally translated 'of bowed age'.

blindness and deafness, the lifeless eyes of tyranny, the dragon's roar of despotism. His extreme cruelty, his condemnations without trial and without investigation, all these banishments 'Dower'd with our curse, and stranger'd with our oath', promises of death for attempting to behave as befits a man – what is elevated, or great about this?

Marcel Marceau does a sketch called *The Mask Shop*: a customer walks up to the counter in order to buy an identity; he tries on one mask after another, puts them to his face and looks at himself in the mirror, takes them off and tries another. But the last one that he tries on he cannot take off. It has grown on to his face. The actor is stricken with terror, he grabs hold of the edges of the mask with both hands, strains with all his might and the mask suffocates him.

Lear tears off the mask of power, and throws it away. Only then does his face become visible: suffering has made him beautiful and human.

I AM NEVER drawn by biblical associations. Neither Michelangelo's Titans, nor Blake's gods, soaring over the universe, give me any help; none of them would have proclaimed: 'Ha! we are all men of little worth'. Titans for this tragedy are a stereotype just as 'Hamletism' is in *Hamlet*.

However in one of Michelangelo's frescoes there is a figure which reminds me of Lear: in the gallery of faces for *The Last Day of Judgement* the painter included a self portrait; he drew his own face on the skin torn from the body of Saint Bartholomew. The mad king's soliloquy about the administration of justice in his kingdom seems to me to be just such a self portrait of his own power painted on his own skin which was stripped from him while he was still alive.

THE PLAY BEGINS with the theatrical – fine dress, pretence, props (the map, coats of arms) contrived speeches and assumed poses. The end of the play has stepped into the real world, on to the dirty blood-soaked earth. The wind has long ago torn the theatrical costumes; the rain has washed the make-up from the actors' faces.

The meeting between Lear and Cordelia after Lear has gone mad is elevated not by their circumstances, but because of what takes place in a human soul when it has rid itself of all that is base and illusory. The scene is full of poetry, and because of this one must film it in the most prosaic, everyday surroundings; the sort of surroundings in which it could really have happened.

There is a war. In the square of the town which has just been captured tired soldiers unharness their horses, light fires and bandage their wounds.

How would an old man travel in time of war? Most probably on an army waggon; they would lay him down on the straw and cover him with a horse cloth.

There is dirt, piles of weapons and horse dung. A young woman leans against an old man.

In the play Cordelia's doctor orders the band to start playing so that harmony can heal Lear's distracted soul. But what about attaching the Fool to the soldiers instead of the musicians – he is ragged and worn out after wandering endlessly along the hard roads of war together with his master? He has finally reached the square, more dead than alive.

The mournful pipe plays; the exhausted, bloodstained soldiers warm themselves over the fire; the stable boys search for a place to water their horses; a very old man climbs off a waggon and kneels before a young woman; she also kneels and asks for his blessing.

There is a gust of wind like the beat of a wing.

All one needs is to get it out of one's head that the woman is the Queen of France and the old man the King of Britain; this does not mean anything any more.

IT IS WORTH thinking about what happened 'before the entrance from the wings', to use the theatrical expression, and one finds that there are no wings left. People walk not on to a stage but into life. Even the most abstract metaphor of the storm can and must become a tangible part of life.

But how? By what method? . . . I saw clearly the possibilities but as yet had not found a way of expressing them.

I found Lear's wanderings among the beggars easier to understand, even down to the details. They are shots containing the bitter truth which the writers of the last century also learnt. They did not use gentle water colour tints for the portrayal of *The House of the Dead*. There is only one colour – the grey of prison uniforms, the gloomy darkness of the barracks, and the impenetrable mud of the halting places.

The content of the tragedy, when I thought about these scenes, seemed to be so simple and clear. Simple and clear like our proverbs. There are so many which fit this occasion.

'We are all people, but not all men.'

'But are there no people among the people?'

'There is a great crowd but no people.'

And here is a definition of the action:

'Through people they emerge among the people.' 'If we have enough patience we will become people.'

There is the less optimistic one, 'If there is rye in the fields there will be lies among the people.'

I HAVE WRITTEN about the scale of spiritual movement in *Lear*, about the power of response, the depth of wounds cutting to the brain. It is like a cry amidst complete silence, a scream in wordless emptiness.

There is no need to treat Lear's speech to the sky and the elements as rhetoric: who else could he talk to in this dumb lifeless world in which he himself threatened men with execution for speaking the truth, for speaking humanely?

So he gets into conversation with a storm cloud, with the wind. His interlocutors reply perhaps a little loudly, but the conversation establishes itself as a dialogue rather than a monologue. There are many similar places in Lear's role: he argues with his grief and exchanges words with the sore in his heart. He has to communicate with someone.

These places should be played as if they were nothing out of the ordinary – naturally and decisively. They establish an important boundary for the image. Dostoyevsky called it fantasy, 'fantastic realism'. This is what translates triviality and thoughtlessness on to another plane.

In art it is not easy to show an interest in everyday trivia; Daumier illustrated 'physiological sketches' and Nekrasov also produced them. The very insignificance of life, conceived as a tragic force, contributed much to Russian art. Vulgarity, boiling up to life's extremities, boiling over the edge into the eternity of time and space, is insepar-able from Gogol's tragic power; the wind in Blok's 'The Twelve' brings both the husk of the seed and fragments of gutter talk, the trivial details merge into 'a single musical pressure' (the poet's own definition) with the mighty step of the vanguard, the vision of Christ.

The whole of Dostoyevsky consists of such links and intangible transitions.

'I grasp at every straw and synthesize all the trivia of life,' Meyerhold wrote.

The significance in Shakespeare of life-like details in their most insignificant and debased form is enormous. When working on his translations of Shakespeare, Pasternak discovered signs of hurried composition in the original: uncorrected slips of the pen and obvious repetition. This fact in itself seemed very important to him, because it allowed him not only to learn more about the author but also to imagine the conditions under which he worked: 'His realism was given birth and first saw the light of day not in the seclusion of a study but in the untidy morning room of an inn charged with life, like gunpowder.'

If one restricted oneself to looking at nothing but the insignificant outward objects what would one see? On the other hand to constrict oneself to the so called breadth of the 'most important' nevertheless shows a poverty of thought. You cannot escape the life which is charged with everyday details; except that its destructive explosive force has left the powder far behind.

The golden crown is a blatant symbol of power, the sort of prop which theatres like to flaunt; Shakespeare treats power like a piece of commonplace inhumanity, the oppressive ordinary quality of grasping for power.

SUFFERING OCCUPIES a large part of this play; sometimes it is evoked by physical torture, sometimes by mental torture. Lear's feeling of shame is almost unbearable. His awakening after his illness is both reality and metaphor: his natural human feelings have awakened and the first of them is shame. He who was once a king finds in himself the courage to kneel down before his youngest daughter and ask for forgiveness.

Goneril, Regan, Edmund, and the Duke of Cornwall are not only heartless but also shameless. Lear's white hair means nothing to Oswald. He would relieve himself in someone's living room if he had not been afraid of being discovered and punished for indecency: for the outward violation of outward laws of decency.

They all lost their shame long ago. The elder sisters harbour not love for Edmund but fierce desire. They are ready to tear each other apart for their lover. One cannot portray this on the stage. On the screen, while the war is raging, one must unceremoniously show dogs mating against a background of fire, steel and blood.

These roles must not be played by handsome young actresses and they should be as far removed as possible from sex-symbols, from sophisticated intellectual sexuality; it would be shameful if these particular scenes contributed to a 'box-office success'. It is better to dispense with attractions; there is nothing attractive about the play – it is dirty, foul and vulgar.

Shame humanizes men. People flock together out of shamelessness.

It is a help in building a career to lose one's shame; shamelessness moves mountains.

In Tolstoy's diaries of his last years the same phrase is often repeated: 'It is shameful to live as I do'.

From a letter to an actor *August 1968*

I should like to discuss with you some of the danger spots which cropped up during the rehearsals.

Even before we met together I told you that it is premature to begin work by reducing the text (and cutting). I want you to discover what catches your imagination in the text, what stirs your thoughts and feelings. But it is not simply a question of finding a number of pegs. You wrote, 'I am overcome by horror at the thought of this mountainous role'. It is a natural feeling. Every actor who has thought about Lear has felt the same.

Climbing a mountain is hard and agonizing. But what else can you do? It is after all a mountain. You can of course take a different course and compare it (in your own mind) to a small hill; then the climbing of it will not present any difficulty. But if you do this the mountain will remain on one side, far away. We will not even reach its slopes.

One must distinguish between genuine difficulties and imaginary pitfalls. You often tell me, 'I don't understand this sentence'. Shakespeare is being staged throughout the Soviet Republics in translations (there is a long tradition of Shakespeare in Russia), but I have never yet heard of a performance failing because it was incomprehensible.

In Shakespeare plays – as in everything created by man – certain aspects are closer to artists of one nation or epoch, others to different ones. The rhetoric and complex metaphors are what I feel to be most alien to us and this part of the text is cut in the script.

The meaning is revealed only through the general action, through the development of the whole; one cannot search for it in individual sentences. Reality and naturalness are essential: who would question this now? However it is the reality and naturalness of a poetic image, not of a mundane character, which is immediately visible as if it had been handed to you on a plate, clear to everyone. It is not a question of the clarity of the text, but of the spiritual complexity of an old man who is 'fourscore and upward' with all the obscurity of his delusions and then of his blinding enlightenment; his childlike innocence and profound wisdom; his ancient superstition and sharpness of contemporary irony.

You are wrong to be worried by 'repetitions'. There are none. If Hamlet had not repeated over and over again 'A little month', 'But two months dead!' and so on, there would have been nothing to act in the first soliloquy. The almost obsessive way his thoughts return to the day of his father's funeral, and the day of his mother's wedding, the swiftness of transition, represent not only an insult to the son but also horror at the signs of a new age, and this is the beginning of the moral and philosophical theme.

Lear asks himself the same question over and over again ('Does Lear walk thus? Speak thus?', and so on). This is not monotony but the long drawn-out process of his awakening consciousness; it is tormenting for him to recognize his mistake; the reality of such relationships, of such a world is even more tormenting. The intensifying of feeling is not like a spring which has been pressed down and then suddenly released (shown by an actor in an outburst, a cry in his voice); it is rather a succession of waves, some rolling in, others rolling out. A great splash is not only unnecessary, but on the contrary would be harmful; crying and shouting are not the best means of communication. We have already talked about how the role is relatively 'gentle'.

You are antagonistic towards the translation and mistakenly. I find neither paraphrasing of the verse nor writing down the underlying meaning at all convincing. In his period of renouncing poetry, Leo Tolstoy accused one poet not only of ignorance about country life (peasants have nothing to be glad about at the onset of winter), but also of writing bad Russian (you cannot say 'jog-trotting along somehow', you should say 'anyhow'[1]); as you will have realized, the poet was Pushkin.

In 'clarifying' the text it is easy to extract the story of a father who has been hurt by his wicked children, who cries on the shoulder of his good daughter. But in this case, where is the sense in turning to humanity, in quarrelling with the universe, the torment of awakening to reality?

From a letter to Virsaladze *October 1969*

Goneril's state costume is the only one I have doubts about. This is my fault. I confused you by talking about the spectacle she presents her father with when she enters for supper with deliberate ceremony, already like a royal personage, the embodiment of power. This situation must be expressed by the scene itself, not by the dress. Everything that is outwardly splendid is offensive to our film. Let her be rather an old woman in her dirty gown. There is nothing more conventional than the presentation of all these 'duchesses' courts'. I am convinced that in any fifteenth-century castle it was customary to have communal living quarters; and there were duchesses who looked no different from the kitchen maids.

I like Regan's obscure, dark-coloured dress very much; it is good that her face will stand out from the black swathing like a white spot. It reminds one of a mask. Her face – the real face without make-up – appears later on. I would like to bring out another contrast – to make Lear's silhouette at his entrance in the first scene even heavier and grander, so

[1] Tolstoy was arguing about the two words 'kak-nibud' and 'koye-kak', both of which are very similar in usage and meaning. Tolstoy is therefore quibbling [trans.].

that in the 'storm', when he loses his outer clothing, it is revealed that he is a thin old man of medium height; small compared to how he looked (or seemed to look) in full dress. Nothing else embellishes him or makes him any different from other people . . .

BEAUTY, EVEN WITH fateful undertones and a taste of the infernal, is death to such characters as Goneril and Regan. Regan tells her father that she has not enough food to keep him and his train; Goneril storms at her husband, using coarse words of abuse like a fish-wife. One must see the horrifying commonplaceness of these obscene heartless old women. Yevgeny Schwarz, a great expert on fairy stories, insisted that witches have not died out: they live on, poisoning their neighbours' lives by their cooking. This is the sort of devilry which is closer to the elder sisters.

I WONDERED WHETHER such thoughts would lead me to the conclusion that the emotional foundation of the scenes, the horror at what is taking place, would disappear.

TALKING OF HORROR films: in one, the audience was terrified by devilish inventions: arms appeared out of walls and stretched out towards the girl who was possessed by some sort of complex; fear was induced by showing the darkness and emptiness of night; one was made to shudder at the glinting of a razor blade, shining in the moonlight . . . It was all there. Unfortunately I turned out to be an unsusceptible spectator. My hair stubbornly refused to stand on end. But then in one of the shots the heroine turned on a tap and, tormented by something evil, forgot to turn it off. Water poured everywhere, the bath overflowed, the floor was flooded . . .

I broke out all over in a cold sweat; the horror at the thought of quarrelling with the people on the next floor down, the unavoidable repairs, drunken painters . . . Nightmares suffocated me. Pictures each more terrifying than the last sprang to life; rooted to the spot, I could no longer tear my eyes away from the screen.

SOMETIMES ONE WANTS to start with action rather than with words. Cordelia's very movements, her rhythm of life must be different from all those surrounding her. She is a being from a different race, with a different nature and a different appearance.

How is one to define the essence of this difference – a difference which should not be demonstrated because it should be so evident? Here people live as if holding their breath, motionless, 'peacefully' as advocated by the propaganda posters. Cordelia is always 'free'; even in the most terrible moments for her she should still be 'free'. Even under the threat of execution she does not fall at anyone's feet or kiss the earth. Her normal state is 'free', not chosen but inborn. This is how nature made her because in this case they did not corrupt, or did not succeed in corrupting nature; nature can be trampled on and destroyed but no one has the power to corrupt it.

There are no grounds for the fear that the role is comparatively colourless. There are so many different nuances in this word 'free'. A natural way of breathing represents indeed a whole programme of life.

Her poetry is literally exactly the opposite of Ophelia's poetry. Ophelia has a fragility, an ethereal quality, a complete absence of the power to protest. She is a pale and gentle hot-house plant nurtured in the steel-framed green-houses of Elsinore. Hers is a tragedy of submission.

Cordelia has no thought of rebellion; such thoughts could not enter her head. But she is herself a rebellion, isolated from the rest by her very naturalness. She is the most ordinary, healthy and truthful girl – and this represents an uprising, a barricade which blocks the palace.

She should be brought to the ceremony by a prim black mannequin, her instructor in the art of pretence; she has been brought up in the same way as Goneril and Regan, but this pupil has turned out to be very unreceptive. 'An unresponsive subject', as teachers bitterly call it, 'a complete absence of natural aptitude'. And she has not learnt one single thing; neither how to behave as befits a princess, nor how to express herself like an heiress to the throne. She should not know how to wear an evening (or rather court) dress – her strides are too long.

As if under the hypnosis of eternal fear, the courtiers slowly begin to move – or rather not even to move, but to shift imperceptibly (like figures in a sum of multiplication). And she comes running down the stairs, falls head over heels like a peasant girl. She is tall, sunburnt and well-built.

What a princess she is already! Of course the King of France chose her; he was not blind.

However this is a special kind of love. The King of France did not appear out of a fairy tale; he is a Head of State. Lear's quarrel with him is an act of diplomacy. Today the news agencies would have communicated the news by telex: 'the entire French delegation stormed out of the congress hall in protest'.

The picture does not form gradually but bursts in on one from all sides. This is how photographs are developed – one waits unhurriedly until more substantial tones appear on the sensitized surface, then softer tones, and finally the whole picture becomes clear. The picture now advances, now disappears, the outlines change and break up in pieces; the dissected surfaces, sections of full-face and profile simultaneously overlap, group together and arrange themselves in a new order, as in a cubist painting.

The intonation of sentences appears in the same way, at first without connection, breaking in from somewhere in the middle of the text, spoken (audibly) in contradiction to the meaning of the passage; the deafening silence of the hall; a movement, begun and never finished; a shadow on the stone wall; an eye visible without the rest of the face; coarse twisted threads, the texture of matting.

I HAVE A particular passion for one character. Clowns have fascinated me ever since childhood. I have a whole shelf of books on pantomime and comic characters; Eisenstein, in his time, was the only person who could rival me with his collection. Two nineteenth-century engravings hang on the wall of my study. Joey Grimaldi ('The Michelangelo of clowns' as theatre critics called him) in fine weather going about in spurs instead of boots and using them to leapfrog over his partner. This was a present from Eisenstein, given to me at the première of *The Return of Maxim*.

And so we have *A History of the Comic Grotesque*, *The King's Fools*, *Clowns*, articles about the itinerant troupes of comic actors, *Masks and Clowns*.

Nothing from any of these books is of any use. Not one item, not even the tiniest detail. However the time spent in searching through source material was not spent in vain. The very fact that the historical material does not fit *Lear* in any way, as far as I can see, gave my thoughts a direction to turn to: not to take any notice of what usually is given most attention.

One must put the oar against the bank and shove with all one's might so that the boat will float away and so that the shore will completely disappear from sight.

One must take away from the role of the Fool everything that is associated with clownery. There should be no grimaces, funny faces, no chequered costume, no coxcomb cap. And a rattle is also unnecessary. There should be no eccentricities, not the slightest kind of virtuosity in the singing and dancing.

The most amazing situation then appears: he is laughed at not because he is a Fool but because he speaks the truth. He is a village idiot – or rather they think he is an idiot.

It is not the King and the Fool, but the strong and the weak, the rich and the poor. The most elevated and the most debased. The debased one tells the elevated one that he is a fool because he does not know his daughters. Everybody laughs; but it is true.

They think that nothing is funnier than the truth. They laugh at truth, kick truth with their spurs for amusement and relegate truth to the doghouse in order to make it a laughing stock.

The Fool is like a dog. He snaps like a dog.

This is how the idea for his costume arose: no attributes of the conventional fool, but a beggar in rags, wearing a dog's hide inside out. He is a boy with a shaven head.

Art in the grip of tyranny.

He is the boy from Auschwitz whom they forced to play the violin in an orchestra of dead men; and beat him so that he should play merrier tunes. He has childlike, tormented eyes.

'All the same,' Virsaladze said to me, 'he ought to wear at least some mark of his profession.'

We settled for the most unobtrusive mark possible: bells tied to his leg. The difference is not so much visible as audible. He is distinguished by sound. Before his entrance there is a soft jingle. Something like a call sign: the listener knows that the broadcast is about to begin and that he must tune in on the exact wave.

I asked Dmitri Shostakovich to compose a short piece for the Fool's bells. He sent me an excellent piece of music for xylophone and bells. I was very taken with it but unfortunately the musical form was too concrete and the piece too self-contained. The result was not a sign for recognition but a musical characterization.

It was my fault. I should not have bothered the composer. All I needed were bells and nothing else. A barely audible sound, soft but persistent, stubborn and continuous . . . A sound heard over the howl of the wind and in the downpouring of rain. The Fool's toy rings out in the storm, resounds over the earth, . . . the tocsin of the Fool's bells.

This is the call sign of conscience.

THE SUPPER WITH Goneril, the Duchess of Albany. A well-trained servant noiselessly draws up the chairs; there is a chalice with scented water for washing one's hands; a towel is instantly offered; at a barely imperceptible sign the soft, soothing sound of music is heard; food is eaten from golden dishes, wine tipped into goblets from huge vessels.

If one does not concentrate one's attention on the utensils, the setting at the supper looks like the 'Carlton' or the 'Savoy'.

The eldest daughter insults her father almost immediately; the father does not waste any time and delivers a frightening curse on her. It is all in front of witnesses, in front of the servants. It is something like the huge scandals in Dostoyevsky's novels : rogues making disgraceful scenes, raised voices, distorted faces. The indecency is just as outrageous as the funeral party for Marmeladov.

Oswald, the duchess's right hand, is not only a palace servant, but a servant with a capital letter, General Grovel, a smooth well-fed scoundrel, a swine of the first order.

In *Hamlet* the link between Hamlet and death turned out to be Osric, a half-wit from Elsinore, a nobody who had a big mouth. In *Lear* Oswald enters history (the history of states) together with the cad. He is the first man whom Lear comes across in the real world. Reality begins with people turning their backs on the old man. After renouncing his power, he has to find out for himself that he is no longer a man. This cad does his job, carrying out an order from his mistress; it is his specialized work; he is a cad with the highest qualifications. A Doctor, and perhaps even a member of the Academy of Caddish Sciences.

The circles of tragedy move outwards; after the museum of wax figures of royal power (Lear's palace) comes the planet of grovellers. A labyrinth of servility in which an old man has become confused and cannot find the way out. In spite of outward brilliance and dust being thrown in the eyes, Goneril's whole court bears the stamp of drab impersonality, the uniformity of illiterate boot-lickers.

Far away from the action on the top floor there is a library. Only one man ever uses it. The picture of the Duke of Albany in the quiet surroundings of his books is important and explains a lot.

Each main character's surroundings are very different.

Lear's train consists of a hundred blue-blooded sluggards. Goneril's servants are a hundred well-grown, well-fed curs; the Duke of Cornwall's guards are a hundred experts in robbery and dirty dealing. The Duke of Albany's surroundings and guard are a hundred books; the number is of course relative; there are more scoundrels and servile grovellers in this story than books.

DONATAS BANIONIS is one of the busiest actors and it seems that he was being offered leading roles by all the film studios. In spite of this, to my great joy he agreed to take the small part of the Duke of Albany. We both liked the part. We were trying to show in detail everything which is only hinted at in the play; his nobility of spirit and unpractical mind. Or rather unwillingness to be practical. There is an important difference between the two ideas. He is certainly not at all weak-willed, but he well knows the price of displaying his will. He does not wish to pay such a price. Goneril of course cannot understand any of this: her husband is a 'milk-liver'd man', who has nowhere to go from under her feet. She understands nothing about his character. There comes a time when, with a heavy heart, he descends from the library into the world: he will judge and consider how the people can be fed, and given shelter.

He had the strength of will to refuse to join in the struggle for power and to stand aside. Then he has to take the power into his own hands. He does everything that not time but his conscience demands. Will the Duke become a good ruler? . . . Hardly. He does not know how to howl with the wolves.[1] He keeps his human voice.

YOU REALIZE THE spiritual closeness of an actor not only when he is acting but when he is listening to you explaining the main character. You realize that the bait has been taken. The part becomes a mutual hero.

IT TURNED OUT that we would shoot in detail some small part of the life of each of the characters, sometimes even a part which is mentioned only indirectly in the play or not even mentioned at all; on the other hand certain famous places in the play would be quickly passed over or even dropped altogether in the film.

This was not just a whim. The people whom Shakespeare wrote about demand this treatment; all we did was to listen hard to their voices. Cordelia insists that we linger over her departure and show her marriage to the King of France; the Duke of Albany thinks that his every change of facial expression is important during the division of the kingdom; the elder sisters do not want to talk out loud about their passion for Edmund, or about their jealousy of each other; they want not talk but to act, to meet with their lover in dirty castle courtyards in the heat of war.

Just you try controlling them.

October 1968

TODAY, AFTER MANY difficult months, after so many unsuccessful tests, I have at last seen the eyes on the screen: the very eyes.

[1] The Russian proverb, 'When with the wolves, howl with the wolves' has its equivalent but less picturesque echo in English 'When in Rome do as Rome does' [trans.].

In outward appearance he did not look the part at all: he was short, with a small head, and very nervous. To crown it all he not only spoke Russian poorly but also only partly understood it.

Inna Mochalova had suggested him for the part of the mad beggar, the prototype for Poor Tom; Edgar assumes his shape when he hides from his pursuers. It goes without saying that he was suitable (and how) for the part of Poor Tom. Yuri Yarvet agreed to play this part although it was a minute one. No problems would have arisen over sound: instead of lines he only had to produce inarticulate cries.

But I had no time now for anyone from the beggar's camp: none of the tests for Lear had come up with anything. I had rehearsed good actors for weeks and sometimes months; we had tried dozens of different make-ups but I had not recognized Lear among them. I had not had the good fortune to glimpse either the bitter irony, born of suffering, or the wisdom, arising out of madness.

One actor had achieved red hot anger, another the eyes of a madman; the outward appearance of a third had weight and a certain strangeness; a fourth looked like a man who was intelligent and well-read. They were all talented people and had successfully acted a great number of difficult parts. But they did not resemble Lear. We parted friends: I had not concealed my opinions; while working with one I had never rehearsed another simultaneously behind the other's back.

And now I began to feel pangs of conscience. I had light-heartedly taken on a film without knowing beforehand who would play the principal part. Had I a right to do this? The costumes were already made and they had begun to build the sets. But there was no one to play the title role. God help any director who finds himself in a similar situation!

My proposal to summon Yarvet for a screen test for Lear met with general disapproval. The production manager said to me, 'All right. There's no harm in wasting the price of his rail fare.' It seemed that no one apart from Mochalova was behind me.

Yarvet told me later that he had not believed for one moment that we were serious when he went for the test. He had said jokingly, 'It's ordinary film routine but Leningrad is a beautiful city; besides I wanted to buy some oranges for my children; I had been told you could get them there. Why not go?'

Our relationship built up in an odd way. There was no interpreter. Yarvet was too embarrassed to tell me that he did not understand what I said, and I pretended that I understood (in general) what he tried to express in a few sentences.

And would you believe it! We understood one another. I studied his face and the liveliness of his eyes with mounting interest; now he seemed a different man: a huge forehead, wrinkles which made his masculine face beautiful, sadness, irony. Who did he remind me of? Of course, portraits of Voltaire, the bitter irony, the wit of Europe.

For the screen test (we decided not to rehearse beforehand) he learnt by heart a few lines from one of the soliloquies. And then we moved the camera closer to his face. There was a dirty wall and a kitchen table in the studio. An assistant put a candle on the table – evidently for the sake of propriety; it was after all a historical film. I asked Yarvet to do the first thing that came into my head – to blow out the candle, and to watch, taking his time, the wick curl up and the stream of smoke spiral upwards and disappear. And to think about death. To be honest, the task does not seem so pointless now. Anyway what else could one have thought of in similar circumstances?

I looked at Yarvet and recognized Lear. Yarvet looked like him.

THE PERSONALITY OF this actor (a man I did not know at all) seemed so attractive that no difficulties seemed insurmountable. The main difficulty was his lack of Russian. Well, we would have to dub. After all his eyes did not have to make any sound. The eyes would be kept 'in the original'. I have to admit that I have always found even the making of a separate sound track a trial. A multitude of elusive nuances of everyday speech which synchronized shooting picks up are inevitably lost on the separate sound track. I prefer extraneous noises, lack of clarity in speech, anything rather than the desiccated words of dubbed film. Now I would have to go back to school and learn a technology which was new to me. The first essential was to get an Estonian text in which the length of each word was equal to the Russian (and in the number of words). We sent our order to the Estonian dubbing studio. Yarvet went home to Tallin to learn this text. I had already had several meetings with him. My mind was at rest: Yarvet understood my every word – I could see this by the glint in his eyes. A translation was being made from Russian into Estonian; Yarvet said nothing for the time being; he was making notes in the margin of his script.

A director must not only explain his intention but bring it close to the actor. He must talk, show and adjust the spiritual link by every means within his power. If he feels he is getting no response, he must re-word it, look for different comparisons. Sometimes I would get so used to the new phraseology and level of understanding that there would come a time – after such an explanation – when I would notice with horror that the poetry was fading, the image which I had loved for so many years, was somehow growing fainter, and drifting away. And I would grow ashamed of my own words which I had used to describe the image. On reflection, it would seem clear that the actor (even a good one) was spiritually incompatible with myself and perhaps even with the author.

Yarvet and I had a complete compatibility of spirit. With every day I became more convinced of this. We loved the same qualities in Lear.

Yarvet arrived from Tallin and immediately presented me with an unexpected surprise: the Estonian text was ready but Yarvet did not want to speak it. In his hurry and agitation, so that the interpreter hardly managed to keep up with him, he explained that technically speaking the layout of the dubbing script was exact, but that artistically, it was revolting and unpoetic. The very task would murder the poetry. He would find it impossible to speak such a text even though it was in his mother tongue. He would have to learn to speak Pasternak's beautiful verse (even if with an accent, and stumbling).

I noticed the beautiful way Yarvet spoke Estonian – it was musical and at the same time perfectly natural.

And so began the inhuman and agonizing task of overcoming alien consonants.

As we left the rehearsal, Yarvet told me with embarrassment, without looking at me, that he would give all his energy to the task. He stumbled as he talked, making mistakes of pronunciation, but he talked in Russian. There was not one of my colleagues who would be rehearsing the play who would not have called me aside and said smiling happily, 'We have a Lear'.

It is good when the respect of colleagues is won over immediately – by talent and hard work, not by ambition.

Chapter Eight

MY WORK HAD had its ebbs and flows. Now it seemed as if it was flowing. Perhaps it was as a result of my month's holiday in Kislovodsk[1], or of working with Yarvet?

During my month's holiday I used to go to the cinema every evening. I had after all to see what sort of films were being made. They turned out to be mostly detective films. What a strange fashion it was and why had it happened at this particular moment?

When conceiving *The Youth of Maxim*, Trauberg and I agreed at once that we would not have 'conspiratorial secrets', or mysterious *agents provocateurs*, or prison escapes in our script. Why? After all, this had actually happened in reality and had now taken its place in the history of revolutionary movements. Of course it had happened. But the same things had happened in the real life of other parties and with even greater effect; and even simply in *The Knaves of Hearts Club.*[2] This was surely not the essence of revolution, its moral significance.

And now what had come into fashion was exactly what we considered to be vulgar. And how vulgar it was! The action completely excluded any spiritual content; there was very little significance left in these films.

'They talk about "the literature of adventure",' Samuel Marshak wrote in his time. 'What is our literature of adventure? In Pavlov's laboratories dogs could be made to salivate at certain recognized signals, and then they were not fed . . . They have learnt to make readers produce saliva at certain recognized signals; the readers produce the saliva but are given nothing to eat.'

He continues, 'What an enormous difference there is between verse which is loaded with imagery and verse which has none. It is strange to think that 'Songs flow over the meadows' (— ◡ — ◡ — ◡ — ◡) is written in the same metre[3] as 'Once upon a time there lived a poor knight' (— ◡ — ◡ — ◡ — ◡). One structure is empty of imagery, the other is loaded.'

[1] A Caucasian spa highly regarded for its mountain air and healthy atmosphere.

[2] *Klub Chervonykh Valetov* – a prerevolutionary group of speculators [trans.].

[3] In the Russian version [trans.].

It would probably be hard to find a better way of defining the differences in spiritual essence. Empty or loaded? Of course this is not referring to what is ingenuously called 'content' (for what art form can be without it?). We are still apt to extract quotations from dialogues, put them together, and proclaim happily, 'Look what an important subject the film has!'

Only the power of response, a depth of feeling, give life to an image. The apples in Dovzhenko's film[1] are not photographed but cultivated with his whole life, beginning with his 'sacred, barefooted childhood' (his phrase). Art is a reflection of life. Of course. But how does this reflection come about? By this alone – the power to awaken a response, by suffering and by sympathy.

Andrei Tarkovsky's landscapes are not photographed but achieved through suffering. The best pages of Chaplin's memoirs are devoted to his poverty-stricken childhood; he recalls all the details of the years of cold and hunger; he writes, 'Picasso had a blue period. We had a grey one'.[2]

IN ONE RUSSIAN film – there was nothing bad in it and nothing particularly good, but it all looked true and lifelike – the hero turned on his transistor in the course of the action. The transmission was supposed to be no more than a background; the action was accompanied by an ordinary radio broadcast, the sort one might often hear. But it was the voice of Edith Piaf. And immediately everything on the screen – the director's observations of life of the sort that anyone could see for himself, characters and relationships all possible in real life, but discovered long ago and demonstrated more than once – all this immediately somehow faded and lost its significance. The criterion had changed: it was the exultant power of a voice.

Obviously there is no point in comparing different genres, talents and so on. But nevertheless . . . we are concerned not so much with construction as with fuel and the possibility of getting into the air.

AFTER A LONG search we had found a Lear; a mountain had dropped from my shoulders. But a new mountain was already building up. I do not mean a mountain (or plain) in the figurative sense, but the sort of mountain one can shoot. The choice of location for this film was particularly complicated. We needed not a location for the action, but a world which would enter into the image of the character – sometimes the main character – and which would in many

[1] *Earth* [trans.].

[2] Chaplin, *My Autobiography*, The Bodley Head 1964, p. 16.

ways determine people's actions. These actions are often explained not so much by psychology as by history. But the earth on which people walked was also history.

People and earth make a complex unity; the scenery of *Lear* changes before one's very eyes: people mutilate the land and then finally depart not to the peace of the tomb but into the earth which they themselves have trampled upon and scorched. I wanted to show this on the screen with the greatest possible clarity and as naturally as possible.

The earth of history has a peculiarly natural quality which is not easy to define; it is the stamp of time by which the material world is marked out. A landscape – even where no man-made constructions are visible – can be historical, or rather it is taken to be historical. There are latitudes of climate and climates of history. You can talk about a nineteenth-century tree, leaden storm clouds of the middle ages, empty primeval sky, scythian steppes – all these are not empty words but poetic images. We transfer the marks of history to nature. Stendhal wrote, 'The colour of the times has changed.' The wind and the snowstorm in Blok's *The Unknown Woman* is different from the wind and snowstorm in 'The Twelve': in the first example it is white and dark blue, with more dark blue than white; in the second it is white.

Many years ago Moskvin and I photographed a frozen, deserted Lake Baikal for the film *Alone*, an enormous expanse of ice – we needed a dark and primeval silence. And as if to spite us, the result on the screen was a gay sugary snow, like a winter sports resort. We had to keep changing the angle of the lens, the light filters, the type of film, before we succeeded in getting the right atmosphere.

If one diligently searches for *Lear*'s scenery in the real world one will find that it does not exist, and cannot exist. Shakespeare does not have its exact details (the unity of geography and history). But one can create it by speculation – by creating a non-existent whole from a montage of fragments. I was not new to this method of working: Hamlet took his first steps in our film on the shores of the Baltic Sea and his second by the Black Sea; there were several hours of flying time between the two.

I have never been convinced by the idea of filming Shakespeare in the actual settings of the plays, neither by Orson Welles' Venice nor Franco Zeffirelli's Verona: historical naturalism is alien to the poetry of *Othello* and *Romeo and Juliet*. I could not have filmed *Hamlet* in the real Castle of Elsinore: it bears no resemblance at all to Claudius' kingdom. It is no accident that the playwright had never visited these places: he had only the most approximate conception of them.

And so one should have as few 'details' as possible and no 'style'; it should be the world of history without external historical characteristics; a world which is absolutely real (filmed on location), without existing in nature, constructed out of a montage which will last for two hours. We began to look for the separate parts, the fragments of the imagined whole. Yenei immediately suggested the Kazantip promontory on the Azov sea; Virsaladze talked of castles in Georgia. Geographical maps appeared on the walls of our work rooms: of Georgia, Armenia, Estonia and the Crimea. We tried to map out the first version of 'the world': fields and boulders in the north, turrets in mountainous Svanetia, the rocks of Kazantip, the ruins of Armenia, castles in Georgia and fortresses in Estonia.

M. S. Shostak, the production manager, clutched at his head: the shooting would evidently take five years.

THE EXTERIORS ARE kind to man only once: when he loses his reason. Then he is surrounded by gay wild flowers and warmed by the sun. The fundamental tone of the exteriors is harsh and desert-like: hunger, lack of shelter, cold, 'unaccommodated' nakedness (about which there is so much talk in the poetry) do not blend with abundance and fruitfulness.

It would be a bare landscape, a country 'almost totally without animal hide' (Aragon). It is as if greatness of deserted, rocky expanses form one pole of the visual poetry. The other pole is also indispensable: Shakespeare's imagery has to have the complex linking of the abstract and the concrete. Both poles had to be present on the screen in their extremes. While we worked, the needle inevitably swung first to one and then to the other; now towards the mightiness of nature (when the studio shots looked too ordinary), now towards the environment of human life (when everything on the screen became too abstract). This is how I usually worked: dashing in one direction and then in the other. There could be no golden mean.

While I was shooting *Hamlet* in the studio I would rush to the sky and the sea; in *Lear* it was essential to have rotting straw on the roofs and to show the swollen dampness of the beams. I awaited with impatience the appearance of horses on the film (harnessed to carts, and certainly not racehorses!), and shaggy watchdogs. They would be real and I wondered how people, costumes and words would look beside them. The testing out of truth by the genuine article is essential in film making.

Shakespeare's words have already more than once been spoken

against an empty landscape or against an abstract background. Even in Gordon Craig's day a lot that was good was done by this kind of expression. The relationships themselves – between figures and space – accentuated the loneliness of the individual in the evil emptiness of an antagonistic world.

We played around with this sort of composition while making *The Cloak*: we were trying to demonstrate the insignificance of Akaky Akakiyevich amidst the deserted night scene in the Emperor's capital.

Now I wanted another kind of tragedy which would be achieved not by clearing the screen of all signs of life but on the contrary by swamping it with everyday life.

There is no 'desert' in *Lear*, the world of tragedy is densely populated. And it was just this – a magnetic field humming with reality – which interested me most of all. Lear, the King, in the thick of life, this is what the camera was needed for, this is what cinema could add to what we knew already, to what the theatre had already revealed. The problem began to take on a clear definition: we had not to take away the landscapes but to move the characters forward into life. As in Balzac – the scenes of courtly life, the life of politics, villages, war – tragedy takes place not amongst landscapes but among people.

The *Comédie Humaine* as far as Balzac conceived it was to be completed by the 'philosophical studies . . . overwhelming storms of thought.' This is also one of the roles of the exteriors in this film – an expanse in which the eternal quarrel between man and the universe takes place. We needed not only historical but also philosophical landscapes.

I WAS LOOKING at a book of Elizabethan pictures: engravings, coats of arms, stone turrets with loopholes, and drawbridges. All this would be for a 'historical film'. But there was one emblem which caught my attention. It seemed truly beautiful. Was it really engraved by a completely unknown artist four hundred years ago? It was a scarecrow in a vegetable patch. I recognized it instantly. We had one when I was a child: two crossed sticks, a shirt made of sacking and full of holes and a squashed and torn hat. When I looked more closely I saw that the hat was a slightly different fashion from ours. But it was just like what people have: a vegetable patch, a scarecrow – the warmth of human habitation.

Within the confines of the Roman Pantheon there was a *Genius Loci*: a local god. Let our *Genius Loci* be a scarecrow.

THE SCREEN HAD to show a cruel stone world. But a scarecrow had also to be there. And a vegetable patch. People are born and must get food. Life. There is no beginning and no end to life.

In order to get the feeling of cold one must also convey warmth. The spark of life still smouldering.

EVEN BY THE time of making *The Youth of Maxim* I had developed a distaste for so-called 'monumentalism'. It is easy to work when the loud sounding epithets and dazzling generalizations are completely cleared away. One must look closely at one's subject, and stand on the same ground: talk about man in the language of men. We are all still deafened by talk of volcanic passions, rivers of blood and tears in tragedy. There are of course rivers and passions. However if one only looks a little closer one can see something else; insignificant bustling about, low dealings and characters worthy only of contempt.

Kent, the King's messenger, is not stabbed or thrown into the dungeons, but put in the stocks. Let us imagine such a scene in a contemporary situation: an ambassador representing a foreign government is dragged off to the police station by doormen who hurl jeering taunts at him on the way, implying that this member of the diplomatic service is a fine example: he got into a fight and used foul language.

Gloucester is blinded in the midst of chaos: a confusion of movement, stamping of feet and muttered curses. It is vile and filthy. They spit on him, swear at him and kick him. A base swarming mass of people. What style should the scene have? Dirty dealing in a back street.

What place has purple and gold here?

It is a grey world. Beggars wander through the mud in a murky twilight from village to village. Soon Edgar, Lear and Gloucester will all join them.

'SHE LIVES OVER some laundry' wrote Bunin of a prostitute, 'She goes out in order to earn money underneath some scum or other.'

> She lives to
> Earn
> Over
> Under
> Some sort of
> By another sort of

This is the whole structural material; neither the houses nor the clients have an image. The very featurelessness of the description is dramatic, the insignificance of the words, a sort of complete removal of artistry.

In Chagall's early canvasses (the Vitebsk period) the very clocks on the walls, the samovars and the kerosine lamps are tragic.

In the ancient theatre the grandeur and epic quality was achieved by the force of the principal character's passion, and by make-up. It would be very simple to change all this for a monumental landscape. But do the Nibelungs recall *Lear* in any way? One should get as far away as possible from oaks of enormous girth and vast cliffs. Overpowering nature is no better than declamation.

The storm has passed. The titanic winds have abated, the cosmic downpours are appeased. And then what? . . . We will try to imagine Lear's wandering, his way of life, the words he uses in living situations. Let us forget about the time and the genre, get as far away as possible from the theatre and find ourselves on ordinary soil, in human (even if also inhuman) situations.

It is something like 'variations on a theme'. The first variation: a queue of tramps stand suffering on a street in the suburbs under the dim light of the streetlamp: it is the entrance to the Salvation Army's night shelter. An old man in rags with a growth of grey bristle on his face stands gulping down his soup and mutters: 'No one can stop me from minting my own money. I am the King after all.'

Variation two: he is asleep underneath a bridge. A policeman gives him a kick.

'Don't touch me,' the old man demands. 'I am wounded in the brain.'

Variation three: lying on planks and talking to a blind man.

'You're a king?'

'Every inch a king.'

The sly old men split their sides with laughter.

And one more: the edge of a village. It is washing day. The dogs are barking furiously. The boys, whistling and shrieking, chase the madman. Lear turns and shakes his fist at them. Those are the challenges I threw in the giant's face.

A cat's chorus. They hurl crusts and peel at the old man.

WHEN WE WERE shooting Elsinore, we decided to break with the tradition of portraying Claudius' palace like a prison ('Denmark's a prison'); the prisoner, Hamlet, was portrayed in a comfortable world in our film; here falsehood had a pleasant face, baseness

3. Act III sc. vii: K. Cebric as Gloucester.

4. Act IV sc. vi: ''Tis the times' plague when madmen lead the blind.' (Lear, Gloucester and Edgar/Poor Tom (Leonard Merzin)).

caressed the eyes. The substance of *Lear* is different. Here the transition is the simple thrusting of people from one condition and situation to another totally opposite one. These are no transitions but gulfs and chasms. A warm place by the fire contrasted with rain out on the heath; velvet contrasted with a bare dirty body. The strata of life do not mingle but collide.

The main scenes would be shot coarsely, sharply, spotlighting the roughness, the coarse-grained textures – sackcloth, rags, dark weather-beaten faces. This is how we shot crowds in the twenties: one could even see the pores of the skin and the pock marks. I wanted the substance of the film to express the motif (important to the philosophy) of the raising of the shrouds; the savageness of life's essence hidden beneath the wrapping of civilization. This is how the 'bare forked animal' looked without adornment.

We had to drag it out into the open and throw light on it. There had to be a density and compression of all that was natural down to physiological sensitivity. The effect of existence was the most important; we ourselves were resting in the evil-smelling hovel where the King and the earl's heir mingled with the beggars. Stench, filth, horror of the 'lowest of the low'.

God help me if a contemporary Gogolesque lady 'pleasant in all respects' says happily in the audience, 'How lovely this is!' They have sores and scabs on their bodies just like a Grünewald painting.

Chapter Nine
RUSSIAN TRAGEDY

DOSTOYEVSKY HAS CONTRASTS of completely deserted and unpeopled voids, as against extreme crowding: seething masses of people, men squashed into minute surroundings, packed one on top of the other like sardines in a tin. In his novels the landscape is often evoked by a character's gesture, or by his behaviour. In his lectures Eisenstein delighted in breaking literature up into shots. He discovered a montage of close-ups and long shots in *Poltava.* To continue with the cinema metaphor, Dostoyevsky is always different: the filming is always of movement, of a panorama; it is rare to find a static scene. The pictures of towns in his novels are formed by the rhythm of the main character's actions. His movements are somehow continued by the streets.

> And with a swift involuntary movement of the hand he pointed out to me the misty perspective of the street, lit by street lamps flickering dimly in the grey darkness, the dirty houses, the pavements glistening with damp, the sullen, bad-tempered and sodden passers-by . . . We were already coming out into a square; a monument stood before us in the gloom.[1]

The pace of the uneven, nervous steps alternatively slows down and speeds up. 'The old man and the young woman entered a large, wide street, which was dirty and full of industrial labourers of one kind or another . . . and turned off it into a narrow, long alley . . . set against a huge blackened wall . . . through gates . . . one could pass into another equally large and crowded street.'

Steps, objects, space are somehow transformed into a unity of moving substance, and elements of reality arise suddenly: 'An impoverished undertaker lived on the ground floor . . . Passing by . . . the workshop, Ardynov climbed up a slippery spiral staircase to the first floor, groped in the darkness for a massive clumsy door covered in rags, found a key and opened it.'

In these novels there is no so-called environment for the action, no

[1] This and subsequent quotations in this chapter are random, taken from all Dostoyevsky's writings. Since the author is demonstrating style, the exact references are not given [trans.].

atmosphere for the events, no way of life which stands on its own outside the spiritual world of the hero (or rather the author). One can of course say that a certain man is living in a town. However the opposite would be no less true: a town lives inside a man. There are no separate houses, streets, thoughts or feelings; no descriptions; there are only impetuous and interrupted actions. Relationships develop not just between people but between blocks of houses and people, between living quarters and people, between blocks of houses and living quarters. This is why the passages stretch out (both in space and time), the alleys turn into blind alleys, ways through courtyards suck one into them and push one out as if they were tunnels. What is the topography of the town? A feverish inflamed brain? An unusual summer heat-wave, stifling to the point of suffocation. What is foremost, where is the beginning hidden?

The landscape is a confused and neglected case history of an illness where a man runs from chemist to chemist in search of a medicine which not one chemist has ever heard of.

Some time long ago in ages gone by they called 'case histories' the 'list of sorrow'. The urban scenery with all its long drawn out tedium is just such a 'list of sorrow'.

Shapes are confused, the functions of the individual parts have been destroyed. In the crowd and the stifling closeness of the Sennaya Market man demands an answer: how is one to reconcile the falsehood of life with life's meaning? The answer comes as an inarticulate hubbub, shrieking and a faceless bustle of activity.

Cinema has tried many times to reproduce this imagery. In Robert Wiene's film *Raskolnikov* (1923) the hero was surrounded by expressionist scenery, the feverish conscience was portrayed literally. But man existed on one plane, and the material world on another: the Art Theatre actor G. Khmara walked on sloping surfaces, appeared against a background of conventionally decorated surfaces. But a united world, the spiritual world of the author, was not achieved. The result was no better when the artists constructed a realistic scenery – the living quarters of just the sort of proportions that are shown in the novel: they had placed the author on the side of the 'naturalist school' where everyone knows he did not linger.

DOSTOYEVSKY'S BIOGRAPHERS have drawn attention to the fact that he frequently moved flats and that the situation of the houses in which he lived was always the same; a corner house near a church. The crossroad and the call of the faith. It is like the proverb, 'If you go to the right you will turn to the left . . .' His friends have described how he often used to wander through the streets alone, waving his arms as he went and talking to himself. Certainly the rhythm of his walk was very significant.

This is how the world of his novels appears, a particular view by a travelling camera shot. Sometimes the hero is walking along with shaky, nervous steps, stumbling and out of breath, and beside him like a double, strangely appearing and disappearing, sometimes walking in step with him, sometimes quickening its pace and running ahead, then dropping back so that it can catch him up again, walks his illness: filthy blocks of flats, houses which look like prisons, houses resembling cemeteries, dirty snack bars, dark beerhouses. It is just like the fairy story: no matter where the man goes, grief is bound tightly to him and plods alongside, never leaving him.

If he notices details as he goes along, they appear one after the other in unnaturally stark outline, leaping out in front of him; if there are general features then there is nothing to see – the darkness of night, the greyness of day, everything is washed clean, it is dark without a line or a feature. 'Rain penetrated the whole neighbourhood, drowned every reflection and every nuance turning it all into one hazy, lead-coloured indistinguishable mass . . . And suddenly a strange and awkward figure was outlined against this cold hazy darkness . . .' 'There was a dense crowd of people . . . He pushed his way into the thick of it . . . they were all making a noise about something, massing together . . .' The contours are erased, the forms are lost, there is only the slimy, fluctuating masses of buildings and people. The crowd has lost all human features, its movements are unnatural: no one is alone, nothing is separate, all crushed together in a herd: 'people seethe' 'thrust'. Sometimes it is as if a spring noisily works loose, the mechanism springs into action without ammunition: 'All the kitchens in all the flats on all four floors opened . . . caretakers walked up and down the steps with notebooks under their arms.'

The same attributes apply to images of sound: there is either dead silence or noise, uproar and discordance. What is thrust into the foreground and is heard louder than anything else is usually nonsense. In the tavern in which Svidrigailov is sitting there is not a moment's peace: a chorus, orchestra, shouts and the banging of balls from the billiard room, the barrel organ and the street singer 'with rhythmic obsequiousness' all together in the same place and at the same time. Nozdrev's barrel organ – squeaking and wheezing, with a meaningless succession of snatches of tune – grew in sound until a whole symphony orchestra burst out.

The seasons of the year are shown only in their extreme manifestations: if there is heat it is asphyxiating; unbearable mud; the unbelievable quality of the white nights. It is as if everything that has been written about the beauty of this town (and how much there has been of great artistic value) does not exist, not even one line hints at it. What influence can beauty have here? 'This is a town of people who are half mad. You do not often find so many gloomy, harsh and strange influences on a man's spirit as you find in Petersburg. The influence of the climate alone is enough.'

'I wanted to put a question as clearly as possible in the form of a novel and to provide an answer to it . . .' (*Diary of a Writer*). Both the question and the answer are inseparable from the material world, the world of history; the climate of the town has a peculiar origin: the capital was founded, built and erected on a swamp; but the swamp has not been exterminated or destroyed; underneath it all oozes mud, marshy vapours gather, filth and disease drown the streets; everything takes on a fantastic aspect. A half-dead figure breaks out of the darkness, shakes his fist and shouts 'Damn you.'[1]

The theme was found long ago in Russian literature. And in both how the question is presented and how the answer is given, the tragic power of history and the grief of everyday life are always inseparable: the tumbledown house by the river where Parasha lives, and Senate Square.[1] Imagery is usual in our literature: the mad clerk astride the stone lion and the coffins floating on the turbulent waves of the Neva.

GOGOL DECLARED THAT a small portrait of an ordinary man could become an historical work of art under the brush of a real artist, and many huge canvasses on historical themes were only worthy to be called wall decorations: it all depended on the artist's depth of insight into the heart of the subject matter.

I RE-READ DOSTOYEVSKY: I was searching for a way of solving the problems which kept appearing every day – they were always new ones and were becoming more and more difficult. It was not for nothing that one of the American reviews of *Hamlet* acclaimed it as 'The Brothers Karamazov from Elsinore'. Alas we had taken a lot from the author of the Karamazovs. I was fully aware that Dostoyevsky's Petersburg had nothing in common with Shakespeare's

[1] A reference to Pushkin's epic poem, 'The Bronze Horseman'. In the poem, Parasha is the girl friend of the hero. The misery of the small man is shown in contrast to the implacability of the founder of the city, Peter the Great, symbolized by his statue, the Bronze Horseman.

Britain. It is hardly worth even mentioning it. We were concerned with something totally different. Great discoveries in art influence not only the future but also the past. One discovers new things in old books from reading a contemporary book. The 'fantastic realism' which Dostoyevsky talked of so much (and which began with Gogol) was not only responsible for and forestalled much in contemporary art, but opened up new aspects of the classics (and perhaps Shakespeare first and foremost) which no one had paid any attention to before. Shakespeare's realism became clearly visible, the tragedy charged with life like gunpowder.

THERE IS NO need to think that the abstract always results in lifelessness. There are different kinds of abstraction. I still remember one of the funniest and happiest productions I have ever been lucky enough to see. Wooden tools were fixed against a plain brick wall background, platforms, a ladder, a revolving wheel (the designer was L. Popova); the actors were wearing everyday dress instead of costumes – it was *The Magnanimous Cuckold* by Crommelynck at the RSFSR Theatre No. 1 (1922). The audience roared and clapped, showing their delight at Meyerhold's production. The young, light-hearted and mischievous actors – Babanova, Ilinsky, Zaichikov – filled the conventional space of the stage – would you call it constructivism? or suprematism? – with the whole fullness of life; Meyerhold's artistry transformed the 'conventionality' with such *joie de vivre* that it took one's breath away.

It was 1926. Meyerhold had invented something new: a sort of materialistic formula for the epoch of Nicholas I, realized on the stage in red wood and real objects. There was no abstract space, nor were there copies of life. It was the expanse of time or rather the author's expanse. It was this which interested me now and made me remember Meyerhold's work. The décor for *The Government Inspector* bore no resemblance to living conditions in Gogol's time. There was no question of a fourth wall let alone the other three. All there was on the stage was the polished surfaces of red wood with doors and empire furniture. The action took place on small sloping 'truck-stages' with screens. Everything was hemmed in by the space and restricted.

Stenographic transcripts of the rehearsals have been preserved; they reveal Meyerhold's train of thought, and make clear the direction in which he was trying to go (much of it turned out differently in the production): 'One must put the whole company of people on a platform measuring approximately five square arshins[1] – no larger. That is, fit them into a very confined space'. 'It is almost impossible to pass between the table and the sofa'; 'he entered, or to be exact he emerged from the furniture because the chest of drawers was in one place, the cupboard and candlesticks in another, and people somehow came out of the furniture.' 'An enormous sofa which could seat nine people' 'they sit close together'. 'The whole platform was covered with a very high trellis . . . faces appearing here and there through the ivy . . . and a nose stuck out.'

From the very beginning of his work on *The Government Inspector* Meyerhold talked continuously about tragedy. It was this feeling of the tragedy of events, within the governmental sweep rather than the provincial sweep of history, which gave the production its tone. The director came in for as much criticism immediately after the first night as the author had in his time. Demyan Bedny composed an epigram: 'Meyerhold is a murderer, he has murdered Gogol's laughter.' As is well known it was not easy to find one's bearings in this sort of laughter. After the first night of *The Government Inspector* Gogol fled from Petersburg in despair. What caused this despair? The fact that no one, not one single person liked his play? But according to the memoirs of the time there was no question of it being a flop. Sosnitsky as the Mayor was excellent (whatever anyone says, the success depends on the main character), the opinions of the audience were varied, but eye-witnesses have recounted a large number of favourable responses; Nicholas the First and his heir laughed and praised the play; the critics began to argue; the people whose opinion Gogol valued were overjoyed. What more could a comic writer wish for? Evidently nothing. But Gogol wanted something else, not louder applause or favourable reviews but a different understanding of the play; in his work laughter was always mixed with something completely different. Later he wrote that a production must have a 'horror at the disorderliness of things' . . . the action must take place not only in a small provincial town but also in the spiritual world of each man so that he thinks again and cries out with the author, "Fellow countrymen, it's frightening!" '

Of course an author cannot always express his own intentions better than anyone else; one must not take his words too literally especially when the author was Gogol; and these words were spoken in the latter part of his creative life. Nevertheless, his words were not supposed to vanish into thin air. He expected not only laughter, but horror as well: the smile should have disappeared; his own face, reflected in the mirror of comedy would have frightened the audience,

[1] About 2 foot square.

made them open their eyes, and look closer at life. But on the imperial stage they were acting vaudeville. And even if one were to qualify it by calling it vaudeville with accusatory tendencies, it would not have measured up to the author's intention in the slightest degree, nor to the inner power which set the action in motion. He had been possessed by great arrogance; he had not meant to amuse, and 'laughter through tears' was already past history; the laughter had to 'sear the heart'. He would not have agreed to less whatever words he might have spoken in conciliation at the time.

Meyerhold threw all the theatrical doors and windows wide open: not even memories remained of the vaudeville spirit, the amusing clerical stereotypes and the harmless caricatures. The very feeling of space was tragic. The oval stage for *The Government Inspector* was removed as far as possible from a comical set-up. A multitude of doors watched the audience. The doors – how many were there? Eleven? Fifteen? A hundred? – all opened at once: a whole world crawled in with its bribes. The crowd of visitors dashed from right to left: a large number of people, gathered together in a group, mimicked the drunken Khlestakov's every movement – his legs no longer obeyed him and carried him all over the room and in the terrifying crush, people pressed against the low balustrade before which he was ticking off the boxes of kringels. Small sloping platforms were wheeled on one after the other; there was a crush of things and people and only once was the whole stage revealed completely bare, with huge spaces in which the figures of puppets, clowns dressed up in the costumes of the main characters stood out – a dumb scene, inspired by the author.

Discovering the beginning of an invasion of madmen on the stages of Europe and America, the mayor went out of his mind, began to leap about, making scenes, and accompanied by a deafening uproar an enormous shirt was brought out as a gesture of conciliation. Noise was also born with Nozdrev's barrel organ, symbolizing the nonsense of discord. Offstage the order which the Mayor had specified in the event of his daughter's betrothal was carried out too late: 'Cry it all over the town, ring the bells and let the devil look after himself!' The audience were deafened by the bells, the beating of drums, the screeching violins of the Jewish orchestra and the police whistles. A white sheet rose up out of the ground: enormous letters announced the arrival of the Government Inspector.

Russian tragedy in the theatre had its own peculiar character. It had nothing in common with the plays of Polevoy and Kukolnik[1]

[1] Both Polevoy (1796–1846) and Kukolnik (1809–1868) echoed European Romanticism in their plays.

(the school of false grandeur – as Turgenev described it). Gogol and Dostoyevsky showed the power of combining history with ordinary everyday life, horror with vulgarity, and laughter with despair.

A new genre was formed which was unlike anything else and which was perhaps more or less accurately described by the phrase 'devil's vaudeville'.

The theatrical aesthetics created by Meyerhold influenced the theatre all over the world. They were developed in the repertoire of the Berliner Ensemble. Both space where only genuine materials and objects give an idea of time and where the poles of dynamic movement and immobility are planned, and slogans are cut into the production like a silent tape – all this has now become a commonplace and does not strike anyone as embarrassing. More than one director in the world has said that he was brought up on Brecht. This is undoubtedly true. But their first teacher, whether they know it or not, was Meyerhold, and the fantastic realism of Gogol and Dostoyevsky.

I WOULD WANT to demonstrate the formula for Shakespearean space entirely in the open air. I wanted to shoot the division of the kingdom in all its visual clarity. Lear and his heiresses walk out on to the highest tower: the father points out to his daughters the land which will belong to each one. I wanted a complete proverb at the beginning of the story, a visual proverb: an old man with his three daughters, and beyond them across the whole width of the screen – their possessions: fields, castles, lakes, villages, herds of livestock, and people. As the King's hand moves, so the riders immediately spur on their horses; the prints of horses' hooves on the ground mark the new boundaries; posts are hewn out as landmarks, estates are divided, and the livestock herded to new pastures.

It is easy to work out a production round a table. You can clearly visualize the shots and things begin to happen. Then other people assess these shots and define the possibilities in terms of production: 'How many objects?' This is what my friend Andrei Moskvin said, and when he read new scripts he always said 'there are rather a lot of objects'. And now we had the same problem. There were plenty of locations but we could not spare a whole year for shooting – it would have to be re-conceived for the studio. Yenei was just as disappointed as I was; he himself prefers only to add to nature, to change it almost imperceptibly; he does this beautifully, the natural expanses are revealed and strengthened by his art; the foreground (constructed from real materials) always gives the feeling of breadth and character. Everyone tried to convince me that the studio scenes wouldn't be noticeable. Alas, I know how noticeable they wouldn't be. One thing consoled me however: whole blocks of the sets would be made of wood which had been roughly hewn with an axe. Some craftsmen had been found in Lithuania and the furniture ordered from them.

AT THE BEGINNING of the revolution they proposed not only to destroy the boundaries that separate art from life and to step across, but to tear them apart, to destroy their very foundations so that no trace or memory of them should remain.

'Now as far as footlights are concerned' Meyerhold wrote (for the production of *The Dawn*[1] at the RSFSR Theatre No. 1) – 'Let us underline with particular embarrassment that in spite of all attempts to free the stage from this revolting phenomenon of illumination from the ground . . . not one of the theatres has wished to throw out this scenic rubbish . . .'

This is how Peter the Great treated the boyar's beards. The degree of ferocity, or rather even frenzy ('with particular embarrassment', 'such a revolting phenomenon') now surprises us . . . What called for such a degree of wrath? The stubborn preservation of the footlights? The conservatism of producers? Were these really such strange crimes? The cause of anger was even deeper: a hatred of artifice which shielded one from life; the illusory footlights accentuated various spheres of life; they symbolized boundaries across which one should not tread. The inspiration of the new art was its complete unity with the real world.

There should be no boundaries between *Lear* and contemporary life. I could distinctly hear the direct speech with which Shakespeare addresses his audience – one should add, the audience standing in the pit – the gallery as we should now say. Those who usually sat on the stage itself and behaved affectedly throughout the production could not have been spiritually close to him. Shakespeare's truth lies first and foremost in his freedom from illusory lights, his stepping beyond the line of footlights.

However it is not easy to achieve justification for a direct approach. 'Here in *The Forest*[2] Ostrovsky is getting at the life of the landowners,' Meyerhold wrote. 'He did not want to bring out either the philosopher or the capricious Chatsky[3] . . . two clowns would shake the foundations of this well-established prosperity.' The heroes of the

[1] By Verhaeren, first produced by Meyerhold in 1920.

[2] Produced by Meyerhold at the Meyerhold Theatre in 1924.

[3] The main character in Griboyedov's *Woe from Wit*.

play in Meyerhold's opinion 'are on the one hand the simpleton and on the other, the tragedian – the surly man in a jacket turned inside out . . . It is not the so-called "positive characters" which decide the fate of the drama, but the clowns – and this device catches us, the audience, unawares, tricks us like game birds. This is the device of artistic provocation.'

It has already been remarked many times that the dialogue between the mad King, the Fool and blind Gloucester is full of strange jokes which would seem to be completely out of place in their dramatic context. In his *The Wheel of Fire* (first published in 1930) Wilson Knight has researched into the malicious humour in *King Lear*: it is a complete comic encyclopaedia from Gloucester's jokes (in the very worst taste) to the quaint retorts of the Fool. The critic shows that cruel humour, or rather the humour of cruelty, is one of the foundations of the play.

I would also like to mention a short and now little-known article. Two pages in minute format were astonishing in the decisiveness of their refutation. This always happens: a new slant on something, the discovery of an unknown aspect of a work (a well-known work) is always strengthened by the complete rejection of everything that was formerly considered to be most important. Victor Shklovsky wrote in this article, 'The most unimportant fact about *King Lear*, as far as I see it, is that the work is a tragedy . . . conforming to type is not important to Shakespeare, it is not important to him why Lear says one thing one moment and another thing the next, or why he breaks out with coarse jokes. Shakespeare sees Lear as both an actor and a fool . . . How should one play *King Lear*? One should act not a type . . . a type is like threads which sew the work together, a type is like a maker of panoramas showing landscape after landscape, or the justification of effects . . . King Lear must be played like a wit and an eccentric.' ('On Horseback')

Victor Shklovsky never re-published this article and it is a pity. The extreme experiment, the testing out of the hypothesis was interesting at the time. Time demanded such tests then, and Shakespeare did not lose anything by them. One thing has remained of Shklovsky's conception today: 'the philosopher' is not given the right to address the audience directly. There is no figure of tragedy without the 'wit'.

MEYERHOLD'S TERMINOLOGY changed so radically that it is not easy now to understand his early articles and speeches. In the foreword to his book *On the Theatre* he wrote, 'I began to work as a director in 1902 but it is only now, towards the end of a decade, that I have begun to uncover the secrets which are concealed in such prime elements as the proscenium and the mask.' There was a divergence of meaning in the word 'secret' in the lexicography of the symbolists and of the artists who belonged to his close circle. The shadow of secrecy fell on Meyerhold's favourite images – the carnival *bauta* (a white half-mask with a sharp bird's beak and a black three-cornered hat) from the paintings of the Venetian Pietro Longhi, or the fantasmagoria of Carlo Gozzi and Hoffmann – but it is unlikely that he discovered any other-worldly spheres in them. His *opera* (as he called his productions) often featured candles, mirrors, playing cards – the symbols of fate. A whole period of similar amusements was crowned by the magnificent and evil *Masquerade*[1]: the proscenium, the Stranger carousing, Arbenin spiralling in a dance of masks. Then in many articles this première was effectively juxtaposed with the fall of the tsardom.

And in fact it seemed as if Golovin's last funeral curtain fell not only on the show but also on the past, and that included the past of the director himself. Everything in his art seemed to change out of all recognition; he was the first to underline the complete change. The director of the October Theatre was not interested in 'secrets' but in biomechanics, conditioned reflexes, constructivism. And what mystery could there be about a platform erected at one end of a hall or about a theatrical mask? . . . It is true that in practice his theoretical terminology somehow did not take root and died of its own accord. The words, particularly his own, confused rather than clarified the significance of his work: he expressed himself not in his declarations but in his images, which form perhaps some of the most complicated in the art of this century.

The simplest objects and technical methods took on a particular depth in his work; as in any true poetry, not much is conveyed in a paraphrase. The truck-stages of *The Government Inspector* on which the sets stood were extremely significant.

Meyerhold paid particular attention to what in the life of the theatre is called décor – whether painted or constructed. He began his director's life with the denunciation of naturalism and the imitation of dwellings; blobs of paint became the basis of his productions. Then he cleared his stage of anything that bore any relationship to painting; he was delighted by the bare and dirty wall of a theatre building; then he crowded the area of the stage with elegantly beautiful museum pieces . . .

Other directors (even great ones) have made innovations in their

[1] Adapted from Lermontov, premiered 25 February 1917.

schematic 'designs': they have often worked with the same artists as Meyerhold did, but in their productions the stage was only a place for the action irrespective of whether it was reflecting life or was merely the foundation for a theatrical jamboree.

Meyerhold created the philosophy of space. In his works it was as if the world doubled and space was broken apart: there was the ordinary sixpenny space of everyday life – dense crowding, smallness (the vision preceding his decade), and behind all this the infinity of the world. These are motifs which are familiar in lyric poetry. Alexander Blok was tormented by the feeling of closeness, the narrowness of the spiritual world which would not accommodate the real world within it; the word 'irreconcilability' recurs again and again in his letters and diaries. A stifling airlessness, and a striving to break away and enter space 'out of the darkness' (even if also 'of the universe') to 'God's world'. Blok wrote in a letter to his father that his realism borders on the fantastic and cited as an example Dostoyevsky's *Youth*. Again the same definition. Everything was far from simple: there was neither 'darkness' nor 'God's world', but the contrasts between the living (even vulgar and concentrated to the point of horror), confined by time, fettered by time, and the undefined – the beautiful? the terrible? – gave a new character to Russian literature. Romantic irony does not cover it all.

Much in Meyerhold's art began with Blok's *Fairground Booth* (1906). The director and artist, Sapunov, built another tiny stage on the stage – a complete theatre in miniature with its curtains, footlights and prompt box, with little slips through which the scenery was carried. In the little theatre a play was distorted to an unrecognizable extent and its infuriated author stopped the production: he ran out on to the stage wanting to explain to the audience but someone grabbed hold of his coat-tails and dragged him behind the curtain; when Harlequin jumped through the window – he tore the paper: the window turned out to be painted on to the wall of the scenery; beyond the little theatre was the theatre, and beyond the conventional space, the world. The action revolved on three planes: a play (the author himself remained as a real part of it); the 'show' with the masks of Pierrot, Harlequin and Columbine; and the world outside the conventional space of the 'little theatre'. What was this world? Real? A Blok-like eternity of dark blue and snow storms?[1] Who knows. One thing one can say: even in those times the author and director laughed at mystics, joked at their talk of 'other worlds'. Their jokes were not without some malice: Blok's close friends considered themselves insulted and broke off all relations with him.

[1] A reference to Blok's long poem 'The Twelve'.

The simultaneous existence of different spatial dimensions and the impossibility of reconciling one with the other was also present in Blok's *The Unknown Woman*; the boredom of the tavern (on Gislyarovsky Street, portrayed as it turned out with complete accuracy), the gossip of society drawing rooms – and outside the walls of the houses, the flight of stars in the eternity of night, and falling snow, covering everything. The theatre censor racked his brains trying to discover the meaning of the play. And so, without understanding at all, he wrote 'decadence' and, latching on to the name of the heroine 'Maria', banned the play for blasphemy.

A few years later the twelve Red Army soldiers arrived in the indistinguishable whirling of the snowstorm which carried them across time and space; and amidst the abstract intersecting surfaces, built on the empty desolate stage of the RSFSR Theatre No. 1, they performed *The Dawn*, half play, half political meeting.[1]

The truck-stages of *The Government Inspector* – worlds populated with Gogolesque characters – floated out of the murky darkness, out of the blackness of space, as if from immeasurable time. The cells of life – furniture, people, things, sounds, gossip, fear, all crowded in on the audience, just as Gogolesque images crowd in on the reader, as each dead soul[2] takes up the space in order then to recede into the distance, to give way to the next dead soul which is also approaching, moving across space. Really Sobakeyevich is both man and house – he is the chest of drawers, the whole world is Sobakeyevich.

These worlds, terrifying in their narrowness and insignificance, are revealed in Gogol, like a travel novel with movement, if you like 'filming in motion': the coachman gives the signal, the horses go faster, the horizon disappears and the outlying villages of the estate appear, the entrance to the park, a multitude of objects, and the landlord himself comes out to meet them; boundless space gives way to an accumulation of objects, the walls contract, the ceilings are lowered – it is the sixpenny space of the theatrical truck-stages.

Meyerhold's light projectors lit up not a copy of reality, but the reality of the heart of things, concentrated essences. Secrets of the theatre but also secrets of Gogol's art. What did these strange formations mean? People bunched together with candles in their hands, the reading of a letter for 'Tryapichkin's soul', closed in an

[1] Verhaeren's play depicted the transformation of a capitalist war into an international proletarian uprising. Meyerhold made the most of its relevance to political events in Russia and the theatre had more the atmosphere of a meeting hall. Admission was free and the audience were periodically showered with leaflets during the performance [trans.].

[2] This is a reference to Gogol's epic novel *Dead Souls*.

arbour, gilded and cheaply illustrated trellis work. Red wood, Karelian birches, porcelain and crystal – all crammed into the space of a sixpence, and then the bareness, emptiness of a harshly illuminated expanse of the whole stage – not a thing, not a sign of life, only the sound of galloping hooves – a fool's carnival covering the whole world.

The proscenium is not only the architecture of the theatre area, but also Meyerhold's own footsteps, his irrepressible movement forwards, beyond the portals, the bounds of the theatre. In his art the 'proscenium' was always an edge, a spatial boundary between reality and the theatre. Here on the very edge he manoeuvred and pushed worlds together: he arranged mirrors in different corners so that the reflections doubled, tripled, and doubles grew up behind the characters, and the space stretched out into eternity. And what about the mask? He did not mention Harlequin and Pierrot any more. During the months while he was working on *The Government Inspector* he talked about other characters: he would call on his troupe to learn from Charlie Chaplin and Buster Keaton. They learnt with dedication: the stupefied immobility of Garin's face as Khlestakov was akin to Keaton's look of frozen sadness. The masks of the ancient folk theatre were preserved not only in the stylized theatrical pantomime but had to be transferred through vaudeville to the screen of Mack Sennett.

Unusual structures in art alternately disappear, and then are regenerated in a different form. Are they secrets of the theatre or secrets of life? At odd times some phenomena are condensed; the living significance disappears – the nonsense bundles together, and you get an absurd squash on the tiny sixpenny space of the stage. And then for some reason, behind all this is suddenly unexpectedly revealed the threatening expanse of history: tragedy is followed by farce. And then you get farce until you are sick of it.

The proscenium and the mask. But there is no proscenium in the cinema and the mask would look theatrical to the screen. Then one must say it another way: Lear – King, father, old man, tyrant, wise man, martyr, Shakespeare himself (how many more masks are there in the role?) enters facing the camera and walks forward into a close-up; there must be no reflection of footlights on his face. No separating line between Shakespeare's people and the people in the audience; between the grief on the screen and the memory of grief in real life.

IN 1925 WE FILMED *The Cloak*.[1] In defining the role we once imagined Charlie Chaplin in the part of Akaky Akakiyevich. It

[1] Based on Gogol's short story *The Overcoat*.

turned out to be a stupid idea: what similarity is there between a small tramp and a clerk, debased and destroyed by 'a department of baseness and rubbish'? . . . But all the same the shadow of something similar flitted across our minds; there was some almost imperceptible likeness: a small man in the vastness of a world that was alien to him. Nothing is ever rejected without some trace being left behind: a few sentences were printed from an interview conducted in the heat of the moment. I found them later in an American film magazine. All this would have been forgotten, would have completely vanished from one's memory had not . . .

There is complete justification for the direct approach, as Meyerhold understood it, the eccentric in the space of tragedy – a white-haired eighty-year-old . . . Yes, perhaps Meyerhold would have made the best Lear of all.

Chapter Ten

PETER BROOK REGARDS contemporary theatre as an almost completely dead organism; he is searching for the seeds which will save it. One of the seeds, as he always maintains, folk theatre, changes in form but unfailingly preserves a single characteristic which distinguishes it and gives it life: roughness. A chapter in Brook's book is thus 'The Rough Theatre'. 'Salt, sweat, noise, smell', Brook enumerates, 'the theatre that's not in a theatre, the theatre on carts, on wagons, on trestles, audiences standing, drinking, sitting round tables, audiences joining in, answering back; theatre in back rooms, upstairs rooms, barns; the one-night stands.'[1]

This is how I began as a boy: screens, puppets, red calico and tin foil, battered top hats, clowns' noses, beards which hooked on, painted green, red, agit-sketches[2] on lorries, platforms made out of planks set up in town squares, on railway wagons, showbiz, shouting at the top of one's voice . . .

This was my training; it taught me to be revolted by grandiloquence; I look back on it with nothing but happy memories. The first agit-sketches ran on high quality fuel: a simplicity of faith, the enthusiasm of youth, and the fuse was a hatred of academism, a feeling which was common to all leftist artists. One more thing can perhaps be added: the very poverty of revolutionary art was beautiful – plywood, colour washes, and canvas were noble materials. One could not sit around for long in this school. The agit-sketch ended its short life not because of artistic poverty; there was another reason – the world ceased to appear simple; the desire to understand its complexity brought to life completely different forms. As far as artistic qualities were concerned – energy, invention, a concentration of method, directness, and a feeling of love for life – they were particularly strong in these first productions. But the spontaneity, the strength of feeling began to fade and the profession moved onwards. And then velvet, marble and bronze appeared in the warehouses. A different kind of scissors were at work: feelings cheapened but the materials grew richer. Speaking figuratively the peep show entertainers began to compose in hexameters: this business produced its

[1] *The Empty Space*, MacGibbon & Kee 1968, p. 65.

[2] 'Agitki', short propaganda films or playlets made or performed during the first years after the Revolution of 1917.

own 'academicians'. Mayakovysky laid down the paint brush of ROSTA[1] and wrote:

> One thing I fear
> For you and me
> That our soul will
> become shallow
> That we will carry into
> the communist order
> The cheapness of the entertainer
> and the rubbish of their verses.

[1] ROSTA – The Russian Telegraph Agency – the centre where the latest information and propaganda was pinned up in poster form. Mayakovsky joined the artists who painted these posters in 1919 [trans.].

Chapter Eleven

PREGNANT OPHELIA

FRAGMENTS OF MEYERHOLD'S ideas still keep breaking out either in someone's memoirs or in their correspondence. One can distinguish the hand of an architect by his favourite building material. Meyerhold's was gunpowder. So to this day you will find the first signs of one of his productions: a fragment of a play, but containing an explosive charge, with a Bickford fuse protruding from it – the tell tale sign that he had a hand in it. Terror would seize the unprepared, the unwarned – run, run as fast as you can, they would cry! I read in N. A. Belevtseva's memoirs: 'Meyerhold invited me to work with him in the theatre, but after I had met him, I must admit that my desire to join vanished.' What can have frightened the actress? 'He portrayed the character of Ophelia to me in coarse, naturalistic terms. "Ophelia loves Hamlet", he said, "but she loves him with earthly love. She is carrying his child and here one should not apply any lacquer. She is pregnant, heavy, simple, without any clouds".' There is no doubt that the conversation is reported accurately, that these are his words. Who besides Meyerhold would be so stern, even harsh towards Polonius's poor daughter? If she had still further wasted time with her flowers, the chief Commissar of the Theatre[1] could have called the armed guard: then there would have been no time for joking. He used to wage war, to go into the attack. 'Belly' (If you have 'earthly love' then you have the word belly as well) was like a millstone to him; you tied the stereotype to it so that it would sink as deep as possible. One only has to look at old photographs of theatrical Ophelias to see what he was getting at. He tarred these Ophelias like the gates of prostitutes in old villages. And he stripped off the lacquer, this is where the brilliance would have come from! Rehearsals grew like a treatise called 'pregnant women in the history of art'; but what about Pushkin's letter to Natalya[2] (as a footnote)? this is true lyricism! and the death in childbirth of the little princess in Tolstoy? Is this not true tragedy? He would have illustrated his words with quick gestures and then, taking off his

[1] The Russian word *Narkompros* stands for *Narodny Komissariat Prosveshcheniye* (The People's Commissariat for Education). In 1920 Meyerhold was appointed head of the Theatre Section.

[2] His wife.

jacket, would have come up on the stage . . . Applause would have broken out in the auditorium – a stooping middle-aged man with a hooked nose and untidy hair would have become in the eyes of the company the irrevocably pregnant, undoubted Ophelia. And all other Ophelias would have perished – Gretchens with flowers in their long curly hair. Away with 'clouds'! No more 'clouds'!

The next day he would have said to the actress, 'Pregnant? Why pregnant? Who ever thought of such an idiotic idea?'

I stored this memory in a safe place. Similar instances often happened in his work as a director. The story of the green wig in *The Forest*[1] is famous: at each discussion Meyerhold would think up a complicated explanation for having green hair. 'Why green?' they would ask. 'It's the colour of youth . . . the emblematic significance of make-up even in the Kabuki theatre' . . . but once no answer to the question was given.

'Take away that wig', he said irritably to his assistant after a performance. 'And who on earth could have thought up such an idea? Green! Why green?'

Fragments of pottery – the traces of some ancient experiments – which someone had forgotten to clear away from the laboratory table.

Here is the transcript of one of the rehearsals for *The Government Inspector* (they are talking about Khlestakov's appearance).

Meyerhold: How do you visualize the head?
Martinson: He evidently wears a powdered wig.
Meyerhold: Oh no . . . he is bald. As bald as a coot. He has been bald since childhood . . . But they always make Khlestakov into a beau . . . But anyway all women love bald-headed men. Bald-headed men are tremendously successful with women. Gabriel D'Annunzio[2] for instance. I see Khlestakov as a Gabriel D'Annunzio of the thirties.

Later, it further transpires that the Mayor's appearance is a match for Khlestakov's: 'The meeting of two bald-headed men – Khlestakov and the Mayor . . . This is interesting. An abundance of hair is boring.'

Neither the bald head of Skvoznik-Dmukhanovsky nor of Khlestakov/D'Annunzio saw the light of day in the actual production. So what was the point of these flabbergasting suggestions? Was it really only a matter of deliberate provocation?

This was not the only point. It was the abruptness of the move-

[1] The play by Ostrovsky [trans.].

[2] The poet and playwright whose play, *Pisanelle*, Meyerhold produced in 1913 in Paris [trans.].

ment: a break with tradition – with the links in a chain of vaudeville fops with powdered wigs – Duras[1] (the subject of Gogol's despair). As far as the dumbfounding novelty of the suggestion is concerned, this too was not a bad method of shaking the actors, and pushing them as far away as possible from what lay on the surface. He did not want to take anything at its face value; he wanted to find everything out for himself; to discover without repeating what had been discovered long before; everything was first-hand, nothing was inherited. In school repetition is the mother of learning; in art, it is the mother of the artisan, of routine.

Explosive techniques in industry have long since become not only a method of destruction but also a method of construction.

CAUTION, A LOOKING back, boasting of perfection (something thought out seven times) is the sclerosis of the director's profession; without experimenting with all possibilities, and that means often coming up against brick walls – in front of one's colleagues but also with one's colleagues – rehearsals will wither and die; only artisans fear for their authority (the director is an erudite man, a pedagogue, and foresees all possibilities). Of course there comes a time when one has to choose with firmness, to throw out the superfluous and to reject what does not relate to the essential. But without the 'superfluous' in the course of working, the most important does not emerge. Here one can quote Lear himself: He says to his too unreasonable daughter:

> our basest beggars
> Are in the poorest thing superfluous:
> Allow not nature more than nature needs,
> Man's life is cheap as beast's.

I read (in M. Knebel's memoirs) that when the theatre was on tour, Mikhail Chekhov and Vakhtangov (they shared a room in their hotel) had a morning routine on first waking up of playing the game of 'unscrewing' themselves limb by limb, that is with the complete exactness that mime actors show in portraying an act without objects, acting as if they gradually unscrewed their fingers or their feet from their legs; once the limb was completely unscrewed, they would carefully place this imaginary part of their own body on a table or chair. They observed meticulous accuracy down to the most minute gesture and there was a complete illusion that this invisible

[1] Duras was a celebrated actor in Gogol's day [trans.].

action was indeed taking place. The pantomimes were acted seriously with absolute concentration. Vakhtangov won: he took a long time in painstakingly unscrewing his head, eventually lifted it intact from his neck, carefully carried it away and put it on a shelf in the cupboard, and then he began to unscrew other limbs with great precision and without losing the feeling that he no longer had a head. I do not know whether this was only a joke, an amusement, or whether it was a professional preparation, a training without which the artist would lose his form.

IN 1934 MEYERHOLD again – for the hundredth time – talks of *Hamlet*. There is no mention now of anything to do with pregnant Ophelia. 'Looking into the distance, Hamlet sees his father (his father's ghost) coming out of the mist with the waves running up against the shore, laboriously dragging his feet out of the oozing mud of the sea's bottom. He is in silver from head to foot.' Here there are already clouds of some sort. But let us turn our attention to the ghost's walk: the silver feet of the spirit in the wet sand. However this is only the beginning; later we discover or rather see, 'Water has frozen on his armour and on his beard. He is cold and distressed.' The son sits the father down on a rock and himself sits beside him, and – the detail! – Hamlet takes a large cloak from his shoulders and wraps his father up in it: frost, a ghost wearing nothing but armour has grown cold . . .

No, there is still a trace of pregnant Ophelia.

Lomonosov[1] wrote in his *Rhetoric*, 'The more abundant inventions the composer of a work can enrich it with, the quicker will be the power of expressing with one thing imagined in the mind other things which are somehow related to it; for instance, when you imagine a ship, you also see the sea . . . with the sea a storm, with a storm – waves, with the waves – noise against the shore, with the shore – rocks, and so on.'

To discover the region of the 'related' is one of the main tasks of the director and is perhaps the most difficult; what once strengthened and deepened life-like qualities may at other times kill them. The work dries up and wilts when its images can be 'wholly expressed' not with living phenomena but only with artistic images.

This is the danger of a film production of a play: one can break out beyond the confines of the theatre and find oneself in a different but equally confined space; something like Blok's hero's jumping out of

[1] M. V. Lomonosov, 1711–65, the great scientist, also considered one of the forerunners of Russian literature [trans.].

a window which was only a drawing; beyond the theatre lies not the depths of life but the flat surface of the screen. Space is not a biosphere of time (that is what one would wish for most!), but the illusory reality of the cinema: the screen has made a tight covering over life. Horse radish is no sweeter than radish. Only it is easier to deceive on the screen: cinema reflexes have already worked themselves out, are achieving artistic harmony; the simulation of life looks like the truth but in actual fact it is just as conventional as, if not more so than, declamation against a background of cardboard décor.

Real art more often than not begins outside the bounds which contemporary aesthetics designated for it. The circle of deviants grows. Technical developments (in terms of the cinema) not only broaden art but at the same time make it contract: each new method is assimilated by the production line. What was once a subject for scientific fantasy – the invention of self-propagating robots – has become a commonplace in the film industry: films beget films, until you have an entire witches' brew of self-conceived and self-propagated editing combinations – eyes of heroines and snatches of dialogue. Film festivals can send one mad: films are doubled, trebled, reproduced a hundredfold. The film critics, it is true, find differences, weighing up the nuances. In just the same way the circus horse probably thinks that it has galloped round the whole world from pole to pole: the joke is that, almost every evening it has trotted, galloped, and the carriages have changed during journeys and the stalls in the stables have been different. And in reality it has only galloped inside the circus – it was the façades of the circus that were different, but the circle is the same, measured accurately to the world standard of 13½ metres, neither more nor less.

Meyerhold was one of those who broke out beyond the confines of the theatre, so far beyond the 'small area of expression'[1] that one catches one's breath at the strength and daring of his breaking away. This is also how his pupil began. The screen shook from top to bottom with Eisenstein's ideas – which have now become world standards.

I HAD GOT an insignificant word on the brain and could not get rid of it. Its very sound was irritating: 'screening'. 'The basis is the title of the same name'.[2] 'Where? what basis? There are no bases, this title with the same name must come to life, begin to live with the fulness of life. And for God's sake don't translate this into cinematic language; cinematic language must translate it into human terms,

[1] To use Lomonosov's terminology [trans.]. [2] i.e. *King Lear* [trans.].

full of thought and feelings, such feelings as are contained in 'the title of the same name'. Well what is the cinema there for after all? For me it has been my habitual means of expression since childhood; there is more space on the screen.

I HAVE MORE than once looked over my notes (over many years) on Meyerhold, rearranged them, corrected them, trying to bring out, to make clearer what seemed to me to be the most important about his art, what effected his whole life in spite of the apparent complete disparity of form. In recent years collections of Meyerhold's own articles have been published, his unpublished speeches, transcripts of rehearsals, reminiscences about him – all this has given me the opportunity to re-check my notes, and I sat down to work again . . . What was the meaning of his work? What task had I set myself. Why did I keep so stubbornly returning to his productions, or rather not to individual productions, but to something much more important than theatrical hits and flops – to certain aspects of life, to movements caught by his expression. My aim was certainly not to describe his *mises-en-scène* (with all possible accuracy), and still less to judge them as either 'true' or 'false'. I saw *The Government Inspector* in its day (and still think about it now) not only as one of the audience in the stalls or the circle – I had a different viewpoint: 'from my own ivory-tower'. We had only just finished filming *The Cloak*, and from that time onwards (and even earlier with the turbulent FEKS production of *Marriage*[1] in 1922) the Gogolesque images never left me. On our screen Akaky Akakiyevich was moved into the inhuman emptiness of enormous squares; bronze and cast-iron giants – monuments to emperors – towered over him, worthless midget that he was; in the shots the monumental piles of buildings were outlined in black, and then a snow storm blew up. Without thinking about it and not imagining that such a task existed, we tried (by feel) to include the story in the space of tragedy; now, after long years of work, this aim seems even clearer to me (in words) but to attain it (in reality) is even more difficult. While shooting *Lear*, I remembered the landscapes of Dostoyevsky, and Meyerhold's crowding on the 'truck-stages' (as it really was on the stage or how I interpreted it adding or taking away certain details) not because they resembled the castles and roads, the kings and dukes of Britain – what could one find that was remotely similar here? – nothing. There is literally no likeness even in a single characteristic or a single visible detail. But in the very depth of portrayal there is a feeling of the breaking apart

[1] A staging of Gogol's play [trans.].

of the epoch, 'The time is out of joint' (*Hamlet*); it is all charged with everyday life like gunpowder and unless the world changes it will burst into the air, into the immeasurable void, will scatter as ashes, and the black whirlwind of history will take the harvest from the charred earth in its iron hand. It is the same feeling of tragedy.

The wide sweep of space, the unity of the ununitable. Are these lessons from Meyerhold? Yes, they are his lessons and a lot of other lessons as well. It is a confused school. But this confusion helps one to understand a great confuser – Lear.

WHEN YOU WORK, whether you like it or not the whole of your life gets involved: what you lived through, thought about and suffered; there is no order – the memory takes and pushes to the fore what would seem to be unnecessary; things get woven together and absurd links are forged. By some unknown route (as so often happens in everyday life) Meyerhold was linked in my memory with completely different things. What role could aesthetic memories and harlequinades by Doctor Dapertutto (Meyerhold's pseudonym on the eve of the First World War) play here: the railway stations during the war were the beginning of my life, the beginning of art; the crush of bodies, the colour of the soldiers' uniforms, the musty smell of carbolic, shag, burning, grief, typhus (I have forgotten so much, but one thing I do remember clearly is my own feverish delirium when I had typhus); and then the heated carriages, overcoats, footcloths, children howling, peel, lice, the dim shroud of smoke from the self-rolled cigarettes (this is when I was on my way from Kiev to Petrograd to study with Meyerhold, and he as if deliberately turned out to be in the south!): Petrograd – not finding a place for myself in the consciousness of the enormity of this frozen city, the year 1919 . . . And all the same I found myself in Meyerhold's school, to use a contemporary phrase, as an external student. It was a strange education, not like other people's. I thought (there were phases like this) that it was pointless to study with him any longer, and that I had studied long enough anyway: we sat at our desks and studied on our own. But then time would elapse and one would have to turn to him again; not even to his work but to his destiny. Eisenstein – his true pupil – had a complicated relationship with his teacher. Meyerhold was a difficult person but when Eisenstein began to write his autobiography during a serious illness, he wrote 'I am not worthy to lace up the strings of his sandals.'

Whatever he began (and rarely brought into order or finished) is still developing and will continue to develop: time will reveal not only the significance of his innovations on the stage, but the meaning of his prophecies; his head which looked like a ruffled bird, proudly and sadly thrown back, will remain in the memory not only as the image of a director-innovator, but also as what he himself celebrated; the mask – the immortal mask of tragedy no less beautiful than those which the heroes of Sophocles and Euripides performed before the crowds in their thousands.

In his last speech in 1939 (in the Stanislavsky Opera Theatre) he said, 'I'm not going to start defending four columns with you. I'm used to being persecuted. You can persecute me from pillar to post and I may leave. But I'm not going to start preserving columns.'[1]

The transcriber wrote 'applause'; this was the last applause that he heard.

Often something that is now considered to be a generalization, was in its time real, and was talked about not at all as a concept of deep principle but as a practical reality. The four columns were not figurative: Meyerhold had in mind not the ghost of classicism but the most realistic columns which were in the auditorium of that same Stanislavsky Opera Theatre. In the production of *Eugene Onegin* they were used as part of the décor and then became a habit, sometimes taken as a whole, sometimes once more in separate parts; they were introduced into the staging of other productions and transferred to other buildings. They were held as if in reverence in as much as they had a connection with Stanislavsky. 'The art of the founder of the studio', explained Meyerhold 'is not contained in these columns, and being true to Stanislavsky does not consist in having to sing against this background.'

The conversation turned to everyday topics and the four columns stood there for every one to see. This is how it was at the time . . . But now it all seems symbolic: the preservation of the columns, doors banging shut.

[1] This translation is taken from Edward Braun, *Meyerhold on Theatre*, Methuen 1969, p. 300.

Chapter Twelve

A YEAR HAD gone by in the search for actors, the rehearsals and the screen tests. Now the whole team was going out on to the field; the game was about to begin; if the choice had been right they, no longer actors, but characters, would lead the way for me. They had already gone beyond my control in a lot of ways; they had to move, talk, and behave towards one another in a certain way and no other; 'no other' occasionally flashed on the screen – it did not belong to Shakespeare or to *Lear*. And at the same time, emerging of their own accord and assuming first place were the eyes of Lear, the enormous and very bright eyes of Yarvet. Speaking in theatrical terms, they upstaged everyone else. A form began to emerge: a concerto for piano and orchestra.

AT FIRST I did not want to be concerned with the production side of the film; I was interested in another kind of complexity. But it transpired that it was impossible to escape altogether the humdrum details (and what details) of film production: a director's work is the continuous overcoming of difficulties and there is no end to them.

The fact that we had to transfer the 'division of the kingdom' scene (and a number of other exterior scenes) to the studio destroyed a lot of what had already been planned. It had been easy for me to tell Peter Brook that I was going to shoot the whole film on location. But what else could I have done? It is impossible not to be confident at the start: everything seems easy; the sea is up to one's knees; but once the work starts one is suddenly up to one's neck in water, struggling with all one's might to avoid drowning. We had re-take after re-take. And between sessions we hacked off pieces of the sets, not because they were poorly conceived (Yenei's sketches, as always, were excellent), but because, in the course of 'rationalization' the size of the acting area was cut down ('line production of studio scenes', the next one was already under construction); they changed the shape of the walls which we had settled on after a lot of experimenting (a more economical method of working); the proportions were ruined and the deception was obvious . . . And there I was gloomily wandering through the sets wondering how it would look if I took away another piece. We hacked, cleared and carried away: we were cutting through the 'palace hall' to some completely unknown building. Every night Yenei would give it some sort of shape with coarse wooden coverings (hewn with an axe); only one thing remained from what had been there before – a coat of arms, a stone lion on a stone wall; provided there was a coat of arms, that meant it belonged to the King. Virsaladze walked into the studio. 'But do you know' he said, 'I rather like it; it is turning into some sort of shed or barn. This shed is a good thing.' And then, looking at a hide which was on the floor, he quickly added: 'How about me taking this hide? This is just what I need for the Duke of Cornwall...'

Were there ever (anywhere) halls looking like this? Who knows. We would try to convince people that there were. One of our advisers visited us during the filming and I watched him. There was silence. Then, as if in answer to a question (I had not asked him anything) he said, hesitating a little: 'No, why . . . it would have been possible during the Stuarts', and then he looked away, smiling guiltily. As a rule consultants quickly get attached to a film and are ready to sell their historical soul to the cinematic devil; what didn't they have to justify in our film . . .

'Now it is clear what we need', said Yenei, 'One man and a piece of "truth"' (by 'truth' he meant genuine material).

But the date? The epoch? The epoch was the character of the figures, their faces; we would date the action by the faces of two stereotyped old men (here were our 'architectural details'); I had been admiring them for a long time; we had persuaded them (almost a year beforehand) to grow grey beards; they were to accompany Lear, to be near him all the time like statues at the entrance to a tomb. I took less care over many of the characters in the film than I did over these two dumb witnesses. Where we had cut down the arch (framing the halls), we built up a line of guards – dark tanned leather and steel (helmets and weapons); this was the impassable boundary between two worlds; the ranks stood aside to let the chosen through (Gloucester, Kent, the King of France) and immediately closed in again behind their retreating figures. This was the architecture of the King's castle. We set up the shots so that man was always in the foreground. We could film any one of them without make-up and in close-up. The space behind the characters had to be rather felt than be visible; here there was nothing to look round at, nothing worth studying closely; neither architectural details nor ornaments woven into the material. Only people – individual figures and individual groups – stood out clearly; there were no links or common characteristics between them; each man (or group) existed apart, on his own merit, in a vacuum. This sort of planning is of course conventional, but the convention belongs not to the theatre but to life – life had adapted itself to the plan; the inhuman geometry was set up (from above), the hierarchy of power was defined; this was the royal order of things. The eldest daughter, Goneril, comes out and stands in her appointed place, Regan follows her and then Cordelia. And then, observing the same order, each must take a few steps forward (counted) and say how much they love the king; first the eldest, then Regan, and then order breaks down: the youngest daughter does not say anything. Then there is a general sharp movement, a break in the ritual; everyone immediately steps back from her.

I wanted to express this geometrically, to make it visually obvious; this was important not only for the scene itself but also in contrast to what was to come; what appeared firm and unshakeable collapses in an instant, turns to chaos, a seething mass of bodies: they all rush from their places, from their chains – to get away as quickly as possible! Where? Why? They do not know themselves. The chain is broken, it could not be otherwise because order is already dead, an illusion. Underneath lies total collapse and everything is rolling, tumbling, turning to confusion; the rhythm of Shakespeare must take hold of the camera itself, move it along behind the hurrying crowds of people; someone is pursuing someone (or something?) and is in turn being pursued. Space and people are at one in this commotion, the perspectives become confused, doors bang, courtyards and roads follow one after the other and the sky moves to meet the earth. Now the energy of the verse carries the shots along with it, charges the cinematic fabric with electricity – this is what I wanted to achieve on the screen.

And then I remembered the end of Peter Brook's letter: 'How? . . . To what degree?'

'IT MUST', 'it will turn into', 'it will' – I think that in these very verbs with their worthy intentions is contained if not the road to hell (too exalted a definition!) at least the waste-film-bin into which discarded film is thrown. Everything which embellishes historical box-office hits – even in the most modest doses (even in the small degree with which we used details of the time in *Don Quixote* or in *Hamlet*) – is incompatible with *Lear*: this is what we had learnt so far by harsh experience. A sort of severe yardstick gradually began to define itself: nothing was allowed which showed the interference of the artist, and no ornaments. A distinct 'epoch' does not go with this tragedy; it is all less than what it embraces, simpler than what it is talking about. But the opposite is no better: a studied emptiness or abstraction immediately turns it into theatre.

The saddest part about it is that we started in the studio: I am convinced that on location we would have found a mode of expression more quickly. And for the moment we were occupied in cutting out as much as possible of the 'artistic', taking away all signs of 'style'. Only Yenei was capable of such a task.

What pains Virsaladze had taken so that his work should not be noticeable on the screen! What was his work in our film? . . . I found it hard to define it. 'Costumes?' No, his art went far beyond the boundaries of these matters: he created not costumes, but whole ensembles, the face of worlds of tragedy. This time there were practically no sketches. Nothing was done in addition to the living man, the character, and the thought which was contained in the role: the Duke of Cornwall's costume had nothing in common with the Duke of Albany's (men belonging to the same age and of the same rank). He had succeeded in attaining the reality of a historical world stripped bare of everything that belonged to 'historical costume'.

Yenei consoled me: everything would take shape and fall into place in Kazantip (his proposed location).

We achieved our 'pieces of truth' like grains of gold; on the other hand the slag heaps grew into mountains. These grains of gold are revealed – in the plastic art of Shakespearean film – when one finds a link in the combination of things which is not naturalistic but poetic; when the significance of the object in the shot is not literal but metaphorical. In order to overcome naturalism by 'living photography', one is looking for the points of gravity of a varied collection of elements, for their inner unity.

During the production of *Hamlet* I experimented with several film versions of the soliloquy 'To be or not to be'. The problem was not to find a place (which would be natural for the action), where the main character could speak these lines, but to reveal the link between the hero's spiritual life and the material world. At first I thought contrapuntally. Hamlet was walking along a very long corridor in Elsinore; it was as if he were walking through life, the life in which it was better 'not to be': soldiers were being drilled in the courtyard of the castle, they stepped back and from a distance hurled their spears at stuffed dummies – Denmark was preparing for war; he walked through halls where children were writing dictations, one could hear the teacher's voice, and the scratching of pens. A new generation was being brought up in accordance with Polonius' ideas (from his sermons to Laertes) ('Costly thy habit as thy purse can buy . . . For the apparel oft proclaims the man').

The beating of the drums, the roaring of the soldiers and the tedious dictation all merged into one. The sound, sometimes soft, sometimes threateningly loud, accompanied the words (the inner monologue) – and the result was a peculiar sort of dialogue: between the voice of life and thoughts about it. This version seemed like an illustration and I rejected it.

I began to think in terms of a walk through a forest, part of which was on fire: from the living trees to the blackened and charred and finally to the scorched earth . . . No that was some sort of symbolism. Perhaps it was worth basing it all on the rhythm? Hamlet in a ship's cabin during a storm, everything was rocking, the waves were rolling on to the deck, the words rose and fell amidst the roaring of the storm and the creaking of the rigging. Or perhaps one should lengthen the time of the action: Hamlet is walking at the same pace but in the same sequence day turns into night, it grows light again, dark, and the weather changes. How long did he go on thinking – for hours? days? weeks? . . .

Then in the old part of Tallin we found a long, very narrow alley; in a single panoramic shot Hamlet was to walk along the walls; the smooth surfaces were almost imperceptibly shaded with dried plants growing out of the stones, pieces had been chipped off, and what was most important a thin ray of sunshine (coming through a hole in the opposite wall) fell on one spot, the only one in the otherwise monotonous grey of the stone. We rehearsed several times in this street but the sun clouded over and we had no time to wait any longer.

The last version (the one which appears in the film) was found in the Crimea, on the sea shore. The rocks formed huge blocks and in order to find our way to the sea we had to displace them and negotiate more piles of rocks. The camera followed behind Hamlet – the cold, grey-black surfaces towered over him, and one impasse followed another.

The whole point was to link the rhythm of the cine camera's movements with the main character's train of thought.

LEAR'S FIRST SPEECH (the renunciation of power, and the division of the kingdom) turned out to be a hard nut to crack: the solemn constitution of the speech, the unfolding of the content, based on words alone, none of this lent itself to expressive shooting. The result was something like falling between two stools; because of cuts the strength of the verse was lost, and the camera was disassociated from the main events. It was not going to work. Of course the very character of the hero spoke for itself, but here perversely he used conventional language and it was, after all, his first appearance. We overcame the conventionality. Attention was directed by his words to the map: was the division fair? Were the heiresses' portions equal? Half-way through Lear would bend over the map in mid-sentence; the pauses gave a naturalness to the text, the words seemed more life-like. But, at the same time, the words somehow faded and the image grew dim. Life-like details (in this particular instance!) murdered the poetry. But the poetry was also rhetorical. What were we to do? We changed the underlying thought; Lear's map was not a piece of parchment with topographical markings (allegorical drawings on ancient maps) but a living memory; the king was parting not only with his crown but also with his past (something like Othello's saying farewell to the 'plumed troop'): this is the fortress he won, here were the fortifications he built, and here they were pulled down by his order. There are no bounds to his power. Should he not change the course of the river? Was that hill in the right place? To think of moving a hill! . . .

It was a strange, childish and rather malicious game: the king's finger added curves to the river; as if gathering the forest into the palm of his hand, Lear transferred it from the south to the north. Should he make new plans, for fun? Did he believe that he was really master of mountains and seas? But while the first citizens of the kingdom are in the halls, the crowds of people at the castle walls wait for their fate to be sealed. Here perhaps the camera would have found something to do. And the falling between two stools was averted; it was possible to settle more comfortably on one cinematic stool. But this stool did not belong to the author; we had invented the business ourselves. Shakespeare's poetry was different here. One could try to convey it by other means (even without words), and one could not do anything that was against it. This was not because certain laws protected the classical heritage (the 'people's possessions') from infringement – there are no such laws in art. It was much more simple: there was no point in it. It was not worth it.

I read recently in a newspaper article that, in the opinion of the critic, any director who undertook a production by Dostoyevsky had to solve a difficult problem: he had to enter into an argument with the author. I was astonished at reading this: why 'had to'? The difficulty is not of course in engaging in some argument; he can of course engage in an argument if he has really taken it into his head to do so. You can engage in other arguments : for instance, on meeting a boxing champion, get into a fight with him, in order to see, as Gogol said, what sort of man he really is with his fists.

I did not want to quarrel with Shakespeare. I collected together all the Russian translations and compared them with the original, studying the English text. The absurdity of what I was trying to do became evident.

I had been trying to empty a bottomless pit with a bucket labelled 'life'. In the rehearsal room, distracted by the actors, I had lost the feeling of the whole. The poetry did not touch the sphere of what we call the characters. Of course people are very important in tragedy, very important, but far from the only thing of importance. And the text does not always belong to the character, even though in the theatre it is spoken by the player of that part.

The text of *Lear* is astonishingly uneven : there are biblical tirades, bucolic sayings, rhetoricisms, witticisms, sophisticated curses . . . What does such an abundance of styles mean ? Why does Edgar need so many proverbs, songs and lamentations, when he is pretending to be a holy fool ? Is it so that he should not be recognized ? Silence or muttering would have attracted less attention to himself. Maybe those who accused the author of violating the proportions, of despising life-like truth are right ? If you hear nothing more than the voices of the characters in these passages the critics are right. But if you can only make out in these words not only the voice of one man, but also the voice of life itself, a part of its enormous strata, it takes on a different aspect. *Lear* is not only the drama of a particular group of people who are linked by the plot, but also a stream of history. Whole structures of life, social situations are carried along and tumbled together. Not only single voices are heard in the din of tragedy (lifelike in the fullest sense of the word) but combined and mighty ensembles, whole choruses. It is not Edgar pretending to be a beggar in order to hide from his pursuers, but poverty itself – the bitter village woe – which howls, laments, treads the earth's surface with nowhere to shelter, no strength to endure . . . If these words are only Edgar's, they are superfluous; if they contain images of the unjust life, then they are not only essential but are worth their weight in gold; this is where the high waves of tragedy are gathering strength.

With Edgar's transformation into a beggar, the whole expanse of grief is introduced into the poetry, in all its breadth, revealing the geography of the country of poverty, endless and boundless disaster – pathetic hovels, devastated villages, trampled fields : the homeless and debased are everywhere . . . If this stream becomes material – a scenic reality – the words can be left out, and Edgar need only pronounce what the living drama demands, what is just, beyond argument. But one voice must pick up the general chorus, otherwise the wave will turn into a pathetic trickle.

BUT WHAT ABOUT Lear's first speech? How is this nut to be cracked – this place in the play which attracts either declamation, or worse, thoughts of 'underlying currents' alien to the text? Is it not these lines which disposed the tragic actors to assume the make-up of 'titans'; with white beards down to their knees such a speech would be even more natural. However the same character's mode of speech is completely different in many other places whether he is angry, suffering or ironical. In order to uncover the essence of a speech, it is sometimes more important to understand not what it means on its own, but to look at what it contrasts with.

The play begins with Gloucester's meaningless chatter: jokes about the 'sins of youth' (like the conversation in a gentleman's club, as one critic has suggested). There is immediately not a transition but a precipice: instead of prose there is poetry; the tone and rhythm change sharply. The events open out on to the cold expanse of royal power, here there is a different account, a different path; the speech is no longer an expression of human thoughts and feelings, but a declaration of will, of decisions to be carried out; this is not a soliloquy but a manifesto . . . And then I had a dangerous idea: what if this very documentary style were purposely not smoothed over but, on the contrary, accentuated. It should not be spoken but read. It would be read, of course, not by the King (that would be out of character) but by one of his officials – in some fifteenth century he is doing the same work as our radio broadcasters. While the other man is reading the royal manifesto, Lear can behave according to his essential character.

Shakespeare created the image of Lear in such a way that from the very first moment his every action is unexpected: it is impossible to guess what he will do next, what tricks he is capable of. It is not possible to predict anything beforehand. This is because of the jerky flow of the poetry itself, the fantastic changes in rhythm and imagery. We would shoot it in the following way: the unexpectedness beginning not only from his first appearance but from the first sign that he is about to appear.

In sound cinema silence is very effective. We were trying to create a magnetic field of silence, an expanse of fear – and praying to God that no-one's boots would squeak, or their breathing be audible.

There was not a sound, only the oppressive silence of enormous buildings. Only a change in the expression of a courtier's eyes: the moment was approaching, any time now . . . and the silence was broken by a fanfare, signalling his entrance? No. By a drum roll? No. By a canon salute? No. In the dead silence, the fool's bell sounded – a long way behind the door, but quite distinctly. The important old men (the same ancients with ossified faces) solemnly moved forward, approached the wrought iron doors and stood at either side. The bell was coming nearer, now you could hear laughter too, the door creaked: in the far depths of the room two laughing figures were playing some sort of game, one was a boy-fool, the other (his back was turned) had white hair. 'Always with one foot in the grave' Voltaire wrote once, 'performing leaps with the other'. Fortunately (or unfortunately?) my time for daring experiments was over. It was not for me to create Lear 'the old eccentric', but in the very heart of the image I wanted the Fool's bells to ring out and peal as a salute to FEKS (The Factory of the Eccentric Actor)! I do not think I was entering into any quarrel with the author over this.

In trying to find at least some traits belonging to the image, I studied a large number of portraits, remembered people – philosophers, scholars, poets – anyone who by their external appearance, size, oddity of mind could in any way (even if by the most distant association) help me to grasp something of our main character. I studied photographs of Andrei Bely,[1] his grey hair, eyes, and remembered the verses Mandelstam wrote after Bely's death: 'I put a tiara on your head – on your fool's cap . . . teacher, tormentor, tyrant, fool . . . incomprehensible, comprehensible, inaudible, confused, easy. The collector of space . . . fledgling . . . of fools' bells!' It is a succession of ununitable, impossible machine-gun fire: every bullet is wide, but taken all together they are exactly on target: the sharpness of the definition is like a report, but the next one is a refutation of the one before, another report, another refutation. The rhythm is marked out in the rain of reports, the rhythm contains the step, the gait, the sharpness of the unexpected movement, a change of intonation in mid-sentence.

The Fool's bell is like a beginning, the first note which calls the tune for what is to follow. The bell is a tongue stuck out at pomposity and grandiloquence; a contempt for 'geometry'. Lear is the only one who is outside the general 'plan': without looking at anyone he walks forward, passes the steps up to the throne, passes by the frozen dukes and lords – not to the highest place, the centre, but to one side, to a simple stool by the fire. He has no attributes of power.

[1] The Russian symbolist poet.

What does he need a throne, crown or sceptre for? By lifting one finger every order will be carried out.

The plan – Lear sitting by the fire – was very important; the visual motif began from this point, one of the 'points' which Blok wrote about – a premonition, a support for the poetry; we threw one end of our visual texture over the point of this shot. The arrangement of the figures is not only in space but also in time: a movement backwards into the heart of the centuries. This is how the texture of the imagery is woven together: the fireplace is a hearth, a home. Lear, the oldest of the family, gathers the young ones together; the family are grouped together round the fire; the light from the patriarchal flame falls on their faces. The shot should be just as simple as the sentence from the folk tale: 'Once upon a time there lived a king who had three daughters'. We shot the hall through the fire (the far depths were dimly lit); the logs were burning at the base of the shot; an old man warms himself by the fire; out of the dim background (of the hall? of time?) three women walk forward (gradually becoming clearly visible); the daughters walk up to their father (four figures across the whole width of the screen); the fire burns and the logs crackle; Lear speaks his first words, completely lacking in any rhetoricism: 'Tell me, my daughters . . .' The smoke, as the shroud of time: a spray of sparks fly up into the air.

The answering 'rhyme' is the hearth in Gloucester's castle; there everything looks perfectly ordinary: the modest dimensions of the fireplace, a smaller flame; here in the warmth and quiet, sitting in a peaceful armchair, the master rests from the anxieties of court; it is a comfortable place for an old man. And here also they gouge out his eyes after binding him to the chair with ropes – the very same favourite place by the hearth.

Fire played a significant part in the overall plan of our *Hamlet*; in *Lear* we devoted even more attention to it. I was drawing up (for myself) a dramatic motif: the fire in the hearth; the wandering flames – the torches of the King's train of carts: the soldiers' bonfires in the town square; Edmund set fire to the thatch on the roof – the sign for the soldiers to burn down the village; catapults hurled barrels of burning tar at the fortress; the town was on fire; the earth burned. Ovens stood out from the waste left after the fire – the end of the tale of the king who had three daughters.

The great sweep of movement from the flames in the hearth to the devastated world; from Cordelia's barely audible 'Nothing' to Lear's weeping over her body, to the howling and clashing of the expanses enveloped by the flames. A memory of the museum of Hiroshima: man learnt how to make fire in order to make his life easier.

Of course these are no more than inner links, the attraction and repulsion of visual cells – something like visual 'alliteration'. These links must not come to the surface, to be revealed like white threads of 'significance', otherwise the scanty allegories and shallow juxtapositions would mean that Shakespeare had not been present.

MORE ABOUT THE 'motif of fire'.

We shot a number of takes against the background of burning logs, but once, as I was on my way to a shooting session, I saw the fire brigade in our studio; they were setting up some kinds of burners in the fireplace and there was a smell of primuses. I was told that we would not have any more burning logs: the fire authorities had forbidden it, however the 'artistic quality would not suffer, it would look just as if real logs were burning'. The reality was only the stink of petrol. Symmetrical flames of gas rose over the untouched little logs. The actors gathered in the studio, already dressed and made up (some of them had travelled to Leningrad for a single day): the centre of attraction became not *King Lear* but the studio's fire brigade. At a given signal a strange activity would begin; the burner was turned on, the fireman lit the smoke-box, set the ventilator going, smoke wafted into the room, but the burners lived their own lives separate from the logs . . . The room was aired, and the smoke box was carried away, so that the ventilator did not have to be turned on. The smell was enough to make one feel ill. New suggestions for rationalization were offered . . . At such moments I am conscious of my utter superfluousness. Why was I there . . . ? All the same, one shot, taken before this transformation, got into the film; I experience almost physical pain whenever I see it on the screen.

I have always been interested not only in the material but also the inner link between people, things and space. Mikhoels told me how the layout of the play *Tevye the Milkman* (he played the main part) was linked in his mind with two places; the door and the oven. Bad news came from outside: Tevye learnt about it while standing in the doorway with a draft coming in from the street. Everything that made him happy took place by the oven; good was linked with warmth, bad with the cold. Parallels like this are a commonplace in folk poetry.

As an example of Meyerhold's art Mikhoels quoted the *mise-en-scène* in *La Dame aux Camélias*. Armand threw Marguerite on the gambling table as if she were a stake. These set-ups did not look contrived: an oven and a door leading on to the street are natural in a poor milkman's room and the situation in the play by Dumas-fils allowed Armand roughly to reject his mistress, and the table at which the gamblers were sitting happened to be near at hand. The metaphors did not seem artificial.

IT IS ANOTHER matter when the plan is subservient to the setting. The commercial cinema has fabricated complete sets of atmosphere: love against a beautiful poetic background, murder in particularly mysterious surroundings and so on. Cinema art has often begun with the breaking of such links, with a parody on them. In *Greed*, the film made in 1924 which anticipated much in the history of cinema, Stroheim furiously turned inside out all the Hollywood stereotypes: the lyrical sequences were played in deliberately prosaic surroundings (a love scene in a dentist's surgery during the filling of a tooth), on the other hand, the vile murder was shown against a sentimental background of a Christmas tree decorated with toys and candles.

I do not think that Stroheim was influenced by contemporary poetry and its preoccupation with antipoetic vocabulary; the war was approaching and with it fascism: the sentimental convention looked offensive on the screen.

THE TIME OF the action (the signs of a particular epoch) are only a part of the 'time' element in Shakespeare's poetry. It is well known that *Lear* has no trace of chronological sequence. A historian with the keenest nose will not be able to pick up the scent of actual dates; however other readings are easily recognizable: the hands of the clocks move and the leaves of the calendar are torn off. This very day (in a matter of hours which can be counted), Lear suddenly leaves his castle for ever; he is already eighty; it is not difficult to calculate the time it takes the main characters to come and go . . . But apart from the timing of human deeds and lives in the tragedy, there is also the growth of thought behind the play: sometimes it belongs not to one of the characters, but to mankind, to the long periods in man's development. I mean not carefully worked out philosophical systems, but layers of poetry.

They are clearly evident. M. L. Lozinsky told me that when he is working on a translation from Shakespeare he sometimes thinks that what lies in front of him is like a long poem written simultaneously by Blok, Derzhavin, Mayakovsky and Baratynsky.[1] Lozinsky

[1] All these poets have sharply contrasting styles: Derzhavin wrote at the end of the eighteenth century, Baratynsky at the beginning of the nineteenth, Blok and Mayakovsky, although contemporaries at the beginning of the twentieth, had nothing in common in their poetry [trans.].

mentioned other names as well: it was not so much the names themselves, as the impossibility of associating them together. Lozinsky's translations were works of virtuosity: in order to convey the contrasts in the original he introduced language of the eighteenth century, slavicisms, into the Russian text. I have an enormous respect for his work but I felt closer to Pasternak's translations (or rather the Russian versions) in natural contemporary language. However I too wanted to convey the difference of the poetic layers. What could these layers be compared with? Perhaps with the deposits – the thick ocean's bottom – which scientists analyse after bores have drilled into the bottom. Oceanologists find not only material in the form of organic and mineral substances, but also time – whole epochs. The Academician L. A. Zenkevich has written, 'the deposits from the Don are original chronicles of the earth on an enormous scale'. It is this that I want to show in the poetic texture: a chronicle of thought on an enormous scale – deposits from the Don of beliefs, errors, prophecies, denials – strata of centuries.

The image of the family at the 'patriarchal hearth' appears only for a moment (it must be allowed to take its course without destroying the natural outward pace), and then – in different shots – the 'sharp point' of another layer appears: in the open air we dug into the earth a coarse wooden crucifix at the crossing of two roads; Cordelia and the King of France kneel down and a hermit marries them, but in the far distance lights begin to flicker and the pagan magnificence of the King sets out on the journey with dogs, falcons, guards, servants and carts weighed down with valuables.

The 'rhyme' to this sequence is echoed some time later in the film in the shots showing the halting of the French army; Lear and Cordelia, kneeling (as in the original) by a simple soldier's wagon. And the last echo of the same stratum is when father and daughter appear with their hands bound together with rope in the midst of the heavily armed soldiers; the steel of the helmets, shields and swords. Maces with nails made to crush skulls, halberds with jagged edges for inflicting lacerating wounds – all the weapons of murder and destruction, and two defenceless people, the victors with smiling faces.

Often, what are only cues in the play become the scene in our film: the cycle of shots continues, showing not only the lines of the poetry but also a whole layer of poetry, not only Cordelia, a character in the play, but an active poetic idea: a light spiritual strength which is capable of conquering the material world.

Another layer brings a different view of the world: the hunted, naked Edgar in the endless expanse of the earth – the free conversation of a free man with the wind.

It is in such visual images that the very movement of the tragedy, the sweep of its poetic ideas is contained. Barefooted Lear in a smock amongst the outlaws on the bare, stony ground: a heretic revealing the sins and vices of life . . . One should not look for a literal interpretation of such images whether Christian, pagan, philosophical stoicism or anything else. This is impossible: Shakespeare is antagonistic towards all dogma but often the material he uses in constructing his plays has been abandoned and burned by history. And I want to convey this baked remnant, the stamp of centuries, as well, to deepen the poetic texture with it, and give character to the movement. Which direction is it going in – into the past? Towards the Old Testament? To early Christianity? Shakespeare does not retell history but re-creates it in the movement of life – there is no end to it and you cannot find a beginning. The curtain falls in the theatre but in history it all continues. The texture builds up layer after layer swelling with the blood and tears of generations . . .

Take the year in which I was working on *Lear*: there was war first at one end of the world then at the other; every day without fail people were killed, there was arson in world capitals, whole districts were burnt down; grenades of tear gas flew about; students revolted and troops stormed into the universities; it was the hour of the Kommandants, the tanks rolled into the town. Martin Luther King was murdered – the fighter against violence. Photographs appeared in the newspapers of a new police uniform – a steel helmet covering the head with only a narrow slit for the eyes; the whole body was covered with armour, like an enormous shield . . . What century was this?

The so-called 'epoch' in the tragedy is not confined by historical time, but is an expanse laid open by history; it is all movement, there is nothing at all of the past; the primeval darkness creeps into the future; the extinct light of hope is set alight, and flames; everything moves forward. Where? . . . The roads behind lead backwards into prehistory; the way forward is longer, steeper, beyond the horizon. At an undefined point the times intersect: the past threatens to become the future, and the future has already happened. Who said that the author was reflecting history? He is interfering with the present.

It is as if the play were wound on two springs, two courses: the external events and the inner life of man. As far as the first 'main spring' is concerned, the story of Holinshed (the author was brought up on it) is usually quoted (as one of the sources); I think another comparison is appropriate, not with chronicles but with newspaper reporting (the gutter press alas). The headlines are hurriedly extracted from the gossip and ferretted out: forgeries, crime, intrigues, bloody murders, incredible weather disasters. All you read is 'Under sentence of death!' 'Saddle the horses!' 'At once, double quick!' Doors bang, thrones fall, horsemen gallop away, powers are overturned. And there is another winding mechanism, a different movement which has no account of time: how many hours (centuries) did it take for this thought to mature, for these copies of reality to fix in the memory for the minutest details to accumulate and the enormous circles of generalizations to disperse; the thought was handed down from man to man, crossed over the borders of the epochs and forced the men of the new age to rethink the essence of development.

'Time' in *King Lear* is not the measured pace of minutes but the shop of a mad watchmaker: how many clock-faces and hands has he got here? There is both the uninhibited movement of the memory back in time, and the sudden bursts forward – the thought touches the future as well.

When such thought appears in the film, the events, the space must disappear behind the outer limits of the shot leaving eyes alone on the screen, nothing apart from the eyes. The form is a concerto for piano and orchestra, the part of the piano being played by Yarvet's eyes.

TWO SCHOOL GIRLS, the daughter of the lighting cameraman and her friend, had come to the studio to watch the filming. I could not help feeling nervous – they were after all our first audience. It was of course pointless to be nervous: what could you understand from isolated shots? The sets were obscured by apparatus, the camera unit were at work and the actors were doing a few re-takes. Even I had no idea what it would look like on the screen. And what a subject for ten-year-old girls? . . . All the same, pretending that I was looking for someone – I turned round and as if by accident looked at the school girls to see whether they were finding it interesting. Alas, half an hour later our guests were making their way to the exit. So soon? I ran after them and asked, 'Well, girls, was it that boring?'

'No,' they replied, 'it's interesting, only it's difficult to breathe in here. Do you mind if we go for a little walk in the fresh air and then come back?'

The first practical and truthful report that I had heard from the studio.

Chapter Thirteen

THE TU 104 TAXIED towards the terminal. At last I had torn myself free of the studio. Or more truthfully, the studio had been torn away from under me : our sets had been dismantled piece by piece and destroyed. We had barely finished filming the last shot of a certain point in the play when the whole area was immediately transformed into a seething mass of activity: destroying and re-constructing. 'Goneril's dining room' was pushed out by 'the bedroom of frenzied love', into Gloucester's estate crept 'the chief of the militia's study' (the next film was a thriller). The capturing of Shakespeare's view of the world, difficult enough under any circumstances, was complicated by hammering (which stopped only during the actual shooting): we were driven out of the studio, hustled towards the exit, and through the open doors we could see lorries setting off for the station (the costumes and props belonging to the film were packed up in wicker boxes marked *King Lear*). I fought – with my last ounce of strength – for a close-up of Yarvet (against the background of a wall which was still standing) and then surrendered.

Now we were on our way to our first location; the last part of the flight was off the main air-routes. We searched for a U-2 in an overgrown airfield. Some of the passengers lit cigarettes, or picked wild flowers while waiting for the pilot. How marvellous that the aeroplane was just standing in a field and that the field had not been weeded, covered with asphalt, painted with lines, figures and signals, and that no computer had been programmed to come up with the flight number, but that this young man had just walked out of the hut, pulling on his jacket as he came and shouting cheerfully and unceremoniously, 'Come on, we're off!' I had not had such a good flight for a long time : instead of faceless clouds against an anonymous sky (the landscape out of a jet is all the same wherever you are, whether it is Japan or the centre of Russia), directly below me was a minute human world – low houses, a man cycling along the road, a herd of cows, and a little boy in a garden looked up and waved (to me!) . . . It was the same in very ancient times when you could travel unhurriedly and comfortably around the Crimea in a Tartar carriage under a canvas shade. I wished I could do the same now, skimming low over the world, pleasantly rocking, and look about unhurriedly and far from the glass piles of airports, the crowds, streams of incoming and outgoing flights, the incessant double-dutch of announcements; numbers, hours, flight numbers, minutes, and, like a refrain, some name asking for another name, and then more flight numbers, delays, departures, the thunder of engines shuddering with frenzy . . . It is interesting that you can go even further like this in stages, flying in a peaceful and leisurely manner from one green pasture to another where hobbled planes graze while waiting for arrivals, and pilots drink tea in tiny huts. An excellent way of having a holiday, almost like going to a sanatorium? The surroundings soothe and distract one from anxiety; and the peace – my goodness it is welcome! . . . But what all the same had we achieved? Before we left I had shut myself up in the viewing theatre: we had just about achieved a mediocre quality in what we had filmed so far (a 'mediocre quality' is a fine thing to boast of for *Lear* of all plays!), I thought that the actors were good, and well cast, but . . . the answer was in this 'but'. There wasn't that growing underground force which is constantly moving with the whole – the incessant blows of the 'iambic whip' which Alexander Blok wrote about. In the theatre this is the pressure of the whole textural rhythm. But on the screen there is another unity, different rhythmic laws – the rotating of life in all its reality. The wide open spaces of landscapes, the might of nature give a different character even to sequences shot in the studio, a new world opens up beyond the walls. Perhaps when these sequences appeared the scenes with the actors would acquire a certain scale. Perhaps . . . But one thing was certain: without these scenes the characters of the people they were playing (however hard the actors tried) would seem insular and the gaps where cuts had been made would show. They were depressing thoughts. It was time I stopped thinking. Everything had already been thought through so many times. I wondered what I would see below the wing now.

Some sort of escarpment appeared under the wing – an outline differing sharply from the rest of the region: lifeless, tawny-coloured brown earth, with dark zigzags cut across it like brush strokes, spots like blobs of ink on a piece of blotting paper. Salt marshes? Clay deposits? An abandoned quarry? It was a desert but not at all like an Asian one; the ghost of a lifeless world, a canvas by Kandinsky, which had been stretched over tens of kilometres. The last wedge had disappeared and meadows and fences appeared once again.

'The Sivash lagoon,' the pilot told me, turning round.

WE SPENT THE the whole day bumping about on roadless territory; no one knew the way, the driver refused to go any further for fear of ruining his car. Finally, exhausted and covered in dust from head to foot we reached a dried up river bed: great expanses of dead earth; there was nothing growing, apart from thorns and weeds. A succession of low hills and hummocks, dark divides and hollows created their own rhythm, waves of repetition, a surrounding of emptiness, the horizon, eternity . . . And for some inexplicable reason I became convinced that Edgar, the unfortunate outlaw, could have led his blind father here, and perhaps Lear and the Fool could also have wandered here after the storm. What linked their destinies, their figures, with such a landscape? Evidently the fact that it was an expanse which was harsh, cruel and devoid of geographical features. This was neither the surroundings of an estate nor a field near a castle, it was a different sort of territory: the land of tragedy, and we were standing on it. This was already very different from the floorboards of the Lenfilm studios, quite a different kettle of fish . . . But how were we going to organize the shooting here? There were neither roads nor houses; it was drizzling and if the lorries got stuck they would never get out again. Morale was high all the same: we had seen land on which it would be possible for Shakespearean characters to walk; the most important thing in our profession had appeared – faith and the feeling that what had been conceived could be realized; it meant that it was possible after all to film a world which didn't exist; it meant that it did exist somewhere; even if only in fragments, and that it would be possible to grasp its natural laws, to discover the links between the fragments, and to populate it with characters.

THE GIPSY LIFE of a filming expedition had begun. From early in the morning we would drive round the shores of the Azov sea, and climb hills. We all grew younger. Catching sight of something in the distance which looked interesting and suitable we would race each other to the top, scrambling up steep paths and startling snakes and lizards, and would then discover that the likely place was no good at all, was not at all what we were after. We explored bays from the sea, questioned local inhabitants. The places one is looking for are very rarely 'laid out on a plate' as if specially prepared. Things don't happen that way: a film landscape is concealed, hidden under another sort of covering. At first you do not so much see it as feel it, guess the possibility of its existence. Here at the moment a collective farm lorry was bouncing over the potholes, barefooted children were running about with fishing rods, some 'savages' had put up their tent, a visiting town dog was barking, and bathing suits were hanging out to dry on a line . . . But over there behind those trees and the thick bushy scrub was a heap of different varieties of rock. They looked like the remains of a gigantic explosion . . . Perhaps we should cut down all this dried wood and burn the scrub?

After the studio (I had lost the habit of working in studios) what a joy it was to sit there on the edge of the sea and make plans for the next moves. Yenei drew a sketch in the sand with a twig: 'the world after the catastrophe'. There was a great deal of work to be done of course, but what was the alternative? The game was worth the candle. 'This of course will be the scale[1]', said dear Yenei who after fifty years (since becoming an artist after his release as a prisoner of war from the Austro-Hungarian army) still had not managed to master Russian stress.

The 'savages' approached, saying to each other with delight, 'Here come some actors. Let's watch the filming' . . . Poor things, little did they know that early in the morning of the next day the smell of hydrochloric acid and burning would poison the sea air and the brush would be producing a hot flame; cranes making a roaring sound for miles around would arrive and begin to move the gigantic rocks about.

YENEI'S SUGGESTION that we should film here on the Kazantip promontory was an excellent one: the outlines of Lear's country began to stand out, to shine through the surrounding scene of collective fish-farms. We found landmarks in the scenery which reflected traits of his character. Herzen wrote of the 'ancient rocks of Europe': I often remembered these words now although he was talking about quite different rocks. Ancient rocks are the earth's chronicle, history written with boulders and outcrops; each one has its own brand, the impression time has made upon it. Round boulders had sunk deep into the sand, rough piles toppled one on the other, pitted as if from the pox . . . Leonardo da Vinci taught artists to study spots on a wall: the mould concealed sketches of battles, outlines of sea-storms . . . One only had to walk round these rocks and to look at them from different levels and their inner content, the particular significance, if you like, a whole biography, was revealed. All one had to do was to realize what stood in the way, what 'had nothing to do with the job in hand'. If one were to remove from this stretch of land the few rocks which were of a different shape from the others the rhythm would become evident, one would see the succession of

[1] The Russian word 'mashtab' is here marked with the stress incorrectly placed on the first syllable [trans.].

identical vertical outcrops. They became fragments of gravestones, an abandoned cemetery. It wasn't clear? . . . It would be clear; Yenei was digging in a tenth-century (northern) *bas relief* in the foreground, with the same shape and of a similar construction – so far the only sign of the times . . . If one looked at it standing still it was a formless and inexpressive ridge of enormous outcropping rocks, but one only had to walk along looking at it from the side without taking one's eyes off it, and the general rhythm of the movement would give it all a meaning: broken off columns of tombs moved towards one, high tables with some kind of runic writing on them, and a stone tower rising above the ruins of the fortress. There was not one single historical monument there but the whole scene was a monument to towns laid waste by war, to the destruction of fortresses and castles.

This was a Shakespearean landscape, the power of reality devoid of everything specific, of the boundaries of time, a reality which allowed one to invent, compose and imagine to the full extent of man's powers of fantasy. We could have filmed the whole of *Lear* here.

The meaning of Shakespeare's historical geography becomes clear if you take Dover as an example: in the play this is the place where the French army disembark (the natural beginning for a military campaign) and towards which (for understandable reasons) the characters hurry, but it also symbolizes the ends of the earth, beyond which lies emptiness, the eternal sea. This is the boundary of Britain. And it is a boundary which people reach, the boundary of life; the limits of strength, the end of the century. And how many times before this did they come to an end . . . This is what we needed: the ends of a civilization. This was how our landscape would begin: the road to Lear's castle, a way through the ravages of epochs; a stone chronicle.

From morning till night we scoured the surrounding countryside in cars and walked miles untiringly, studying the face of the rocks for the signs of catastrophe.

Lear has nothing which is at all peaceful or easy: the characters go through the fire of suffering and its heat is inhumanly powerful; it is not just the physical torture but also the mental torture which is unbearable. And even when the limits of deprivation are approaching it would seem that still worse is to come even after everything has been lost. Banished, slandered Edgar recognizes the blind man as his father. Lear, after discovering the whole gamut of grief, finds the gentleness of Cordelia, only to see her subsequently hanged. Suffering passes over the whole world like a spasm and even the rocks have split and fallen in ruins, a cleft has appeared in the rocky mass. The torments of men have surrendered to the torment of the material world. It is an unfriendly, ruined and distorted world: there is nothing to eat, nowhere to sit and nowhere to shelter; a mean, cruel and heartless nature. The very earth is dry, stony, and the beggars find it hard to walk on with their bare feet . . . And so, step by step we discovered the land of tragedy.

HOWEVER HARD YOU try, nothing happens in the correct order in this profession; even if you achieve some sort of system, it is arrived at in an unsystematic way. Just think: a Soviet film director conceived the production of an English play while flying to Japan. There's no escaping the facts; that is how it happened and that is how I had to begin these notes: I tried to convey in the first pages the powerful impression produced on me by the ancient town of Kyoto. Not all that much time had passed since then (one-and-a-half to two years), and yet it felt as if I had lived a whole life-time. I had lived through and experienced so much . . . And after long months of working on *Lear*, scrutinizing or rather contemplating the rocks of Kazantip (which to me were Shakespearean), the ridges, boulders and outcrops, I understood that the art to which I was dedicated and for which I lived, was utterly devoid of peace. Not only was the power of silence, which had so struck me in the Japanese garden, impossible, but everything in the art was without peace (even silence). It was all words, veneration of words, faith in words. And time was everything; and far from curing you, taking you away from worldly cares, it dragged you by the scruff of the neck, bundling you up with your characters towards the 'wrack of life'. This is why working on this tragedy was unbearable (you cannot compare it with *Hamlet* either, there was a lot of light and warmth in the Prince of Denmark); *Lear* furiously demanded an answer, a response. *Lear* was not a film on which I was working but a life which had entered my own and from which it was too late to escape until, for better or for worse, the film had been made. And it would be a long time before the frenzied and heartrending howl of the old man would fade from my mind 'O, you are men of stones!' This is why I heard those words and visualized the epoch in that very place, amongst the silence of the stone ridges. I felt that this shape of the landscape had not been created by the forces of nature – the sun, wind, rain and snow, but that the grand torturer of history had wandered maliciously about the world, doing his indefatigable work; the architects of hate had amassed fragments of altars, ruins of libraries, slabs from defiled cemeteries, the ancient rocks of Europe with sledge-hammers, axes and crowbars.

Whatever anyone said, the harmony was perfect, but in order to produce *Lear* one needed not a feeling of measure but a feeling of grief.

IN CHOOSING THE location for a film you have to consider every possibility. You go on fantastic journeys; while looking for one thing, you find another, but on the screen . . . it would be all right if it was a third element which appeared, but usually the result is some completely unknown thirty-fifth or even eighty-fourth (you have long since lost count). After all, where was I going? We had begun by fighting the theatrical, trying to find means of showing reality on the screen – not copies of historical ornaments but the everyday life of history – we had cleared the décor, leaving only genuine material. This is how we had found our way to the rocks of Kazantip. Now we could begin the real work: this was not a case of overcoming the conventionalities of the studio, but of uncovering nature's hidden significance. We had already come a very long way. Of course everyone develops in his own way, and every epoch influences a human being in a different manner, but nevertheless the same stages of life remain whatever happens: childhood, youth, maturity . . . death. Art has the same degrees, only these degrees succeed one another in a peculiar way. It could happen that they are born an old man, or yet another way: dying, they suddenly come to life (and how many times); it is not easy here to find the beginning of the road and to foretell where its end will be.

To some extent our road to the rocks of Kazantip was not the beginning of the journey. The road had begun to push its way through a long time before. The efforts had been various; and it seemed as if both man's thought and the ideas of the time had nothing in common with our contemporary aspirations, and yet . . .

Chapter Fourteen

THE TURNS OF THE SPIRAL

'HERE IS SOMEONE you might find interesting,' said Isadora Duncan to Stanislavsky, in recommendation of Gordon Craig (the conversation took place in Moscow in 1908) – 'He is the man who has been rejected and misunderstood by everyone; this is because he is original and is too great an artist.' In the great brotherhood of art these words are praise indeed. The Moscow Art Theatre invited Gordon Craig to produce *Hamlet*. Much has already been written about the production. At first, without researching into the subject in any special depth, our critics simply gasped: what could the psychological realism of MAT and dreams of über-marionettes (from one of Craig's articles) have in common? A demon confused them, and so successfully, that they were confused long afterwards: the theatre suffered a defeat and returned to its well tried-out highroad. The scheme was a simple one and was indeed quite unlike anything they had known before. It was not Craig who produced *The Drama of Life*,[1] *A Man's Life*[2] (the demon interfered with these productions no less). 'The more I read *Hamlet* the more I see your image before me', wrote the 'defender of über-marionettes' to Stanislavsky.[3] 'I cannot believe for a minute that anything besides the most extreme simplicity in the portrayal of this character could raise it to the heights on which Shakespeare stood. And I have seen nothing closer to these heights in your theatre than your interpretation of *Uncle Vanya*.' In 1935 – years later! – after seeing Mikhoels' Lear in Moscow, Craig called his performance a 'song'; he discovered a deep tragic significance even in the actor's individual gestures. But was this 'song' sung in a wooden, puppet-like voice and his movements determined by a string by which some hidden person pulled the marionette's arm?... Stanislavsky understood the crux of the matter immediately: reminiscing about the production later, he wrote, 'Craig's rejection of the actors and actresses did not stop him from going into ecstasies over the slightest sign of genuine artistic talent... On the other hand at the sight of lack of talent on stage he would work himself into a frenzy and begin to dream of marionettes

[1] By Knut Hamsun, produced in 1907 by Stanislavsky [trans.].
[2] By Leonid Andreev, produced in 1907 by Meyerhold [trans.].
[3] In 1909 [trans.].

again.' An artist who had made his stage debut while he was still a child, Craig knew and loved the theatre too much not to be discriminating and not to despise pale imitations of the real thing. He hated 'theatricality' as much as the directors of MAT did; it was better to have marionettes than that sort of actor and that sort of 'acting'; I put the last word in inverted commas because Craig (as well as Meyerhold) expressed great delight more than once over free-style acting, appealing against theatricality, but at the same time he also demanded 'the inner fire' – the spiritual force without which any form is powerless and despicable.

I think that the story of the Moscow Art Theatre production of *Hamlet* is marvellous for the very reason that because of the daring decision to invite Craig, because of the sharp clash of opinion, the decisive re-appraisal of experience, it was full of that 'inner fire', of spiritual strength.

According to Sulerzhitsky the theatre had begun preparations for *Hamlet* long before. The designer V. Yegorov, their own man who knew the theatre intimately, was sent off on a long expedition (as an insurance in case Craig was a failure). The project was approached in earnest, in the same way that the production of *Tsar Fyodor Ioannovich* was prepared in its time, in keeping with the most up-to-date historical findings. Yegorov travelled round Denmark, then Germany, studied museums, architecture, drew landscapes; an enormous collection of material was gathered . . . And nothing from these riches was used, not even the minutest detail. Craig's theatrical ideas won the directors of MAT over.

New sets usually come about not because the artist sees the possibility of improving on what has already been achieved, what is already familiar, but because of a desire to turn the tables on the familiar as decisively as possible. Why? Is it because the usual forms have worn thin, art has fallen into a rut and everything has become commonplace? It can happen. But it is a different matter when we are talking about productions which have become chapters in the history of the theatre. The very concept of the words 'production', 'theatre' (in their contemporary meaning) seem debased and insignificant; life, time demand something 'greater' from artists. But what? This feeling of dissatisfaction is not simple or easy to grasp immediately in words; time itself can uncover the significance of such movements after it has compared different developments in various regions of the arts. If one looks at the sketches of Yegorov and Craig now, one's first reaction is of astonishment: could they really have been intended for the same work? It is not only the talent and taste which differs between the two artists, but even the most fundamental conceptions about the play. It is difficult to believe that the artists had the same play in front of them. And the theatres for which they were working were evidently different: the floor of the stage, the lighting technique and the changing of scenery had nothing in common. They were different plays and different theatres. Yegorov was planning a regular production for the professional stage. The sketches would have been easily realized: small buildings (a stylization of the medieval north) with low ceilings and niches; brick arches, behind which one could see the walls of a fortress, chequered floors: the small world of a small country. And the play seemed small as well. Why? Could you really maintain this on the strength of the sketches alone? Yes, you could. It was not difficult to find traces of style, hints of the overall plan, the method of showing the sequence of scenes. One thing was completely absent from them – a sense of mystery. There was not one gleam of that elusive significance, that depth of content (which never revealed its deepest layers), into which it was impossible to delve to the deepest point – qualities which went far beyond the bounds of the 'play' and which had provoked artists and thinkers into re-reading the story of the Prince of Denmark only to find a still deeper significance in it. You could have performed other plays on Yegorov's sets provided the time and place of the action corresponded to the historical and geographical details. You would not have found any history or geography in Craig's sketches. There was no 'place of action' or 'epoch'; they all expressed one and the same thing – mystery. Masses of unknown constructions in the darkness, figures of men in empty spaces, single platforms, bare geometrical shapes. It was all infinite, disappearing into the distance beyond not only the stage, but beyond reality. A philosophical epic? Attempts to grasp the music of visual art? It was a new as yet unknown theatre. A new as yet undiscovered Shakespeare.

DURING THE SHAKESPEARE centenary year a collection of articles was published in England called *Shakespeare in a Changing World*. Would it not have been truer to call it *Changing Shakespeare in a Changing World*? . . . History has shown us these great figures dancing a fantastic quadrille – and cutting all the varieties of steps. Up till the nineteenth century the plays were at first considered hopeless (even if they were written by a genius), and then to a large extent old fashioned; in the subsequent years when dramatic art was developing and becoming increasingly successful, they were regarded as works dating from the ancient heathens. They were of course adapted, the fierce and coarse elements omitted and noble elements introduced. In an age of enlightenment one could not allow a pile of corpses on the stage or let fools interfere with events of seriousness! ... Civilized people corrected and rejuvenated the ancient primitives. The 'changing greatness' of Shakespeare was twisted round to become 'changing times'. For a moment it was as if they had become united. And a moment later these adaptations were being laughed at, so naïve and old-fashioned did they seem. A certain Ducis[1] (the author of the adaptations dating from the second half of the eighteenth century) suddenly dropped Shakespeare, and for heaven knows how many centuries, and then time threw Ducis on to the rubbish heap of antediluvian curiosities: 'Could it have been true that our grandfathers and grandmothers took such archaic stuff seriously?' gasped the 'changing times'. But 'changing Shakespeare' has already entered our life today, living all its interests to the full. The emendations fell away of their own accord; the living substance of the original text was restored. However, the original itself, while remaining somehow untouched, had indeed changed: the underlying meaning (the thoughts and feelings of the 'changing times') gave new meaning to the words. The engine of time had begun to break down: one wheel revolved forwards, another backwards; Shakespeare grew younger, but the theatres which acted him (contemporary theatres, fulfilling the demands of the times) were growing older; the life of runs grew shorter and shorter – in ten years they traversed the path from a stormy birth to sclerosis. They declined not only because of the evil times, but also because of the plays which were written in an age when neither trains nor aeroplanes had yet been dreamed of. Shakespeare overtook the age of steam, electricity, the splitting of the atom, but the theatres, equipped as they were to the last word in advanced techniques, were trying to find a way of catching up with him or at least getting a little nearer.

FROM HIS VERY earliest conscious years Craig grew up in close contact with the best theatre of his times. The expression 'suckled with his mother's milk' would not have been figurative in describing his childhood. Ellen Terry was considered one of the most talented of Shakespearean actresses; Henry Irving's company was distinguished by a serious and cultural approach. In his younger days Craig played the Prince of Denmark himself and his performance was considered a success. His childhood home was the theatre. But not

[1] Jean François Ducis (1733–1816), author of the first adaptations of Shakespeare for the French stage [trans.].

very many years later he left this home without regrets; it all seemed to have become moribund. He had to forget his lessons and reassess his achievements – the relationships of the 'changing values' had altered once again. This man of the theatre began to declare that it was impossible to produce the theatrical play of *Hamlet* on the stage. His claim was not new: several times before Craig it had been said by people who were moving forward towards Shakespeare and who did not want to go back to the theatre of their time.

Something that was most important and of the deepest significance in the play had completely disappeared and evaporated from their contemporary stage. What had been mere speculation had become a theatrical reality and had destroyed the spiritual value of the play. To the new generation the essence of the tragedy seemed ever more complicated and massive, but the methods of reproducing it on stage – unashamedly coarse and vulgar.

The discord between *Hamlet* and the theatre began. On the other hand, how much earlier, about three and a half centuries before, in the very play itself there had been mention of the fact that theatrical affairs do not bring joy: tragic actors 'saw the air too much with their hands', good plays are flops ('caviar to the General'), and comic actors pander to the low taste of the public with gags. But on the other hand the arrival of the comedians is a joyful event, and who knows, the play may suddenly startle the murderer's conscience (was there ever such an occurrence)? And in the same work there is another debased form of art. I am referring to the famous dialogue:

'What do you read, my lord?'

'Words, words, words.'

The debasing of the words was expressed by the words themselves.

A few years ago Andrzej Wajda sent me Stanislaw Wyspianski's work on *Hamlet* (Wajda thought very highly of it); the Polish poet attributed particular significance to the fact that the hero wandered about the castle with a book in his hands; a lonely young man in an alien world; a student, inseparable from his book, living by its thoughts. What was the book? It was probably a volume of Montaigne.

Jan Kott, following close on Wyspiansky, occupied himself with solving the same problem: 'If you tell me what you are reading, I will tell you who you are.' 'In Shakespeare's time it would have been Montaigne, but the times change,' Kott wrote. 'And if we want to see not an old play but our own life, then we must change the book that the hero is holding: the lonely student wanders through the Western World holding a volume of Sartre – the Hamlet of our times.'

And now I wanted to play the same game in my turn. After all what was Hamlet reading? Would I too dare to look over his shoulder. However strange it may have seemed, I thought that the author of the book he was holding was . . . William Shakespeare. And that it was not at all the Prince, an actor in the play, talking about someone else's work, but the man of letters pronouncing his opinion on the state of literature. The writer, forgetting about his hero, is talking about his profession, 'words, words, words . . .'

While working on the production, I could often make out and distinctly hear the sound of this voice interfering with the voice of the hero, and sometimes completely drowning him – the voice of the author himself. Of course it was the Prince and not Shakespeare who dedicated the mediocre verses to Polonius' daughter, but this line, 'Words, words, words' expresses a feeling of the powerlessness of art, the bitterness of the author's feelings. Perhaps this line would help one to guess what provoked the poet to lay aside his pen and abandon the theatre; it was better to trade in plots of land than in empty words . . .

Life, reality, business. And they are all nothing but empty words . . . And there has been more than one book which has refuted or upheld another book, or has pointed to the fact that in the author's opinion the work of the writer was illusory: his basic structure was worthless, unreal. What can you construct out of a book? A cardboard house. A castle on the sands . . . some thought which will later be taken up, continued and developed with many variations (religious, political, philosophical) by other writers? Perhaps the most radical opinion is called for: is there a more perfect form of poetry than a blank piece of paper?

Now let us imagine the same dialogue, but the place of action is not the castle of Elsinore but the theatre stalls, and Polonius' companion is not a young man dressed in black, which seems out of place amidst the gaiety of the court, but Craig (or Stanislavsky):

'What do you read, my lord?'

'I act, act, act . . .'

The theatre had developed a hatred towards itself. It was a situation which I think was very important: there was a decisive rejection of everything which would seem to be the very basis of art and which in time had burnt itself out, had lost its connections with reality, had spent its living content, and had become no more than an outer shell; empty words; a sound, not at all full of spiritual movement; an aimless gesture; convention.

The cinema has a far younger history than the theatre and literature, but the same processes are evident in it as well.

'What are you thinking, signor?', the actors in 8½ ask the director, who is idling his time away at a seaside resort.

'Films, films, films.'

An affirmation grew out of the rejection. Art broke out of the enclosure into which the profession had dragged it and hidden it away. The enclosures were broken down. With a flourish and a full enquiry it emerged, breaking the bounds of the possible (or what had been thought of as possible), the attainable, the familiar. Where was it to go? The direction of the search, the line of development was not immediately defined and often it was not by words but by the conflict of different works or by the conflicts within a work.

'Film, film, film . . .' said a man in a wide hat, shrugging his shoulders, having in 1915 decided to show on the screen all aspects of intolerance in the history of man. The place of action for his film was to have been the universe; the time of the events – from the fall of Babylon to the strikes in contemporary America. The director was convinced that after the appearance of this film, wars on earth would cease and all people would become brothers.

In the years during the production of this film David Wark Griffith personally paid each actor (in dollars) when the filming came to an end, but differences were settled right there on the sets with fists: this was the reality of cinema at that time.

The full span of *Intolerance* (the first edited version) was to have run for eight hours.

The 1924 film *Greed* (in the version edited by its director) was about the same length; Eric Stroheim filmed not only in the most ordinary rooms with a view on the street, but also in the desert beneath a burning sun – conditions which in those times were considered impossible for professional work.

Eisenstein began his revolution in the cinema by despising the cinema – the 'stars', the film scripts and the studios.

'Performances, performances, performances' seemed dull and insignificant to Craig: designs painted on canvas which swayed in the breeze; the smug 'darlings of the audience'; the box-office, dictating its own laws – a commercial theatre for the men of commerce in the stalls. Stanislavsky and Craig were not the only ones to turn away from such a theatre. Komisarzhevskaya and Duse left the stage; everyone was talking of the 'theatre crisis'; it became common to compare the theatre with a brothel. Innovators turned to the past: they searched for new life in collected plays, medieval productions, Italian improvised comedy, the ancient traditions of Japan, China, marionettes . . . Anywhere you like, only not in the performances of the beginning of the twentieth century.

Shakespeare grew younger because the world was on the threshold of the iron age and time broke down once again; a crevice seared its way through history and through the heart of man. What had happened to the theatre box-office before this? The playwrights, their hands full, and the broken-down actors knew how to mind their own business; they had no wish to poke their noses into places they had no business to be in. As is well known not even Hamlet's friend from university advised him to concern himself with this business ('if philosophy could find it out').

In the same year that Craig came to Moscow, Blok wrote in his diary: 'There is a feeling of catastrophe, disease, alarm, explosion (mankind is behaving as people do when they are about to be bombed).'

A slight man of medium height in a soft hat and light coat stepped off the train into the Moscow cold. Florence suddenly moved to Kamergersky Passage[1]: Craig brought with him photographs of the Arena Goldoni (the minute open-air theatre in Florence where he was working on theatrical experiments and publishing the journal, *The Mask*), and a few drawings and engravings. Stanislavsky, Sulerzhitsky, Craig – what could these three have had in common? But they quickly understood each other. They dressed the newly arrived guest in a fur coat from the wardrobe of *Woe from Wit*[2] and felt boots; they put a fur hat on the mane of greying hair (as Denis Bablet describes in his monograph).

After their very first meeting Craig and Stanislavsky were openly delighted with each other. What could have united them? First and foremost their contempt for Polonius and his theatrical tastes: Ophelia's father, as is well-known, favoured performances of the 'pastoral-comical, historical-pastoral', farces and bawdy anecdotes. They wanted to purge the stage of everything that debased and betrayed it. They sought ways of showing what was concealed in the depths of a work, what was higher than 'words' or 'acting'.

A new method of production emerged. Performances often began not on the stage but on paper. Stanislavsky wrote expositions of productions like prose; his ideas were nearer to a novel than to the performances of those times; Craig created series of engravings. Eisenstein drew shots – hundreds, thousands of rough sketches on pieces of paper, in the margins of books. The prose, engravings, sketches of a director . . .

Craig considered movement to be the basis of theatre. It was not the performance of the actors (as in the contemporary commercial

[1] Where the Moscow Art Theatre was housed at that time [trans.].

[2] The satirical play by Griboyedov [trans.].

theatres) nor the subject (*Hamlet* had been turned into a Romantic melodrama), but the conflict between general categories: the first of these was the visual. This is what made me study past theatrical ideas in such detail. One of Craig's books was called *Towards a New Theatre*. What kind of stage was this director dreaming of, who did not succeed in finding a place for himself in one single European theatre company?

On this stage of the future he visualized *Macbeth* extremely simply: he explained that there were only two elements in the tragedy, rock and mist. The rock was the place where all the soldiers were crowded together; the mist was the shelter of the ghosts. The mist was an accumulation of moistures; the moisture undermined the rock, the vapours ate away the stone. The rock collapsed.

Two elements are quite enough. The whole trouble is that directors feel that they must show that they know what Scottish ferns look like and the latest findings from the digs at Glamis and Cawdor Castles. Two shades are enough – brown (rock) and grey (mist). You don't need anything else.

Stanislavsky was very impressed with the sketches for *Macbeth*: he had already long since (by theatrical standards) lost interest both in naturalistic detail and historical household ornaments on the stage.

One can reconstruct Craig's starting point (by his sketches and by the reminiscences of those who were present at the time). There was no division between the stage and the auditorium. The dividing line, the curtain, had been taken away. There were 'screens', as if a continuation of the auditorium. Sometimes this word is put in inverted commas sometimes it is simply: screens. Cloth and screens – what contemporary director would give a second thought to such words, who would be able to hear something in them? They are outmoded and bare forms of stage design. But in its time the appearance of the screen seemed like a stage revolution. Theatrical battles were fought over it. This was not a part of the décor but a means of attaining wide expanses, of discovering whole worlds of expression.

At the same time as Craig (without knowing Craig's work) the Swiss Adolphe Appia was creating his stage architecture – abstract, three-dimensional, bare constructions; but the similarity was only external. Appia destroyed only the shape of the scenery – the traditional slips and back drops, the naturalistic imitations of life; his architecture was also nothing more than scenery for a production (Wagner Opera). For Craig the space itself was inspiring, full of movement and feeling. In his engravings man often only underlined by his minuteness the enormity of the universe. Craig, a true-blooded artist, chose series of engravings as the place of his productions : the conflict between the primeval powers of darkness and light, the relationship between three-dimensional space and flat planes.

For him the 'screens' became units of consecutive, constantly changing three-dimensional space. They moved, changed shape, and light transformed them. That was how *Hamlet* was to begin : the audience would grow silent having settled in their seats, and then with majestic, triumphant movement the 'screens' would shift their positions. They would move apart and disappear into the darkness – a dance of architecture, of light and shadow. Rays of light would appear from unknown sources, spots of light falling, and the flat surfaces of the 'screens' would come to life : reflections would begin to flicker, and the shadows deepen.

Was it Denmark? The North? . . . All the richness of detail, the patterned cloth, the different shapes of weapons and the character of the objects, everything that Yegorov had copied down from the museums of Europe turned out to be superfluous. In Craig's opinion, all this had no significance for *Hamlet*. An unknown space unfolded in all its greatness in the alternating three-dimensional spaces and in the fantastic play of light and shade. It was the world as Hamlet saw it, only not with the physical organs of sight but with the 'mind's eye' about which Shakespeare wrote.

Base vanity, worthless pomp smothered the whole world, the king's robe covered life. This was the director's idea behind Act One Scene Two. The place of action was the robe. The crowned overlords sat at an unattainable height. A golden robe fell from their shoulders, occupying the whole expanse of the stage. It was the space itself and the courtiers were no more than heads protruding through cuts in the fabric. An innumerable quantity of heads, insignificant points at the foot of the throne, gazing upwards at the shining magnificence. An unfathomable sea of gold, shedding dark and gloomy specks. The heads swam on the golden waves like sponges. Was it a mystical vision? Or perhaps the realization of a Shakespearean metaphor. The prince called Rosencrantz and Guildenstern sponges : 'he keeps them, like an ape in the corner of his jaw', he explained to them, 'first mouthed, to be last swallowed : when he needs what you have gleaned, it is but squeezing you, and, sponge, you shall be dry again.'

The stone-coloured costumes of Tishler[1] contained a similar metaphor; he dressed the main characters of *Richard III* in them – people with stone hearts were indistinguishable from the castle walls.

[1] A. Tishler, a contemporary, who attended the same art classes as the author in Kiev [trans.].

But what about the heads themselves? Wasn't there something a little insulting to artistic merit in such treatment? It is a difficult question to answer. Although perhaps one can answer for one of the heads: there was one participant in this scene who according to Craig understood his intentions even better than Stanislavsky. This is not surprising since the head was Y. B. Vakhtangov.[1]

'I dream of the theatre', Vakhtangov wrote to Sulerzhitsky about Craig's production, 'and it is already drawing me.

To sit in the stalls and gaze at the grey columns.

At the gold.

At the gentle light.

I will ask the management to let me watch all the rehearsals of *Hamlet*.'

Stanislavsky called another scene 'unforgettable'. There was a long corridor winding without end, and the tops of its walls disappeared upwards beyond one's line of vision. A lonely dark figure stood in the slanting rays of the spotlights. Hamlet walked out of the depths, his reflection shining against the golden surfaces, as if they were mirrors, and behind him, in the far distance, the golden king and his lackeys spied on him. A play of outward effects? . . . Or should one believe what Stanislavsky said? According to him the scene 'revealed the whole spiritual content of the moment being portrayed down to its deepest limits.'

Whole worlds in miniature rolled on to the stage on Meyerhold's 'truck-stages', tight, stifling cells representing the malicious vulgarity of *The Government Inspector* in the seething concentration of things and people.

Craig's 'screens' contained another form of expression which was in many ways diametrically opposed to Meyerhold's. There was a man lost in the enormity of the alien world of Elsinore, a small figure amidst the malicious glitter of gilt in a world which contained nothing that was human or genuine.

What interests me about these productions is not the philosophical aspect. My attention is attracted by something else: the two extremes of expression, the one by concrete objects of everyday life, the other by the abstract. In both cases there was a rejection of imitation, props, the stage in its usual proportions – the treatment of space was different from what is possible on stage, space was conceived like a form of tragedy.

Meyerhold wrote that it was as if he and Stanislavsky were tunnelling from two opposite ends. It is well known from descriptions

[1] The founder of the Vakhtangov Theatre in Moscow and a great Soviet director [trans.].

how wonderful and ecstatic are meetings between the two sides who have laboured so hard in order to combine their efforts. Does such a meeting ever happen in art? I doubt it. There are an infinite quantity of such imaginary meetings – spanning the centuries in the different spheres of art and of life. There are meetings, moments, followed by tunnelling in new directions, new efforts, blows of the hammer against the solid mass which must be broken down in order to move forward.

One should also add that Meyerhold was often unjust in his opinions, but that there were only two people about whom he always spoke with the greatest respect: Stanislavsky and Craig. 'If I had returned to Moscow', Craig wrote in his turn, 'I would have with pleasure tied myself (figuratively speaking) to a chair for several weeks in order to watch the rehearsals and performances in Meyerhold's theatre . . . to observe and understand this theatrical genius and learn from him.'

IT WOULD BE difficult to find a production in the history of the theatre which provoked so many sharp clashes of opinion: it appears that each participant had his own particular point of view, quite different from the man who worked alongside him. Stanislavsky was thinking about the nature of an actor's creativity (or rather about man's place in the art) not only in a different way from Craig, but – and at that very same period – in a different way from most of the company and even from the actor in the title role.

'The inaccessibility for the actor of the heavenly heights which Konstantin Sergeyevich (Stanislavsky) demanded, the impossibility of reaching its boundaries – all this was a great tragedy for my father', Shverubovich (Kachalov's son) described later in his memoirs[1].

Stanislavsky used his 'system' in practice for the first time. The actors were muddled by his analysis of their every movement and confused by the terminology. A wall grew up between Stanislavsky and the company – according to his own description of this period; the actors drifted away to other directors; he accused them of sluggishness and of being slaves to routine.

Everything was discussed from every angle: Hamlet was compared with a purifying sacrifice, Jesus Christ; the early humanist in a barbaric world – the skins of wild beasts, pools of blood, fighting for

[1] I found extracts from these memoirs in N. N. Chuchkin, *Kachalov's Hamlet*, the only serious and well-documented account of the 1911 production.

a mate (Nemirovich-Danchenko); a soul in a world of hostile substance, Craig affirmed; 'a living man of flesh and blood' was how Kachalov wanted to play him. Opinions did not even remain constant in one man; it also happened that they changed beyond recognition during the course of rehearsal. Every achievement was the result of great difficulties, in a fight not only with old customs but with themselves. They were not satisfied with half measures: in Shverubovich's memoirs you often come across the word 'extremism', 'with blood and tears'. The production of this tragedy turned into a personal tragedy for many of its participants. Everything was different: the tradition of acting (of one of the best companies in the world), and the stage techniques (which were considered perfect by contemporary standards).

The model which they accepted and which the most experienced theatrical experts believed could be realized, turned out to be impossible. Craig's worlds when built to scale were transformed into nothing more than clumsy constructions: they toppled over from their own weight, turned into broken pieces which could neither be stuck together, strengthened nor reconstructed. Screen after screen collapsed, the fragments threatening to behead the actors.

The material mocked the ideal with malicious delight. It was the old paradox: the flight of dreams against the pull of the force of gravity; the boldness of the idea and the inert nature of the means of realizing them. Craig insisted on having genuine materials: there were to be no imitations, painted scenery or props. Stanislavsky was his ally over this and they experimented, changing the method of construction untiringly. The original ideas of using iron or stone vanished after the first calculations: the weight of the raw materials excluded the possibility of such constructions; they changed to wood, choosing pear, oak, lime (Craig demanded old uncut wood) – but it was too bulky; they substituted plywood – it bent; they turned to cork. Nothing worked. Imitation bronze? Craig agreed on condition that it had first of all to succeed in deceiving himself.

'Why is the human mind so inventive in matters concerning methods of butchery . . . or concerning the bourgeois comforts of life?' – Stanislavsky cried bitterly, reminiscing about the painful experience with the 'screens'. 'Why is technology so coarse and primitive when man is striving to satisfy not his bodily or animal requirements but his most elevated spiritual aspirations.'

They settled for coarsely woven peasant sackcloth and cheap gold paper. Constructions 8¼ metres high were built, but they too turned out to be unstable: on the day of the première there was very nearly a catastrophe. The movement of the 'screens' had to be abandoned.

The dress rehearsals turned into a field of battle – ranging from petty brawls to large engagements. Craig insisted on pitch darkness at the end of the 'mouse-trap' scene, Sulerzhitsky sent a letter to Stanislavsky saying that without light, without the faces of the actors – the audience had to see them – the play would be a flop. Even the most harmonious relationships grew strained – the actors could hear the raised voices of Craig and Stanislavsky floating across the auditorium. Much was changed at the last minute when the audience was already arriving in the foyer.

Was it a muddle? A clumsy mistake in inviting a director who did not know MAT? Many thought so.

I AM AFRAID that there have already been too many digressions from the subject in this book. But what can you do? When you study biographies of artists and the history of their work which you find particularly interesting, it is difficult to refrain from giving yet another summary of their work from an unusual point of view. Among the critical articles on Craig, Stanislavsky, Meyerhold and many other innovators, there were a number of compositions of a peculiar kind which it is worth being reminded of.

Here for example is a subject for research which would certainly be instructive: the history of critical snorting and hooting. There would be enough material for whole dissertations. Opening nights in the theatre, the facts would prove, were often greeted not with triumphant fanfares but with another sort of music – snorting. There were of course many nuances of the sound; you could even draw diagrams – plot graphs ranging from the amateur's mockery of a single voice to the carefully planned derision of the whole company of critics. And this would concern not only the more extreme manifestations of contemporary art – the beginnings of naturalism were just as much laughed at. The sight of real carcasses of meat or the steam from washerwomen's tubs in Antoine's productions were greeted with howls of laughter. There was an uproar and shouts of 'It's just like life!', and just as much noise when something was 'not lifelike'. The everyday details in Chekhov's plays, abstract scenery, and the artists' arrival at the Revolution were equally mocked ('Meyerhold is awaited in Lunarcharsky's kitchen', wrote Averchenko, with hilarious amusement in the last issue of *Satyricon*. 'Comrade Narkom[1], why don't you frame the 'Internationale'[2] in a cubist background.')

[1] Meyerhold had been made Commissar of the People's Culture.

[2] The anthem of the Revolution.

The forward movement of art (where to? why?), the substitution of the new for the out-dated ('they are trying to be original') were received by the common man as rubbish, material for common derision. The clever critics, the masters of anecdote rose up in their thousands in defence of the tastes of the common man. There have always been plenty of jokers. The feeding troughs of witticisms generously spilled over with the deliberate intention of spreading the merrymaking far and wide. The herd of trotting jeerers laughed at art – after all they knew, whatever sort of theatre you gave them, whatever the respected public paid money to see.

The press of the day reaped an abundant harvest of caricatures from *Hamlet*. No one was spared. I will quote one of these compositions, an article in the newspaper *Russkoye Slovo*.[1] A parody sometimes gives one a clearer view of its subject.

> Mr Craig sat astride a chair, and, focussing his gaze on a certain spot, said, as if letting fall an enormous jewel on to a silver plate:
>
> 'What is *Hamlet*? . . . Ophelia, the Queen, the King, Polonius . . . Perhaps they don't exist at all . . . they are ghosts like the ghost of his father . . . Hamlet alone exists. All the rest is like, a ghost! . . . Perhaps even Elsinore doesn't exist. It's all Hamlet's imagination . . .'

Stanislavsky fared no better: in the article all he did was to ask every now and then, 'Don't you think we ought to have a Great Dane so that it will at least be established that the action does after all take place in Denmark?'

The wittiest part began further on:

> 'Stop the rehearsal', Craig shouted after a few days. 'The point is not Hamlet but the people who surround him . . . They have committed crimes and – they are confronted by Hamlet. He is like a retribution! . . . It must be acted with strength, with juice. Give me juicy, succulent décor. The essence of life . . . Turn the picture over! Laertes goes away . . . There is probably a lady among the courtiers who is in love with him . . . and a courtier who sighs for Ophelia! . . . Dancing. A feast! And somewhere in the background, glinting through all this . . .'
>
> 'Don't you think that you could have the Great Dane here?' Stanislavsky asked hopefully.
>
> Mr Craig looked at him delightedly.
>
> 'A dog? We can have a cow in the graveyard!'
>
> At first Kachalov walked about in the graveyard; ate only Lenten food and then took part in a wedding – and then it was all changed again. 'But this is farce!' Craig began to proclaim . . . 'We will play it as farce! A parody on tragedy!'

[1] Literally translated, *The Russian Word* [trans.].

It was undoubtedly an amusing article. In its time it probably made its readers laugh. Now it seems even funnier. The most amusing part of it is that ten years later such interpretations were indeed realized on the stage. And what a lot of passion was stirred up! The joke is that it was all over the new reading of Shakespeare. Theatres later presented it as 'all in Hamlet's imagination' (Mikhail Chekhov at the Second MAT), as 'farce', 'a parody on tragedy' (Akimov's production at the Vakhtangov Theatre), and as all of these mixed together (the Shakespearean collage of Charles Marowitz), and 'glinting through all this' (The National Theatre's production of Tom Stoppard's play *Rosencrantz and Guildenstern are Dead*, which literally showed Hamlet and Elsinore as a gleam behind a gauze curtain); they also built 'juicy, succulent décor' (the king and queen's Flemish bed in Tony Richardson's film: the gay colours of the bed coverings, pillows, the abundance of food on golden dishes, chalices of wine, even hunting dogs on the bed).

What had seemed a pointless exaggeration, an absurdity, became part of theatrical tradition. Why was this? It was because this is what the play itself is full of – dissimilarities which are irreconcilably various. The dialogue between Hamlet and the Ghost, the grave-digger's puns, Polonius' sermons . . . Are they different styles? They represent the Shakespearean unity of life. It was as if Craig and Stanislavsky tried out the sound of the whole keyboard of the play, getting carried away by different tonalities one after the other.

Many of the latest interpretations, though complete and perfect in themselves, have been forgotten and many more will be forgotten in the future; great 'successes' have vanished from our memories, but the 'flop' of the 1911 production is still alive and will go on living.

WHAT DOES IT mean to say a production lives? Why was it not revived in the following seasons, why is it not revived now? To live in art does not mean the same thing at all as to revive. Sometimes reviving is only a means of killing. This is what happened when Meyerhold's *The Warrant*[1] was revived many years later. People who had known the production inside out and had genuinely loved it, remembered every detail: the general plan, the sound effects, the make-up; everything was meticulously reproduced. But it was to no avail – it all seemed different and not at all like the original.

Meyerhold's *Masquerade*, or *The Magnanimous Cuckold* could not

[1] By Nikolai Erdman [trans.].

be revived. It would be impossible and unnecessary: these productions are still alive, have become part of a new art, and will continue to develop with it, and with the changes in life.

It is certainly not only the successes that live on in art, the examples of completeness and harmony, but also daring experiments, decisive attempts. Nothing is complete, much is out of harmony, but the very thrust forward, the strength of artistic will, sometimes taken up and continued, sometimes refuted (which means, in quarrelling with what has already been done, a living quarrel with a living art), continues to develop and to influence other forms.

AND WHAT WAS the aim of this experiment? What were Craig, Stanislavsky, Sulerzhitsky, Kachalov striving after? Can it really be true that all that remains of their *Hamlet* is the example of the incompatability of certain blood groups? And it is such a simple schoolboy's howler, so obvious does it seem: 'screens' and 'a system', the actor walks among 'screens' and acts according to a 'system' – this is the failure, the mistake.

Craig? And who was this Craig? The review by V. Doroshevich is footnoted (in the new edition) so that the reader can understand who was being mocked and what for. Craig is described as 'a typical representative of decadent art'; and what about Stanislavsky? Of course in his case footnotes are unnecessary. Everyone knows that he was a typical representative of realistic art. And so it was the meeting of two representatives, two 'typical' ones, and of course they could not possibly have come to an agreement.

But perhaps what was more 'typical' about this production was the fact that there was nothing 'typical' about it and that there were no 'representatives' either. Each was peculiar, unlike anyone else, the only one of his kind, unique. It was an unforgettable game of chess: there was nothing but kings on the board; a pack of cards consisting entirely of aces. The very calibre of the participants, the enormity of each of their personalities not only divided them but united them as well. They all had one thing in common, not a theatrical service record, but a destiny in their epoch.

Sulerzhitsky was always re-reading Shakespeare; he was a friend of Leo Tolstoy and of Chekhov, a man who stood up against injustices wherever he found them, who was deprived of his rights, put under surveillance, and organized the underground press and the colony of Russian Dukhobors in Canada; was he really only a technical assistant? A man who realized other men's ideas? Craig was a wandering genius, dreaming of a theatre which would be like Bach's

Passions, the creator of theatrical Utopias which they still vainly try to realize even today (Peter Brook writes that one or two productions which Craig put on in untheatrical buildings have influenced the whole of European theatre). Stanislavsky represented the legacy of Russian prose, the wind of change in the theatre, the legend of *The Seagull*, *The Cherry Orchard*. Kachalov means Brand, Ivan Karamazov, the 'guardian of the thought' of the younger generations . . .

The feeling of the rift between the theatre and the times united them; they despised the box-office sale of entertainment, nothing more than public houses with a curtain. According to Craig's conception the vastness of space carried the theatre on to another plane of thought; behind the plot and the characters, behind the external events towered the threatening, eternal powers of existence. The changing times had carried away the repertory play (in which the touring companies had an excellent role); Craig discovered in the very music of Shakespeare's poetry, in the abundance of its generalized images, in the mysteries of its meaning, the loneliness of the human soul in a world of commerce and industry, the falsehood of civilization's outer covering, the depravity of its emotions. In the production Fortinbras was like a retribution. He stood on the very top of the construction. A shining sword was in his hand, the body of the overthrown king lay at the foot of the throne, he was like 'an archangel who had descended from heaven' (Stanislavsky). Behind him – there is a photograph of it – shone a fiery light.

The image is a familiar one in Russian art: Pushkin's six-winged seraphim demanded that he pluck out the sinful and 'idle and cunning' tongue (of the acting profession? of the theatre?), not in order to entertain, but to shake and to burn the heart.

Who knows, perhaps the fur coat and the Russian hat from *Woe from Wit* in which the Russian artists dressed their English visitor were also not just warm clothing but symbols as well? It was no accident that the meeting place not only for Craig and Stanislavsky, but for Shakespeare, Craig and Stanislavsky, was Russia. 'A mystery', the first word that Craig spoke, was no empty sound in this instance. Paul Mochalov 'burnt his heart' over Shakespeare, and Pushkin called himself Shakespeare's son. Here they had for a long time dreamed not about the action but about the production. 'Light filtration', 'light conception' – Stanislavsky's terminology of that time – was under the influence of the fluid lines reaching upwards towards Craig's designs.

In those days the 'system' was still a heresy; it was a heroic time of renunciations and manifestos, of ascetic sermons, stern calls to chase the money-lenders from the temple. Stanislavsky recalled later how he locked himself into his artists' dressing-room, alone, little understood, alien to the majority – just as prophets used to go out into the desert.

A chain was established: Gogol – Tolstoy – Dostoyevsky – Chekhov – Stanislavsky. The 'link' was not only in their inner action, in the unity of spiritual life between partners on the same stage, but in the connection between the stage and the auditorium, the link between the theatre and life, unifying all people, their demand for complete truth, the search for ideas capable of uniting mankind. Their search was tormenting: it was impossible gradually to resurrect the past, to make minor corrections; the idle tongue did not cease of its own accord, it had to be plucked out – the right hand of Pushkin's six-winged Seraphim was covered with blood.

TODAY YOU CAN read good advice in articles and reminiscences: what Craig and Stanislavsky ought to have done for their joint effort, the 1911 production, to have become famous, to have been a resounding and complete success, met with deafening applause so that you could not have counted the number of curtain calls. And so that this production would have gone down in the history of the theatre as a triumph, a model production. Perhaps Craig should have assimilated the 'system', have renounced his false ideas about marionettes? Or, on the contrary, Stanislavsky should have sought special ways of playing Shakespeare rather than turning it into Chekhov or Tolstoy? Or, better still, to have sat them both down at the director's table rather than dividing their work into idea and realization . . .

It is of course sensible advice. But the complication was that these artists were not striving after a 'good production' but after something much greater: after a 'mystery', 'complete truth' – they were truly unattainable boundaries, heights which were above the clouds. The 'screens' were enormously heavy and how was the production team to manage these constructions, to control them on the stage? But the burden which these artists loaded on their own shoulders was even heavier. Would it really have been possible not to have given way under its weight, to have found the strength to carry it? . . . And 1911 was a difficult enough year without it.

WHEN I AM putting my old notes into some sort of order, bringing together random remarks, adding new pages in order to develop and clarify the thought behind them, unsolicited memories of places and events which would seem to have nothing to do with it suddenly come to mind.

What do film festivals have in common with what I am writing? I have never wanted to write about Cannes. In spite of the fact that every time that I have been there I have been lucky enough to see some good films (among a mass of bad ones) and to meet some interesting people (in all the noise and bustle), I have always had the strange feeling as if I had accidentally walked in on the shooting of a primitive film about 'the seamy side of capitalism'. There was a time, an eternity ago, when such films (silent) were being shown in Odessa: caricatured types of businessmen, over-acted bustle, the vulgarity of the 'publicity'. . .

Everyone knows this already. But there was one circumstance which few knew about and this is what I want to describe. Quite near, next door to the film market, a lonely and very old artist was living out his last days. Would it have occurred to any of the crowd of reporters to have asked to interview him and would any of them have heard of him? He had long since served his time and was no longer talked about. Producers would not have given a cent for his ideas, and newspapers had not devoted one line of type to him. Everything that he despised – the shamelessness of the acting profession (especially among women), the empty imitation of life (technically perfect on the screen and so much the falser for it), commercialism, the 'box office' – all these celebrated their success here in every corner and in every way.

How unlucky I was; I did not know then that only an hour's distance away it would have been possible to shake him by the hand.

Seen next to the 'show' of the film world, his strangest ideas did not perhaps look so very odd; having watched one's fill of 'stars' one could have said to him in all truthfulness – 'Master, you were right all the time: long live marionettes'.

HE WAS A theatrical reformer and director, but towards the end of his life he had neither the theatre which had become like a home to him, nor even a house. He had a room in a small hotel. What had he come to, what lessons had he learnt in all these years?

'If I could start life all over again, I would have learnt to sing, so that I could give pleasure to all around me,' he wrote to Chekhov's wife from Vence,[1] 'I would have sung in the streets, in cellars, on river banks, in boats, and in the fields during harvest time, only not in the theatre.'

[1] Probably in 1956 when Olga Knipper was in France [trans.].

'I don't feel very well, but I am very old, much older than you. I am 84. Well don't you find that insulting? . . . I live by the sea between Nice and Cannes (where Isadora departed) . . . For the last four years I have been living in a single room. It would be better to have two rooms.'[1]

An ivory tower – this style of life does not command respect now: who has a right to hide from life? But there are different lives and different towers. And artists usually retreat not from some sort of everyday life but from the sort of life which they believe to be worthless: they want neither to sing its praises nor to occupy the place of one who takes pleasure in it. You must look at ivory towers in the light of the complete architectural structure of the times. Sometimes they are erected simply because on the other side of the street there are too many commercial exchanges and dens of vice.

It is worth adding that ivory is most often used as building material by those who have not enough money for a second room.

AN ERA PASSES and it is already difficult to glimpse the living features of its people, of its art. The wind unwound the long woollen scarf round her neck, the end caught in one of the wheels of the car and the chauffeur could not brake in time. Isadora was dead. Could one show now the legend of Duncan's dancing in reality? . . . tape-recordings of Kachalov's Hamlet still exist in the broadcasting sound archives: I have listened to them many times. Is it truly a reality of the art of the time that sixty years ago it was accused of being too lifelike, too much like every day? Neither the enunciation of the lines, nor the sound of the voice itself has any connection with such concepts now. From earliest childhood Craig was used to seeing respectable bronze deifications in English squares: magnificently bosomed, round-bellied ladies in tunics crown heroes of the colonial age with laurels; at their feet are heaped the treasure both of the Gothic era and of rebirth; there also are the Queen's cannon, and in the same group they have added her new subjects, the proud camels. Eternal riddles were simply solved: the sphinxes were dug out of the ancient sand and put on a chain in the British Museum; the world was wide open and familiar. Everything was materialistic, compact and unshakeable. The enormous body of the empire spread over the map, dragging down new territories with its own weight. The keepers of the museums had enough work building monuments, glorifying the heroes, entertaining the conquerors.

[1] This is a translation of the Russian translation. Craig's original letter is unfortunately unobtainable [trans.].

Craig found his first hiding place from his times in Florence: a narrow street not far from the Gates of Rome; it was approached through a low door which led into the yard behind. There was a miniature theatre here in the open and here Craig constructed his models, sketched and wrote. What did he write about? Perhaps the main theme was the loneliness of the spirit in a satiated world. He answered the conceit of positivism with a contempt for everything material; he turned the hands of his watch forwards to eternity.

Other times came and went, new decades. What remained of the corpulence of the colonial empire? The bronze of the monuments, made to last for centuries, seem to us today not even like the shadow of a vanishing body, but as Shakespeare puts it, 'a shadow's shadow'. On the other hand the fashions have remained: in the West, boudoirs dating from the end of the century and kerosine lamps are once again in fashion.

Craig could not settle anywhere. In some towns he was frozen with cold in the autumn, others were too noisy. Italy went to war with Ethiopia and he moved to France. At the age of sixty-eight he was interned; the fascists occupied Paris.

And now an old gentleman walked about the town of Vence in the South of France. He wore a white arab burnous[1], his head shielded from the sun by a wide-brimmed straw hat, and he leant on a stick which had belonged to Irving. He always carried his leather brief-case, his pencil, paper, pens at the ready just in case he suddenly needed to write something down or to make a sketch.

The hazy spectre bathed in gold light which was to be brought on stage in the MAT production while Kachalov spoke, 'To be or not to be' and which kept slipping from their fingers – neither the magic lantern nor the gas lamps in the wings managed to catch it – visited Craig when he was ninety-four. He was incapable of creating real theatre, and did not even carry through to the end those few productions which people were foolish enough to entrust to him; his ideas were never realized to the full; only isolated thoughts, certain aspects; a feeling expressed in special relationships; a thought barely suggested by an engraving or a sketch . . . A dreamer, fantasist. And what happened to the MAT production of *Hamlet*? . . . Anyone who is familiar with the day-to-day running of a theatre can easily imagine. The play was put on less and less frequently, more successful productions took its place and there was no longer any need for this already antiquated production. *Hamlet* was dropped from the repertory – it was probably not even fit to be called repertory; the screens were carried off the stage (there is no longer need for

[1] A cloak with a hood [trans.].

inverted commas – they had become simple screens), and taken to the storerooms; the gold paper had probably chipped on tour and the sackcloth had been torn – the materials were fragile and not lasting; and then other scenery had to be stored; the carpenters made an unsuccessful sort of corner and the poles broke (it didn't seem to matter much as there was no question of a revival), and then the time came for a review of the store: should an inventory be made? There was not enough space? It was decided to clear the building of rubbish; there was no shortage of material and to keep warped and dirty screens was impractical. The sackcloth was torn up, thrown on to the rubbish heap, and the wood sent off to be chopped up.

I WAS NOT even remotely thinking of the production which had its première at the Moscow Art Theatre on 23 December 1911 (5 January 1912) when, uncomfortably ensconced (but is there ever such a thing as a comfortable angle in filming?), I lay on a dirty platform which ran on rails and putting my eye to the camera lens, watched the stone outcrops appear in the shot and then disappear from my field of vision. And why, in any case, should I have remembered that production? What similarity could be found between the rough natural look of the pock-marked crags, lit up by the sun, and Craig's symbols – representing either false matter, or royal grandeur?

And all the same I shall have to repeat once again the last sentence of the last chapter – and yet . . .

While I was still only a boy, I was astounded by Craig's sketches: space, devoid of any recognizable landmarks, the unification of the emptiness of night and the coldness of ice, sea mist in which anything can be imagined. Lonely figures in the midst of unfamiliar worlds of stone. There is not one detail, not one feature which you can grasp on to in order to find your way to that place, so strongly does the void beckon you. The rhythm of its structure, the shades of grey, the vertical and horizontal lines give it poetry in their own code – it is no longer heard but seen. Next to these engravings and sketches, the theatrical décor seemed mean, insignificant, on the level of provincial Shakespearean productions: wrinkled tights, drawers pulled tightly over them, declaimed speech and howling, and beards made of tow.

I tried to find out more about Craig (at first I had succeeded in finding out very little); then I got hold of his books and everything that has been written about him; and then I started to recognize his ideas in the best English productions ('only two tones – dark brown and grey – nothing else!'). And now, having put aside my diary (the notebooks of the days of filming), I was re-reading *Towards a New Theatre*, and studying his engravings.

It is true that a lot of time has already passed, but does time ever pass without leaving some sort of trace? But the most important thing is this: Craig was the first to insist that Shakespeare's tragedies are concerned not only with human passions and the relationships between the main characters in the plays but, first and foremost, with the conflict of some sort of mighty visual powers; you cannot restrict the poetry within the confines of the subject matter, it goes far beyond these bounds – it is a whole universe! Can a company of actors really convey this?

Of course he also understood the particular individuals excellently: Polonius's family – he said in passing – is worthless and stupid; Gertrude was not born a bad woman – the atmosphere of the court spoilt her and of course Hamlet did not stop loving his mother. This is so obvious . . .

He explained that long discussions about the psychology of the characters are pointless; words can kill live emotion, dry up the poetry. It is better to listen to the music of Shakespeare's verse. It will reveal everything to you. Chekhov replied to the questions of his actors, 'It is all there in the text, only you don't have to express grief with your arms and legs, it is better to keep silent.'

When he was young, Craig asked a friend to play some Bach, while he painted frescoes on the wall to the music. He saw an art of movement and light which was capable of creating an accumulation of equal strength to Bach's climaxes. He sketched out the contours of thousands of people caught up by one emotion – what stage could they be housed in? One of Macbeth's soliloquies? Are these merely spoken words? – this is how he conceived the production. It is a movement forward, a rising upwards; space moves with Macbeth, he climbs up the tower and space spreads out ever wider: lands, hills and mountains on the horizon.

THE HANDING OVER of torches in relays is a marvellous sight; the creative artist hands the torch to the next artist while he is still running, and the second, snatching the flickering torch, dashes forward in order to hand on the gift of Prometheus unblemished to the next artist – a young man, in his full strength, and he . . . Alas, it rarely happens in this way. The artist stumbles, having lost his former speed, and the torch begins to smoke or even goes out altogether. And sometimes a youth who is not in the least noble hurries to relieve him, and a jealous and ham-fisted man trips over the one who is still at the height of his powers . . . It is sad to relate but there's no getting away from it – the picture often looks just like this, not at all triumphant: someone steals someone else's fire for a light – from one who has devoted his whole life to propagating it – and having lit his cigarette with it, spits on the flame, in order to avoid a whole crowd trying to throw asbestos over it . . .

And if the flame does not die but flares up again it is better to search for the cause not on the racing track of art but in the amphitheatre itself.

Ancient conflicts, deep contradictions do not disappear without trace; in unfolding its spirals, history catches the reflections of old fires on a new turn. And those who lit them will, uninvited, enter the new decade. They are often not recognized, and they walk unacknowledged along the edge of time. The real deeds that they performed have no place in the memory of the new generation and they forgot to carve their name in stone.

This track is not a straight one from teacher to pupil, but in the form of spirals – an approach towards a certain point and a receding, in order again, in a spiralling movement, with an ever widening span, to approach and recede. How many times does it approach and recede! . . .

The accumulation of achievements and their decisive rejection, more accumulations and more rejections is still more passionate. And a strange link is established behind all this. Is it conscious or unconscious? An influence which stems from childhood? A family of problems which life itself poses?

WHAT A COMPLICATED concept is the tragic quality of space and how different are the manifestations of life which it embraces.

The enormity of the material world and at the same time the fictitiousness of this world of marketable worth is contained in a single man: Orson Welles' *Citizen Kane*. The expansion of his possessions and the contraction of his spiritual world. Everything is realistic on the screen – the photography creates objectivity of expression, but the wide-angled vision distorts the perspective: space is stretched out and elongated; however the sharpness of the most distant perspectives is retained. It is the tragedy of a man who turns out to be alone in the midst of an innumerable quantity of objects. After mastering the production, multiplying and selling of things – thoughts, feelings also being things – the man himself becomes a thing, a soulless man in an emptiness stuffed full of things.

The film was made in 1941. Is it necessary to explain the link between the phenomena of art and life?

Thirty years later even the wide-angled lens and the most enormous studios were not sufficient: Orson Welles rented a derelict station in Paris which had not been used for many years – and here he filmed *The Trial*. But Kafka is characterized by a different quality: small, stuffy buildings with low ceilings. However, who has taken the measurements of Hell? Welles created an enormity from which there was no escape, and the larger the field of action (of fictitious action), the greater the number of people who were drawn into it. A thousand typewriters on a thousand tables, an army of typists – Hell's office.

In this film there is a panoramic shot of the whole square: there are crowds of people in their underclothes, with tickets round their necks, faceless, identical, and at the end hangs a statue, covered with a sheet: it has neither figure nor face.

What has remained of the king made from molten gold? From the sea of gold – the king's robe – in which the heads of the courtiers swam? The boundless darkness, the mist – through which you can see not heads but tickets round their necks.

The art of enormous generalizations of visual images. Ten years later the most different, opposing experiences were echoing each other: Meyerhold, Craig . . . and then stepping over the stage, solving all the technical complications on the way (is it necessary to turn the 'screens' – it is simpler to move the camera), the screen: Griffith, Stroheim, Eisenstein, Orson Welles . . .

And, at the same time, experiments were being performed which were no less irrevocable and extreme in their decisiveness: their complete naturalness, truthfulness to life – you had to begin not with 'the universe' but with a real man really drinking tea.

It was unavoidable that Shakespeare should have been played like Chekhov in 1911.

After all we too try to act *King Lear* not like *Uncle Vanya* but having read Chekhov. You must be able to see clearly and not to be frightened of what you see: King Lear drinks tea, his eldest daughter pushes his cup to one side – the old man has no control of anything in the house.

Chapter Fifteen

IT WAS THE eve of the most difficult shooting. Four months' work was already behind us. A huge sheet of Whatman paper ruled into squares hung on the production manager's study wall with a number in each square. Every number represented a shot; once the shot had been taken the number was struck out. Once the number was struck out the length of film was calculated. Once the length was calculated, the accounts were made up. Up till today we had shot altogether in usable length of film . . .

If only I knew whether it was going to be usable or not. And usable to whom? To the film? To the accounts? To Shakespeare?

All the same perhaps only I knew that we had not yet touched on the essence of *Lear*, on the particular imagery of this tragedy which was unlike any other. And tomorrow we would.

I had probably exaggerated; we had surely touched on some part of it, but it was no good trying to console myself: the most difficult part was still ahead. I mean the scenes next to which the violence of today's avantgarde looks provincially modest and timid. In Shakespeare's tragedies you come across places which startle you by their very boldness. How is one most accurately to define their attributes and methods of expression? Mayakovsky wrote in an attempt to put in a good word for Yesenin, 'You knew how to exaggerate'. Perhaps such a definition fits here. Shakespeare's text is uneven; it has both beautiful poetry and ordinary passages – rhetoric, improvements on old plays; there are also, whatever anyone says 'exaggerations': a sudden foreshortening, the fantastic setting up of an experiment.

Lear gathers strength when everything is turned upside-down. And it is then, when the world is standing on its head, with its feet in the air, that the essence of the events are laid bare; the false coverings drop to the ground and the common link between one object and another is revealed in its true unmystical form. The most difficult problems are resolved by a topsy-turvy kind of method, and jokes hit their true target.

We began to shoot the meeting of mad Lear and blind Gloucester. Much has already been written about the paradox – the scene's basic contradiction: the one who has lost his reason has become a wise man; the other who has been blinded can see.

The different ways of studying the phenomena of life are quite varied enough. 'Now I will show you a trick' (handy-dandy) – so the homeless beggarly old man (the King of England) suggests to the other old tramp (one of the King's ministers). The aim of the trick is to show clearly the true order of rank in the kingdom. It is as if the old man takes off his battered hat from his grey head and, as in conjuring tricks in the circus, shakes various people out of it: a judge, a thief, a prostitute, an executioner, a money-lender, a swindler. He arranges them in pairs; for instance, he starts with the thief and the judge, and covers them with his cap. One, two . . . On the count of 'three' the cap is lifted: the figures have changed places, now they are indistinguishable. Which is the thief? Which is the judge? Why do they punish the prostitute? For the executioner himself wants her.

All this is in the text.

Towards the end of the scene Lear suggests preaching Gloucester a sermon. Its subject? The point of man's existence on earth from his first appearance on it to death itself. It can be explained in a few words; the point, it seems, is one single item: tears. The human creature enters God's world crying and leaves it crying. No, the word is not 'world', here the author used another expression, not 'God's world' and not some country where yet another soul is added to the population, and not even a world which it enters – no the definition is different: 'this great stage of fools'. One can try to convey the shades of meaning in the original in a different way: a great peep-show, a world farce, a universal stage of clowns. This is the finale – the sum total reached by puns, parodies, and practical jokes.

'The humour of cruelty' or 'the cruelty of humour' (Wilson Knight) has permeated all of this. The old man with bleeding holes for eyes is called 'blind Cupid', 'Goneril with a white beard' and is goaded in his blindness to read out some sort of challenge, or look at the world with his ears.

What is the salt of these puns? It is the same salt which, according to the common expression, is poured on to wounds, one's own, other's, the wounds of all mankind. This is done in order that the wounds should become still more painful, so that they should never be forgotten. A backward kick for the lame, fire for the burnt, icy water for those who are soaked to the skin; these are the kind of practical jokes which are played. Why are they devised and performed with such cruelty? In order that they should finally realize – these blind, lame, burnt, and drenched people – who made them like they are. Everything on which their world is founded – institutions and figures of power from the finance houses to the army, from the holy personage of the king down to the man who carried out his orders – is distorted by puns, embellished with parodies and tripped up with jokes. It is a variety show at all four corners of the earth, a circus ring embracing the whole world. There is plenty of room to gambol about provided you don't slip: at every step there is a pool of blood.

The sermon is over. What remains? The smell of ashes and the echo of crying.

This is where you can see an example of where Meyerhold was right; the foundation of 'well-adjusted contentment' is shattered in the theatre not by the philosophers but by the 'fools'.

THE BASIC TEXT of this scene was kept almost in its entirety in the script. I did not want to cut any of it; every omission would be like cutting live flesh. It is not for nothing that the speeches have become sayings, they have even invaded everyday Russian speech. Many people have not even heard of the play but 'every inch a king', 'Plate sin with gold,/And the strong lance of justice hurtless breaks', 'none does offend, none, – I say, none' are phrases which everyone knows. The strength of the scene is contained in the text. And this is the greatest danger lying in wait for the director. You only have to turn all attention to the text, to the famous aphorisms, and the action stops, the scene loses its significance.

Let us imagine a game of ping pong in which the players are using not balls but jewels stuck on to a pigeon's egg – what would such a game lead to? Would much be left of the game? The precious words speak for themselves; if they are given special emphasis, as if they were treasures, they will seem like glass imitations. Help can only hinder here; it is easy to drop what you are trying to carry carefully to its destination.

How should the text be enunciated? It should not be enunciated at all. One should not act something which acts itself. One should forget about the importance of the words (they are obvious), about the idiosyncrasy of the form (it is in the structure of the speech). Nothing should be shown, underlined, or strengthened. Attention should be paid not to the words but to the circumstances in which they are spoken.

This is what differentiates the cinema from the theatre. On the Shakespearean stage the life-like surroundings (the most important of these is the place of action) not only do not have any particular significance but an attempt to make them clearer, to show them in all their reality would destroy the action. Words and words alone create the scenery here (when it is necessary to imagine it), both the movement of people in space, and the extraordinary jumps from the real to the fantastic, from the tragic to the grotesque.

A realistic scenery on the stage would reveal the accidental and unlikely quality of the meeting of the two characters in the same place, the conventionality of the action. On the screen it is quite different. The lifelike surroundings are dynamic and can themselves become the action. Locality is easily replaced by the abstract: the shot shows both earth and sky. 'A lack of attention' to the words I am writing about means a greater concentration of attention to everything which strengthens the thought. The more fantastic the text, the more natural must be the surroundings in which they are spoken.

Let Lear 'drink tea'.

Of course you cannot have tea here. There is bare ground, stoney earth, boulders. But you can quench your thirst: water has collected in the cavities of the rocks – it poured with rain all night. The old man is tormented with hunger and thirst; he is tired, not being used to walking. He has now become just like everyone else, one of the beggars. He is a ragamuffin among ragamuffins, unwashed and unshaven. The tramps wander about on land which was once a vegetable plot. Might they be able to dig up something to eat? . . .

The business of everyday life. Grey upon grey. Perhaps it is just such a combination which will produce clarity? . . .

It is essential to be able to convince the audience that it really did happen like that. That all this unlikelihood is the absolute truth.

But what about the famous words, how are they to be spoken in such surroundings? An old man in rags gnaws at a frozen beet-top and in between mouthfuls answers the blind man – who recognized his voice – that he is indeed a king, every inch a king.

Between mouthfuls – this is the heart of the matter.

The more unlikely the situation the more it must be played like an everyday occurrence – this is the first law of eccentricity. The illogical must be presented with complete, unarguable logicality.

THE CLOWN ENTERS the circus ring bowed down under the weight of the gate which he is carrying on his back. Before entering a house you have to open the door. The clown does this: he puts the gate down on the carpet, turns the key, opens the door, walks through the gate and closes the door behind him. Then he heaves the gate on to his back again and walks on further with it.

They are natural actions. Only one thing is missing: there is no house.

The clown takes his jacket off his shoulders (a torn piece of cloth), brushes it down, folds it carefully and hangs it up on a nail. Or rather he pretends to hang it up: there is neither nail nor wall; the jacket falls to the ground. The clown carefully wipes his feet on it.

These actions are meaningless taken individually: clothes are brushed and folded in order not to get crushed; before entering a house, you must wipe your feet so that you do not bring mud into the room. Everything in life happens just like that. Only the connection between the actions is distorted; the meaning has disappeared, the aim is lost. The main point has vanished, but the details have been preserved in their entirety.

Lenin was intrigued by the number of eccentrics in London's music halls; Gorky described Lenin's thoughts 'about eccentricity as a peculiar form of theatrical art': 'Here there is a sort of satirical or sceptical relationship to what is commonly accepted, there is a striving to turn it inside out . . . to show the illogicality of the ordinary.'

We are no longer concerned with the humour of shuffling links but with the fact that these links themselves have indeed lost their meaning; the ordinary has become illogical. What seems outwardly impressive is shattered in reality. A picture of disintegration and collapse is revealed.

Marx wrote, 'The disintegration of the consciousness which realizes and expresses one's being – and Hegel wrote of this in his old age – is a cruel mockery of the individual's mode of life . . . and of one's own self. This is both in itself the destructive nature of all relationships and the conscious destruction of them.'

You can read about Leo Tolstoy's interest in madmen in the memoirs of people who were close to him. 'Semyon took snuff and frequently offered it to madmen' wrote S. L. Tolstoy, remembering the fairy story which her father made up. 'Once he fell asleep in the passage with his axe beside him. A madman crept up to him, took the axe and chopped off his head with one stroke. Then he hid Semyon's head under his bed and went off with a crafty expression on his face to tell the other madmen what a funny trick he had played: "When Semyon wakes up and wants to take some snuff he will not be able to find his nose. I have got his nose under my bed."'

This is the sort of film Buñuel could make. One of the funniest comedies of recent years in my opinion was Luis Berlanga's *The Executioner*: the only way the young couple could get a flat was for the husband to get a job as an executioner garrotting criminals. At first it was unpleasant work but he soon grew accustomed to it.

S. L. Tolstoy writes, 'In all stories about madmen the basis of their illness is their illogical reasoning. But the majority of people also reason illogically; this is why my father considered that most people who were regarded as sane were mentally ill.'

Leo Tolstoy wrote in his diary. 'I was afraid to say and to think that 99 out of 100 people were mad. But not only is it pointless to be afraid, you must not refrain from speaking and thinking about it.'

Shakespeare spoke about this very same subject. Lear had lived for eighty years but he did not know his own children, or the kingdom which he governed, or the world in which he lived. The truth was revealed to him when his consciousness clouded over. The distortion of all living relationships became clear to him in his madness.

The culmination of the conflict is contained in this paradox. And it flares up here with all its strength. But it is not the end of the play yet. How are the mad episodes linked with what has already happened and what is yet to come?

Does the meeting with Cordelia take place on the same 'stage of fools'?

The more exactly any of the conceptions (and there are enough of them) are developed, and the clearer the interpretations are defined (by a director or a scholar), the less I am convinced by them. The perfection of logical constructions (extracting the 'essential' from the tragedy) is overthrown in an instant by Shakespeare's live action; static formulas by their very definition are alien to the freedom of action, the unbiased inspiration of the poetic substance.

We can grasp (if we want to discover the variety, rather than just the 'essential') the appearance of the links, and their immediate disintegration, and the immediate striving towards other links, as if another magnet were drawing the links of the broken chain into a new order; for a moment everything is chained together and whole, and then there is another collapse.

When Hamlet is falsifying the order for his execution which Guildenstern and Rosencrantz are taking to England, he says that like an engineer he will dig beneath their mines and place another mine beneath theirs.[1] This is roughly how *Lear* is constructed: there is an explosion, and then another explosion from a greater depth.

What can one read into such a construction without taking into account the abrupt changes of tonality? The very way people walk is significant here. By listening to their walk, their movements and their breathing you will come to a better understanding of both the categories of 'madness' and 'sanity'.

The rhythm expresses madness no less than the words themselves. And what is more important it is often at variance with the words.

[1] Act III iv [trans.].

In the mad scenes, where you would expect sudden halts, discords and sharp changes, peace reigns. At first glance the thoughts are fragmentary, however the hero's breathing is regular. Once Lear has lost his reason the pace of the action slows down. The scenes are written unhurriedly with many different nuances. Before the appearance of Cordelia's soldiers (the horror at returning to normal life) there is neither violence nor melodrama in the portrayal of Lear's mental illness. On the contrary, peace has descended: he is enjoying the freedom to think about life, to sort out his own opinions . . .

But before this there was so much haste! This was where the violence was, in the gathering snowball of madness. The whole of the first half of the play transmits the contagious epidemic, the loosing of his reason, If you detach yourself from the rhetoric of the soliloquies (full of Old Testament hyperbole and heavy, noble speech), and turn your attention to the pace of events, you begin to feel dizzy: the world has slipped off its axis, gone off the rails. Actions, events are performed in the heat of the moment, without premeditation; decisions are instantaneous, ruptures immediate and departures are precipitated. The earth begins to move under the characters, burns beneath their feet and is swept away from under them.

LEAR BEGINS HIS stay with Goneril by going hunting. There is nothing out of the ordinary about this form of pastime. He has plenty of time now for hunting. And so Lear's new life begins in the Duke of Albany's castle, his first days of freedom. Man hunts beast. It is a diversion, an amusement.

And the first blow falls when he returns from the hunt. Are these circumstances important to the tragedy? Is there any point in lingering over them?

In the play the hunt took place before the scene opened. It is only mentioned. There are no more than a few sentences to link the chain of events, to give an effective beginning. Lear opens the door into the dining hall while still in a state of excitement. What else can you extract from this mention? You can probably show nothing else on the stage.

Of course you can show his spoil. In the old production at the Jewish Theatre Mikhoels as Lear walked out from the wings holding a dead hare. He cut off its ear while humming a merry tune. A hunting song, a long furry ear – the hunter's trophy. And immediately something strange and alien encroached on the image. Why? The details were perfectly natural: hares could have run over those fields too and why should the hunters not have sung hunting songs? There was nothing invented or contrived about it. It would have been unjust to have reproached it for not being true to life. However the point was a different sort of truth – the poetry.

In studying Shakespearean metaphors Caroline Spurgeon discovered a different world for each of his tragedies. The constant metaphors in Othello are linked with the sensation of something insignificant, unclean, base and which evokes disgust ('Plague him with flies' – the punishment which Iago devises for Othello); insects, reptiles; if there are animals, they are goats and monkeys. There is no mention of any of this in *Lear*, neither of flies[1] nor of toads: the poetic space is populated with beings of a different calibre – enormous wild beasts, fierce predators, and sometimes by the monsters of prehistory – dragons and evil visions from the ancient forests. There are two main spheres in *Lear*, the images of suffering human flesh, and the figure of the wild beast, the habits of predators, and these confront each other and intermingle; the metaphors are not formed as static comparisons but follow the changing circumstances.

The changes are strengthened by the action. And as always with this particular writer, the metaphors are linked with everyday realism. The apocalyptic grows out of the commonplace. Out of the diversions of the King, the amusement of the hunt, an enormous metaphorical hunt grows with ever increasing strength. It is a hunt throughout the kingdom, throughout the history of kingdoms.

The metaphors, Shakespeare's figures of speech, have been studied. But they are not simply part of the verbal texture, they are inseparable from the movement, the action. The 'Mouse-trap' is not only the name of the play with which Hamlet frightens Claudius, and not only the pivot on which the plot turns, but also the character of the movement of many of the scenes; there is an abundance of hidden games, cunning traps, double games, ambushes; the battle is waged on the quiet, in hiding, in secrecy, without faces being shown, in suspense.

It is different in *Lear*. The hunt carries through the whole tragedy with ever-increasing pace. The metaphorical collides with the real, hunt with hunt, at full tilt, at close quarters, creating havoc and changing its target. 'Come not between the dragon and his wrath' is one of the first threats. 'The bow is bent and drawn' – and Kent is banished (and if he is caught 'The moment is thy death'); Kent tracked down Oswald; Edmund hunted Edgar; Cornwall snared Kent (put in the stocks!); they picked up Gloucester's scent; encircled Lear; the footsteps looped like a hare's – Lear's footsteps

[1] The author has evidently overlooked 'as flies to wanton boys' [trans.].

from locked gates to barred doors; they conspire to kill the Duke of Albany and themselves fall into his net . . . There are more instances than you can recount. At every turn of events there are nooses, holes dug in the ground, snares.

This is not only a verbal game, but the action itself. The nooses really tighten; the brushwood covering the hole gives way under their feet . . . The steel trap clatters shut: someone has been caught! But he got away, leaving his bloodstained skin in the snare. Edgar slipped out of his human identity – naked bleeding flesh, exposed nerves, pain and terror – he broke loose and bumped into his father, the one who set the trap for him and who himself fell into the pit – while his eyes were fixed on the jewels.

Sides in a lather, frothing muzzles, whips, spurs: faster! after him! Who is that in the hollow of the tree: an animal? a man? Or one who was a man. They cover over their traces, leap at each other's throats, tear each other's flesh, and scratch with their nails: fathers, children, sisters, mothers, husbands, wives – all are drawn into the chase, into the snare.

It is a hunt where beasts are not caught, but men themselves turn into beasts. They do not destroy predators but become predators themselves – the whole race of man.

Is it a hunt or a kind of frenzied devilish chase?

What does it remind one of? Whose art springs to mind? However strange it may seem it really does resemble Father Goose – this is what Mack Sennett, the creator of madness on the screen, was called in an American biography, relating him to the fairy-tale Mother Goose. The similarity lies of course not in the characters – the moustachioed monsters of policemen, the bathing beauties, or the simple comedians – we are concerned with something else – the cult of the chase. The madness of pursuit, the unleashing of brakes; a whole world caught up in a frantic gallop – where to? why? Heels flash, accelerators are pushed hard down, bridges are carried away, and this whole muddle, senseless excitement, this abracadabra of scuffles, becomes (it would not of course have occurred to Father Goose) a parody, and not simply a funny one but a malicious one as well, on man and on life; a mockery of everything that is human, intelligent and has a soul. They soak each other in water from head to foot, run, splash each other with hoses, the jets of water knock them off their feet and you die of laughing at the slops from the buckets and the dirty tricks!

Piles of custard pies to be slapped on someone's face one after the other until you can't even see that there is a face there – what a riot! . . . Of even better, a tub of dough emptied on someone's head –

where was the man? The shapeless mess jumps up and down, turns round and round, runs, dashes at full speed, and behind him, without pausing for breath, chases something between a scarecrow and a wild beast; he is caught – who is baiting whom! Everybody pile in!

In *Lear* similar things happen. Only the dough is not white but red; blood spurts out as if from a fireman's hose.

It is a frightening, malicious image. Today, it does not bear thinking about how the merry clowning would have ended, the tricks of the common buffoons, and instead of the fairground farces, the brilliant colours – black and red; two interpretations – the tragic and the grotesque. This is what the endless chain of tragedy and farce had come to – the humour of cruelty and the cruelty of humour, the breaking down of consciousness, 'the self-destructive nature of all relationships and the conscious destruction of them.' (Marx)

Half a century ago we wrote of this art in the manifestoes on 'eccentricity' rather suspecting it than understanding, and then during the war, when Eisenstein suggested that I should write about Charlie Chaplin (he was editing a collection devoted to Chaplin), I returned to this theme and much had become clearer to me. Now I saw links with it and *Lear*.

And the important thing is that this whole burlesque, the boundaries of madness, reign supreme in *Lear* where people act in full possession of their faculties and of their senses; people who govern kingdoms, make up laws, and rule over whole nations.

In his *Index to the Story of My Days* Gordon Craig wrote, 'Farce is the essential Theatre . . . farce brutalized becomes tragedy.'[1]

'The devils' vaudeville', 'embittered farce' – these are the sort of genre definitions which thrust themselves upon you. But what happens when tragedy borders on goodness and tenderness?

I was thinking least of all about how to make all these situations obvious, but it is just as important to be able to see the action clearly in these deeper parts of Shakespeare's thought.

This was how I was trying to travel through the space of tragedy. But it was so vast! . . .

IT WAS NOT difficult to find the place where it was as if the devil himself had given a sign and this hell was torn from its chains, hurtling along in a mad gallop. The kingdom was divided (in the heat of the moment), the favourite daughter had been cursed, the trusty friend banished, relations with France broken . . . What still remained whole, was still standing? The house? The house would

[1] Hulton Press, 1957, p. 125 [trans.].

go too. Let us be off, at once! The road burst into the wide open space, the space where there would be nothing but movement and if on the way a floor appeared beneath his feet and a roof over his head, it would only be for a few limited moments; the doors would close immediately, the gates would be barred, and next – where next? The roads were blocked, the paths obstructed. The hunt was on. There was nowhere to go. It was the end of the earth. Dover, the sheer cliff, the sea.

Chapter Sixteen

THERE IS A peculiar feature about Lear's journey. One hundred and one people set out together, but only one arrives.

A hundred knights; his train – the only thing Lear kept for himself. He divided everything up at one stroke, distributed it and threw it to the winds. Everything except his train. A hundred knights would remain with him and accompany him wherever he went. What are they – a guard? But not one of them defends Lear when he is deeply insulted. Servants? But he sends a letter to Regan by the first man his eyes happened to light upon (Kent in disguise), and not by one of these people. They are neither soldiers nor servants but the halo of power.

Lear, when accompanied by his train is King, without his train no more than a bad-tempered old man; 'Lear's shadow' as the Fool explains to him later.

How is one to portray these hundred men on the screen? To any director who has had at least some experience the answer would seem to be simple: to break them up into groups, and to bring one or two individual characters to the fore, those who were closest to the main character, and to isolate a few human traits. This is what we did. The rehearsal room was bustling with activity; characters and whole life-histories were created; one of the train instantly sized up the situation and walked off in the opposite direction; another hesitated, waiting on events; a conference started up behind Lear's back . . . a great deal of business was invented.

But it was invented in vain. Their work turned out to be of no use. It soon became clear that the details only held up the action and obstructed it. It was not invented but contrived; adding to what was there rather than interpreting it.

Shakespeare created the image of the Officer who killed Cordelia with a few speeches (war had taught him everything, all he had to do was to lead the team of carts and to chew oats); once you have read the lines, the life of the old farmer (who saved Gloucester) becomes clear. Shakespeare has any number of similar minute roles – which are living characters.

He did not give human speech to any one of the hundred knights (not counting the stage directions) – neither names, words, nor character. Is this a coincidence? Of course it isn't. These are not people but a way of life. They are a whole, not individuals. Who is most famous, who lives better than anyone else? He who has 'seven thousand sheep, three thousand camels, and five hundred yoke of oxen, and five hundred she-asses, and a great household' – this is how the story of Job begins. Is it necessary to define the breed of the oxen, or to show exactly what tasks the slaves performed?

One can perhaps risk showing the flag of equality by saying that camels, oxen, she-asses, sheep and a great household of slaves is the same thing as a hundred knights and squires which the King demands for his own use.

It is a general image rather than a portrait gallery – just as Gordon Craig saw the King's robe covering the whole stage, a sea of gold with the heads of the courtiers showing above the surface. Corks or sponges. What sort of characters are these?

In the cinema visual generalizations grow into a movement, and take on a shape and dimension in the sequence of shots. The generalization becomes a movement in itself.

This is how we would shoot it.

On with the sea of gold! To work on the King's train!

This is not a play on words, but if you like, a number of shots in a shooting script, indications as to the place of the expedition and the technique of shooting (the dolly for the tracking camera, the camera button); in the specific directions, mention must be made of the 'sheep, camels, oxen, she-asses', that is the horses, hunting dogs, birds . . . and a great household.

All this together makes up the 'cloak'; we would cut it out and sew it together as we went along. We would display it in full view, unfolding the whole length of the train. The train would drag behind the King, lying about the halls, scraping along the roads, growing threadbare and disintegrating.

And then there were no longer a hundred knights, no robe left. Only one man remained . . . one very old man in a smock, on the bare earth, beneath a merciless sky. This is what we would shoot here in Kazantip.

There were neither camels, nor oxen, nor she-asses nor servants.

> For want and famine they were solitary; fleeing into the wilderness in former time desolate and waste. Who cut up mallows by the bushes, and juniper roots for their meat. They were driven forth from among men . . . They were children of fools, yea, children of base men; they were viler than the earth. (Job 30, vv 3–8)

We would shoot the wearing out of the robe in Estonia which has everything you need for its train. We had already shot how it was cut out and sewn together in the studio.

'Robe', 'train', 'hunt', 'madness' – these are not a succession of separate images, but stages in a continuous movement; they represent a development, a contradictory train of thought, sunk deep into the flow of shots. Space within this movement can contract down to the molecule of everyday life, brought sharply into focus, making it coarse and vulgar; or it can suddenly open out, leap outside the shots, delving into history and embracing the universe. The quality which one tries to grasp in the development of the film turns upside down: nothing is constant or fixed.

The Romantics revelled in the juxtaposition of the sublime and the ridiculous in Shakespeare; the result was like a layered pie. There is certainly an abundance of contrasts in *Lear*, only the different spheres are not named; it is difficult to find the boundaries. The sublime does not alternate with the ridiculous but disintegrates into it. And without anyone noticing, the ridiculous casts off the fool's cap, and somehow appears in the crown of thorns. Characteristics of style? No. These are characteristics of history, of life and of thought – and this is the essence.

This is how one must present a Shakespearean film. This is the combination of elements which must define the tone, the pace and the very substance of the cinema. The screen is not a play where Shakespeare is acted 'taking into account the specific character of cinema' (showing visually what is talked about). The screen must be charged with the electricity of tragedy. Underneath the flow of Shakespeare must appear a texture of dynamic imagery.

IT IS NOT easy to talk of the 'substance of cinema' nowadays. One who lived his whole life (more than simply working) in cutting rooms in the early twenties, knows what this feeling of the warm, live substance of cinema is. I had held it in my hands, my fingers had felt the warmth. It was as if the celluloid had a life of its own: every metre concealed buds of meaning, hints of emotion, springs of thought. Scissors, razor blades, tins of film cement were unsophisticated production tools, but with their help we achieved what was almost jeweller's work. Each frame of a shot was worth its weight in gold (and the frames often realized it). In those days editing a consecutive story line was despised: was this true editing? – it was no more than a trade, a splicing together. Editing was a contemplation, an embodiment of feeling, an animated movement. Metres, shots, frames ceased to have a separate existence; a new reality appeared under one's fingers: the mould of a spiritual world, a rocket shooting towards the area of the screen.

Eisenstein separated once and for all the screen – the sphere of cinematographic art – from the rectangle of doubtful purity on which 'live photographs' were projected. It was only the energy of dynamic movement which transformed cloth into cinema screen.

How many days and nights we spent editing the 'catastrophe' in *The New Babylon*. Fragments of action – all in different places, at different times: the chaos of a closing-down sale, the waste of chauvinist action, the tinsel of gala performances, mad dances all over Paris, a German cavalry attack – nothing existed separately, was fixed in place, or defined by time; everything was jumbled together, one overlapping the next, forming a new quality – the growing upward movement of a wave, the theme of the 'destruction of the Second Empire'. Linking relationships, faces belonging to the epoch, the rhythms of its life, the uninhibited speculation, the uncontrollable growth of general buying and selling, the inevitability of retribution – it was all fused together, and linked by the rhythm and chiaroscuro; this is simply space carried along by its own momentum.

In those days they talked about 'an episode gathered into the palm of one's hand'.

What we did then helped me now in making a Shakespearean film. But I could not work in the same way now. The reason was not that the cinema of the twenties was silent, and that the technology of editing changed when sound film came. A lot of water had flowed under the bridge since then and even more blood. The world had changed. These changes could not be expressed in 'episodes gathered into the palm of one's hand'.

This is why I was studying Shakespeare. Why I was writing this book. The years (marvellous, priceless years) of pure cinema, of straight cinema, were past.

Now we needed a different cinema in order to grasp the complexity of life and of history, in order to uncover their depth.

AT ONE OF the stormy discussions in the twenties the speaker exclaimed (they never talked quietly and calmly in those days):

'A director is a man who thinks in shots' . . .

'But I thought he used his head', interrupted a voice from the floor.

The reply was undoubtedly witty and not without significance. However you cannot dismiss the matter with a joke. What is true poetry: the linking of different ideas, complex associations (summer lightning Tyutchev's 'deaf and dumb demons'); or, on the contrary, the natural intonation (Lermontov's 'Let her weep – nothing means anything to her')? . . . You can find as many examples of both kinds of language in great poetry. But at the appearance of each major phenomenon in the arts and in history we are forced to see poets in a new light. Tolstoy not only failed to destroy Shakespeare but on the contrary made many discoveries about him. When Pasternak was translating Shakespeare, he set himself the task of eliminating 'the incomprehensibility of the rhetoric and the metaphysical Romanticism', which only obstructed the 'real Shakespeare . . . the Shakespeare that is greater than Tolstoy'. He strove to convey as accurately as possible the essence of tragedy, expressed above all by its internal rhythm. Pasternak wrote, 'Shakespeare's rhythm is the foundation of his poetry. The rhythmic basis defines the general tone of the drama to a tangible degree.'

Rhythm is the basis for everything: the spiritual life of the actors, the movement of the cameras, the relationship between man and space, the tension of chiaroscuro. Rhythm is significant above all. It contains if you like both the subject of the tragedy and the pace of events: walking, running, flying, falling . . . walking, running, flying, falling . . . the ebbing and flowing waves of both external actions and the spiritual life of the hero (all those attacks of wrath, then shame, and then more wrath . . .).

A fusion, a unity of movement. At the very beginning you do not hear individual speeches (Kent, Gloucester, Edmund, Lear, the sisters) but the heavy sound of the worn-out mechanism of government. The performance of a ritual, in outward appearance only (belief in it has long since vanished), the conformity to positions in the hierarchy (everything is dependent upon fear). The form of the kingdom is observed without deviation but the kingdom itself no longer exists.

Absolute stillness. A few steps are heard. Someone (almost imperceptibly) moves. Stillness. People exchange glances. Stillness.

This is how we shot the beginning. Then followed disintegration and ruin. The lands are divided, the King abandons his castle. Empty geometry is replaced by a kind of devilish sequence. How is one to define, to grasp its characteristics? By a fantastic 'galop funèbre' or perhaps, by one of Sennett's chases in a minor key?

Action: the King chooses his train – the men who will accompany him on his journey. With quickening step, almost running, Lear passes along the ranks of courtiers. The King points at their faces – you, you and you. Through the halls and the stables – he uses the same gesture for choosing his favourite horses, and keeps up the same pace through the dog kennels: the favourites are the wolf-hounds, Great Danes, black giants with dead eyes – follow me! Birds of prey, eagles, falcons – on the march – you, you, and you! And keeping up the same precipitous pace (the train is already trailing out behind, the 'hunt' is assembled), he goes upwards, running up the stairs, higher and higher to the topmost step of the tower, beneath the sky itself, and there everything that has been forcing its way upwards, seething inside him, and barely held under, now breaks out with a curse on Cordelia and a frenzied cry straight to heaven. And far below on the ground the rabble catch sight of the King and fall to their knees; the rags and tatters fall prostrate before the robe.

Full stop. The precipice.

And the robe sets off. Lear goes to see his eldest daughter. The train must unfold across the whole width of the screen.

It is difficult to shoot this. Difficult because it is easy.

YOU ONLY HAVE to set up the camera to see the most frightening process immediately taking place: 'the shot taking shape'. In other words everything which is on the set arranges itself of its own accord as set out in the pattern. People, animals, things take up their places. But where did these places come from? Was everyone given a ticket which told him where he should go?

No it was simpler than that. Tickets were no longer necessary. Processions, expeditions and departures for journeys have been filmed many times before. It is a well-known technology. The people who are summoned to the studio for these shooting sessions perform what they have already performed more than once before; those who are taking part in the shooting for the first time have seen such scenes in films and immediately begin to reproduce them in real life. It all goes smoothly. The cavalry prances about. In what way is it not the exit of a king? 'How fast should we ride?' asks the riders. 'A walk would not be cinematic. A quick trot if you like? A gallop? That would be cinematic.'

WHEN I WAS preparing for the shooting I worked in the Hermitage Library and stood for a long time in front of the exhibits from the Hall of Facets[1] and from the Stable Museum, but none of it helped me very much. One description did help me – about the departure not of a tsar but of an individual who could not possibly have been less important – the collegiate secretary Korobochka.[2] When I remembered about him I immediately felt better; the masters of ceremony faded away and the heralds evaporated.

[1] A Hall in the Kremlin which Ivan the Terrible used as his main throne-room [trans.].

[2] A character from Gogol's *Dead Souls* [trans.].

. . . 'The squeaking and whining of iron harness and rusty screws, shuddering over the cobbles: fool's wagon, not even a wagon, but a kind of melon bursting at the sides, which had been loaded on to wheels, stuffed with mattresses, packages, bundles, parcels; the coachman gave the sign and the badly shod horses moved forward, stumbling over the stones . . .' All this absurdity, blown up to hyperbole – the irreconcilability of the concept of movement with the fact that one sleepy old gentleman could not apparently be shifted by any means – is not only extremely amusing but also moving: the structure of life is already completely meaningless, full of hot air, has moved off, galloped away and begun to rattle. And it is not just a single landowner but a whole dead world galloping over the living earth beneath a sky full of stars.

The description is as amusing as it could be. But somewhere close by is an undefined area which invokes horror. And it is not only moving but tragic as well.

WORKING ON THIS episode, I would bring out a certain quality sharply to the fore, forcing an individual trait to its extremes. The different versions of the script began to grow (Eisenstein considered that on average the eighth version fitted; this is also what I have found in my experience). Then the extremes are softened and relationships even out. Links with reality are re-established.

As a rule excesses eliminate themselves of their own accord. There is never enough time for shooting, circumstances begin to throttle one . . . One would like to have time to re-shoot. If one only knew what was 'fundamental'.

HOWEVER IT WAS a historical necessity for Lear to have a white beard, in a manner of speaking. The tragic actors knew what they were doing when they stuck an enormous quantity of white hair on to themselves; it was important to establish from the moment the curtain rose that he was an old man, a very old man.

And this epithet is essential to me. Yet not as a description of the King but of his kingdom. Lear is old and young at the same time. His thought goes back into the darkness of time and then suddenly, dispensing with time, flares up with all the strength of contemporary irony. He is at the same time both the oldest and the youngest. But the kingdom is only old. A decrepit world, a sclerosis of ideas, a degeneration of beliefs.

A castle with disintegrating walls, with holes in the turrets and rubbish lying about.

Perhaps not one single king had so much trouble with his exit as the artist V. Ulitko had with Lear's carriage. He made a multitude of versions (sketches and models) for it. Yenei and Virsaladze gave their advice. After many trials they based it on the carriage which Elizabeth Tudor sent as a present to Boris Godunov. After all there was a shadow of Shakespearean times on this exhibit in the Kremlin Armoury. Photographs were sent from Moscow with all the details and measurements. The details were omitted, the frame simplified and coarsened. Local artisans from Narva created a carriage (somewhere between the departure of Korobochka and Elizabeth Tudor). Estonian specialists covered it with raw hide. Coats of arms were etched on the leather. And then the main work was begun: the carriage was weathered. It was scorched with a blow-lamp, scratched with a file and had lamp black wiped all over it.

An enormous string of carts was to stretch out behind the carriage: carts with chests, bare-faced serving-wenches, pack-horses – all heavily laden; dogs howled, dug in their toes, not wanting to go any further; there were wild birds in cages; dozens of languid surly good-for-nothings lagged behind; the mounted servants rode in complete disorder. The gilding had gone, it had been chipped off and scattered to the four winds.

This is what the 'robe' should look like on the screen.

WHEN WE WERE shooting I took to one cart in particular. Very old people wrapped up in warm cloaks dozed on top of their things which had been hurriedly and badly packed; as it went along the ropes untied themselves and things dropped off into the road, but the servants did not take any notice of them. It was a broken-down old cart with unnecessary things, and people who had outlived their time – a good knightly procession.

Of course this particular cart did not get into the shot. We never got round to taking a closer shot of it. Who could ever explain this peculiarity of our work: any carelessness, or inaccuracy always comes to the fore, is thrown in sharp relief, and shown up in a prominent position, but a detail which carries greater significance usually passes by on one side, unnoticed.

WE USED THE most inconspicuous costumes. The historical requirements were not worth bothering about. But there had to be a distinctive character about every thing living and moving which would distinguish it from our own times, our own epoch: the enormous dogs, the short-legged pot-bellied horses. A soloist was suggested, a leopard from the Leningrad Zoo which we had admired long ago. At last the historical advisers gave a sigh of relief – a leopard on the King's hunt would be fine! All the historians were in favour. The only people against were the administrators. At the last minute it was declared ill – anyway we had enough troubles without the leopard.

Wild boars made up the spoil (returning from the hunt). I wanted to start the episode abruptly, with a dense hubbub: flourishes on the hunting horns, bloody hides, and fangs.

The local huntsmen for miles around were given the order, but as if to spite us there was no game. One solitary stuffed bird was dragged along to the shooting. A few shots were taken and then rejected; the disgusting props hit one between the eyes. Some piglets slightly saved the situation; the poor things had strayed into a bog and drowned. We dragged them out on the very eve of the last day of shooting.

I HAVE NEVER before seen such a mass meeting. Directors of establishments, a doctor of science, and a second-class captain – passed in front of the lens . . . there is no stronger pride than that of dog owners. In Hyde Park you only have to stop by some terrier or other and its owner will immediately turn up beside it and say, 'It's a beautiful animal, isn't it? . . .'

The experts in breeds of dogs chose the best specimens available.

On the days we were shooting, several warehouses and shops could have been raided; watchmen who had received passes accompanied the King. The troupe was a restless one: the great danes fought with the wolf hounds; Lear's train was pulled apart by their tails.

THERE WAS A constantly changing instability of quality. There was also a mournful commonplaceness about the shape of the train: the howling and the dog fights, wild ruffled birds in cages; lazy servants; the order grew more and more unruly. The riders drifted off, there were already fewer animals and eventually all that was left of the train was a small chain dragging along on its own.

And at the same time a sort of fantastic quality was strengthened in some of the other scenes. In the dark shaking carriage Lear, turned out of Goneril's home, is overcome no longer by madness alone but also by fear.

'O, let me not go mad, sweet heaven!'

he begs (God, fate?)

'Keep me in temper: I would not be mad!' . . .

Black dogs' muzzles with burning eyes should cross the screen in close-up – like demons of madness.

Chapter Seventeen

METHODS OF LITERARY research have entered a new era. Once it was thought that a poet was the best judge of another poet. Pushkin, Goethe, Coleridge, Hugo all wrote about Shakespeare. Then philosophers took him up. Psychologists studied his characters. Then arriving just in time with their knowledge, came the historians of the Elizabethan theatre, the literary critics, the specialists in rhetoric. Shakespeare's text was explained both as the spirit of the Renaissance (full-blooded and earthy), and as the neurosis of our times – the psycho-analysts delved into the inner meanings. We also produced those who liked to brandish questionnaires at the author: Shakespeare went down now as a champion of the vanishing aristocracy, now as a defender of the rising bourgeoisie. It was all there. Who has the strength to find his way out of all this . . . and then came the era of the precise sciences. All quarrels were at an end. How can you doubt statistics? Mathematical linguistics got them down to work.

Exactitude of research was the first prerequisite. In 1919 Boris Mikhailovich Eichenbaum wrote an article called 'How Gogol's *The Overcoat* is written'. There was a challenge in the very title. Science replaces the usual generalities about the author's humanism. Eichenbaum demonstrated the texture of literature; the language, story, the change of tone. The article is discussed to this day: but where are Akaky Akakiyevich's mournful eyes? The feeling of hurt for the underdog?

Of course the story contains both the expression of Bashmachkin's eyes and the author's pain. Only one must remember that even Chekhov sternly reprimanded his brother for his story about the sufferings of a poor little civil servant – the subject sets one's teeth on edge, it was already shameful to mention it. And the highflown words about Gogol's sympathy towards his lesser brother was stamped with the same seal. Of course Eichenbaum could have given his article an even more accurate name. For instance: 'This is how *The Overcoat* was written'.

Art should not be exhausted by 'methods'. The best definition would seem to be Tolstoy's: 'a labyrinth of connections'. Signposts are not allowed to be put up in a labyrinth: 'turn right', 'keep to the left', 'way out' – it is not allowed for the very reason that it is a labyrinth. Each man must lose his way individually inside it, lighting up the path, trying to come out at new crossroads, stumbling against blind alleys, and again raising his lantern in order to find new directions to walk in.

Where does he get the lantern from? The answer is not a simple one. This is the light of day by which you live (you yourself); and it is the work of other people which has been made accessible to you. Those same people who sought an answer to the question, 'how is art made'? 'how is life made'?

Of course it would be convenient to have clear explanations, simple conclusions. We have all long ago lost the taste for mysterious expressions and highflown turns of phrase. One would like to talk about art in a clear and businesslike manner.

I remember well one such attempt. In 1919 the magazine *Fine Arts*[1] was published in Petrograd. There was a shortage of paper but for some reason two publications were printed on art paper, *The Red Militiaman*[2] and *Fine Arts*. In the first (and only) number of this journal there was an article called 'The Artist and the Commune'. Osip Brik wrote, 'The cobbler makes boots, the table-maker – tables, but what does the artist make? He doesn't make anything; he "creates". It is a doubtful and suspect business.' These stereotyped words made a tremendous impression on me at the time. I was a young artist (very young), and I was ashamed to be spending my time with something that was suspect and doubtful. After all, what inspiration, light from above, or creation *was* there in art, once you thought about it, you chosen few! You had to work properly – do real useful work, make things.

Or show how things were done.

How is the love between Romeo and Juliet made? How many stressed and unstressed syllables fall on Hamlet's doubt? . . .

PROFESSOR MARVIN ROSENBERG (of the University of California, USA) told me how a problem had been programmed: a quantitative analysis of the parts of speech in *Lear*. The verse and the prose were coded. The tragedy was fed into the computer. The calculating mechanism began to work. The first results to come out were, it seems, the conjunctions, 'but, if, besides, however . . .'

It was of course an interesting experiment, but what did it prove? The fact that a condition of hesitation, instability and uncertainty

[1] *Izobrazitelnoye Iskusstvo* [trans.].
[2] *Krasny Militsioner* [trans.].

prevailed in the tragedy? I would not like to judge. There must be an enormous heap of data in the various particles of expression. A whole section of the programme was devoted to such research at the World Shakespeare Congress in Vancouver.

It is pointless to take fright at a machine which has been set up in the world of poetry. It does not dispel the ghost of Hamlet's Father, and Falstaff does not waste away after mathematical investigation. One should add that Shakespeare himself paid particular attention to calculations. Figures had a special significance for him. Prince Hal did a mathematical analysis of Falstaff's notes (on the back of the bill from the Boar's Head tavern) and discovered a lack of proportion in the numerical relationship (of drinking to eating). Shylock's treatment of the unit of weight 'a pound of flesh' is also well known.

I mention all this because I wanted to make an experiment. It also concerns mathematics but it is turned in another direction, perhaps even in the opposite direction. It does not consist of coding verse by means of numbers but on the contrary, revealing numbers in the poetry. *Lear* has its own arithmetic and it also has algebra. There is as well, and I am not afraid to say it, a magic in numbers. The work is devoted to the turbulence of the elements, to the chaos of the universe, but all the same it imitates the universe in that it divides, subtracts, and multiplies . . .

Numbers are rapped out from the very first speeches; the kingdom is divided, words of love are measured and even Cordelia's silence is turned into a formula: 'Nothing will come of nothing.' The division into three parts, then another complication and the division into two. This is how the government expresses itself: 'When she was dear to us we did hold her so', Lear says of his youngest daughter. 'But now her price is fall'n'.

Then Lear's price falls. Goneril demands that his train be reduced by half; Regan takes away another quarter. 'Thy fifty yet doth double five and twenty', Lear calculates, 'And thou art twice her love'.

Is it an arithmetical parody? Or the standards and dogma by which Lear judged life? . . . The parody turns into a formula for tragedy. It is not immediately transformed. At first we are confronted with the age-old problem out of the school textbook: a king and a train of a hundred men make altogether – a hundred and one men; when the train disappears there are a hundred and one minus a hundred: how many are left? The pupil answers without hesitation: one man. Shakespeare reaches a different result: one man is no longer a man. 'Now thou art an 0 without a figure' the Fool tells Lear.

One plus a hundred = a king. A king minus a hundred (train) = 0.

The measure is very much less than a man. A new measure is introduced: Poor Tom is a bare, forked animal, and nothing more. Nothing. An O without a figure.

THE TWO MEASURES act like a scale of relationships, of calculations. The two numbers, the largest and the smallest: all and one.

The King is everyone. Cordelia, in standing up against the will of the King, is alone. Alone versus the rest. They reject her from their calculations with a dismissive gesture of the hands. Kent stands up for Cordelia: now there are two versus the rest. It is again a number not worth reckoning with. Kent is destroyed, banished. A third man appears: the King of France. Three versus the rest. And Cordelia no longer appears defeated.

Perhaps the ratio is decided not by one man but by the crown of France? No it is the man. The servants destroy the Duke of Cornwall's plans; an old farmer saves blind Gloucester. 'All' is by no means a constant indivisive quantity. There must certainly be one amongst the 'rest' who stands apart from the others; a simple digit falls off from the majority. A digit of goodness, truth, compassion – against the mass of evil, falsehood and cruelty.

All the heaviest elements fall on one side of the scales: the crown, the sword, and the other side momentarily shoots into the air. Is there anything which will balance gold and iron? There is, answers tragedy. Another crown? Another sword? No, an altogether different measure of weight falls on the other side of the scales. What would seem to be immeasurable in weight. *Lear* is based on a conflict of measures, the collision of spiritual and material worth.

Nobody and nothing – an old man, seriously ill, comes to his senses (he was senseless for a long time). The world which he rules, and in which he lived for eighty years, is presented to him in a kind of new light, judged according to different standards. Before he did not notice other people. Now he distinguishes before anything else the minute particle of moisture.

'Be your tears wet?' he asks his daughter whom he threw out of his house and cursed – 'Yes, faith'.

I think these are the most powerful words in the whole tragedy.

Dostoyevsky demanded that the history of a state should be measured by the tears of a child. Cordelia's 'nothing' (barely audible) is louder than the resounding speeches to the glory of the King.

The tears, slowly running down Cordelia's cheeks, occupy no less a place in the space of tragedy than the darkness and fire of the apocalypse, the black whirlwind of the storm which was hurled down on the earth.

'ALL' IN SHAKESPEARE is a changing dialectical concept: there is no constancy or stability in it; it is both enormous and worthless at the same time: the greatest number can turn into nothing. Edmund's army (mercenaries) gain a victory: the French are defeated, Cordelia and Lear are taken prisoner. Edmund, now the Earl of Gloucester, has attained his goal. The duchesses are ready to fight for him; he will rule the kingdom . . . Complete victory. And then . . . a moment later – nothing is left, it has all vanished. Not one ounce of power, not a shadow of strength. The army no longer exists (dispersed by the Duke of Albany); there is not one soldier to defend the general. The duchesses are destroyed a few moments later. By whom? Who raised a hand to them? Nobody. They killed each other. They destroyed one another; just as the army drifted apart of its own accord. Nothing remained. And this is the final count. 'All' turned out to be phantom; only phantoms disappear momentarily, without trace. 'All' is not only not the majority, but not even reality: 'all' is an illusion, witchcraft.

The instantaneous reversal, the speed of retribution? . . . Or is it not just a dramatic convention? It is Act Five, one must hurry. The audience cannot sit there all night. This is why the author has to transfer events offstage and to punish evil with familiar patter. Is it worth the director's while making much of this? . . .

The concepts are weighty in the theatre: in this part of the play where there are few words the very rhythm of the action, based on the text, does not give any opportunity for bringing the fates of people to the fore, for looking closely into people's faces. The visual make-up of the stage does not allow it. The screen is another matter: a close-up of the expression of the eyes is often more powerful than a whole soliloquy. Regis Adomaitis and I concentrated the whole role on the last expression on Edmund's face. Edmund dies alone on dirty blood-bespattered soil, forsaken by everyone, like a hunted, exhausted animal (he was the most skilful of the huntsmen) – completely alone in the enormity of the universe. But where are the 'all' – those whom he bent to his own will?

Here in the final scenes the existence of another sort of 'all' is revealed. Shakespearean characters demand an answering call. Lear's call, 'O, you are men of stones' is not unanswered.

Who does he expect an answering call, a reply from? From

everyone. Does that mean from all who enter the stage? No, rather from those who are in the audience. And not literally from those who that same day bought a ticket and came to see the play, but from all those who continue to live; from those who will come in the future; from those who understand; those who are not made of stone.

This one man – whether on stage or on screen – this measure of 'one man' is the prototype not for the imaginary but for the real 'all'. The abundance of suffering created this measure.

This is why a production of *Lear* is so unbearably difficult. The ancient moral lies at the very heart of the tragedy: the story of Everyman in Everyman's life.

Chapter Eighteen

THE ARTICLE 'How Gogol's *Overcoat* is written' was generally associated with the film *The Cloak* which we made in 1926. Starting with the first unfavourable review ('why were its film directors not thrown out after *The Devil's Wheel*[1]) to the last favourable one, our film was thought to have stemmed from Eichenbaum's article.

I knew Boris Eichenbaum well and was very fond of him. His article did not have much influence on our film. What did influence me was the assembly hall in School No. 5 in Kiev. When we were children, in the bottom form, and were arranged in pairs, and a strange bearded man with spectacles led us along corridors and then up the stairs to the first floor and we entered the closed doors – I stepped over the threshold of my former homely life and found myself in a new world; the building seemed enormous, unnaturally high, and in spite of the daylight the chandeliers were brightly lit, a large portrait of Nicholas the Second in military uniform with decorations hung on a wall far away from me. Children from all the classes, dressed in uniform, stood in rows. Nobody made another move. There was silence, emptiness, the tsar full length and wearing boots. A man wearing a formal frockcoat which was buttoned all the way up came out on to the gleaming parquet floor. His voice sounded unnatural in the hollow silence. Here I felt completely alien and vulnerable. Everything seemed to belong to a dream, a bad dream.

This was the first time I had ever felt any sort of elementary relationship between two great peaks – natural life and all that was official and illusory.

I have always looked back with happiness on the day when after Kiev had been bombarded continuously for some time, I went to school one morning and the school was not there any more. You could see right through the ruined building, there were bricks and fragments of metal everywhere.

We are influenced not by articles but by life. Eichenbaum lived the last years of his life next door to me. We saw a lot of each other. He always held his head very erect. When I first knew him he had dark hair, then it grew thin and turned quite grey. Those were bad times for him. Once he telephoned me, and I heard his voice down the telephone saying, 'Congratulate me. My name is in print once

[1] Kozintsev and Lev Trauberg's film which appeared in 1926 [trans.].

again. Here in the *Medical Journal*: the case of patient X. The capital X is me. "In spite of serious symptoms the patient is still alive." '

We are influenced not by articles but by people. The ability people have to hold their head high. We revised the script for *S.V.D.*[1] (written by Tynyanov and Oxman) while we were shooting. Tynyanov was not offended; he was interested in the art of the cinema and not in the rights of the script-writer. What was left of his work in the film? The titles remained which he wrote after viewing what had been filmed. The many subsequent meetings, conversations (not about cinema at all) and friendship remained. Tynyanov is long since dead, which means that all this is past history – but is there really nothing but memories left of it? It is the very friendship which has remained in the shots. And not only in *The Cloak* or in *S.V.D.* but also in the films which I made subsequently.

And then, without one realizing it, much of this is transformed from life into material. Could I have a copy from your archives (I would be asked)? In the old days I had never heard such words. Archives? I swear I threw Eisenstein's letters away once I had read them. What was the point of keeping them since we met regularly. Towards the end of the forties I was approached by the theatre critic Professor S. S. Danilov. 'Have you any documents left relating to the production of *Marriage*[2]?' he asked. Some costume designs had accidentally been kept. 'But these are monuments of the epoch!' he said delightedly as he looked through the sketches. 'You have no right to keep them. It is your duty to hand them over to the Theatre Museum. Your *Marriage* belongs to the history of Soviet theatre.'

I must admit that I was flattered. 'The museum will be deeply grateful to you' Danilov said to me as he left with the portfolio of sketches under his arm. 'Your gift will be preserved for posterity.'

The solemn part finishes there. The future arrived pretty quickly: I discovered my sketches in a book on Gogol's dramatic art; the text was about 'mockery of the classics'. And in other books I later found the happy clowns of my childhood, daubed with tar and heaped in a pile of feathers.

Now I had received a letter: there would be a conference in Venice devoted to FEKS,[3] the showing of the films, and discussions. The title of one of the papers was 'FEKS and Tynyanov'; I was asked to send a photocopy of any documents. What documents? . . .

[1] *Club of the Big Deed*, directed by Kozintsev and Trauberg, 1927 [trans.].

[2] The play by Gogol which was the first FEKS production staged by Kozintsev and Trauberg [trans.].

[3] Factory of the Eccentric Actor, the group which Kozintsev formed with Sergei Yutkevich and Leonid Trauberg in 1921 [trans.].

As far as I could see there was more of Tynyanov's influence in what I was writing today than in the film *S.V.D.*

TRAUBERG AND I were sitting at one of the tables arranged in a square along the edges of the Assembly Hall at the University of Venice, Palazzi Foscari. Tiepolo's gentle Venetian goddesses in see-through tunics floated above us on the brilliant bright blue ceiling. The goddesses were blowing golden trumpets, but down below papers were being read. 'Eccentrism – a linguistic, psychological and mechanical concept . . .' '*The Adventures of Oktyabrina* and the European *avant garde.*' 'The massed spectacle of the Revolution and the Comedy of FEKS', Fausto Malcovati from the University of Milan was describing the production of *Marriage.*

My first feeling was of course gratitude – it is not easy to search out forgotten reviews, to recreate the details which we ourselves no longer remember. Everything that the speaker said was accurate: Podkolesina's speeches and the clowns' replies, the plywood constructions and the gesticulations between Agafia Tikhonovna's suitors, the film shots in the scenes with Gogol and the exit of Gogol himself . . . alas you cannot deny it. Only now, while the paper was being read, the brightly coloured covering had somehow faded, grown dumb, had begun to disintegrate into separate pieces – of cogs and springs. But in its time it had all whirled round with a great clatter.

What made it go? Try to pin it down now – to grasp the pace, the spirit – to put it into words . . . Well, first of all it was a happy kind of art. And it was performed in a happy manner. Shklovsky[1] would use journalistic language when writing critical articles on prose. In one of the recent reviews of the first volume of *The History of Soviet Theatre* one of the film critics asked, 'Why has the company of three been forgotten in whose name Dziga Vertov wrote the manifestos of the Kino-Eye? Who were they? And who chose them?' No one chose them. They were Dziga Vertov, his wife the film editor Yelizaveta Svilova, and his brother, the cameraman, Mikhail Kaufman. 'The company of three' resolved to destroy fictional cinematography as being unnecessary to the proletariat.

Was there really no joke in this . . . Eisenstein told me how during

[1] Victor Shklovsky (b. 1893), writer, poet, critic and script-writer. Originally a Formalist, his theories profoundly influenced such writers as Zamyatin, Kaverin and Olesha. Besides his own original writing, he has written many books of literary criticism and has maintained a close association with the cinema [trans.].

one of the VOKS[1] banquets he remembered that he had directed *Enough Simplicity in Every Wise Man* in the very same hall (a detached house on the Arbat) and forgetting himself, stretched his leg out under the table and began to fumble about on the floor with the toe of his boot. 'What is the matter?', his respectable neighbour asked him with some surprise. 'Nothing', said Eisenstein remembering where he was; he was looking for the ring which the circus trapeze wire was attached to – it was screwed into this exact spot about thirty years earlier.

It was vital to find this ring. Or at least a trace of it.

These productions were conceived in the days when lifts used to get stuck between floors in the black abysses of the stair shaft, apparently for eternity – the houses were like blocks of ice. We composed the manifestos of eccentricism in the dark, lit by a spluttering lamp. In the cold and hunger we invented a carnival in honour of electrification.

Now words are compared with words. Would it not be truer to compare them with scenes?...

The productions did not have a long life – the scene changed decisively. Then, in the years of our youth Gogol seemed one of us, the most 'left' man in art, as we used to say; we had to separate his gay elements from his naturalistic greyness, the languor of theatrical play-acting, the sleepy pace. This was so that the 'unlikely happenings' should come alive, so that the world could fall apart. The nose prayed in Kazan Cathedral,[2] a fish swam out of the Fontanka[3] and started to speak English, and walking up and down the Nevsky Prospect were not people but only moustaches and side-whiskers.

Then a different Gogolesque element burst in on our screen like a whirlwind of ice. We chased Akaky Akakiyevich into the empty squares, looking for just one living soul in the night of the Emperor's capital, in order to be able to talk of his grief. A tongue-tied grief in the dumb world of squares and monuments. There was already less jollity here. All traces of the short story had disappeared on our screen. A different sort of genre appeared. What was it? Dostoyevsky wrote, 'Gogol created for us a terrible tragedy out of one civil servant losing his coat'; he called Gogol 'a real demon' and began to boast about him in a strange sort of way: 'Oh, this was such a colossal demon, the like of which you have never had in Europe and which perhaps you would never allow yourselves to have.'

[1] All-union Society for Cultural Relations with Foreign Countries (1925–58) [trans.].

[2] Reference to Gogol's short story *The Nose* [trans.].

[3] A Canal in Leningrad – an episode also from *The Nose* [trans.].

Demons do not write short stories. And we had not dreamt of tragedies in those days. We tried to film the grotesqueness of history. Gogol created for himself a complicated relationship with history: at first he decided to teach it – his first lecture in the University of St Petersburg was even brilliant, but then for some reason it went sour, chaos ensued, his studies lapsed, and he had to resign his chair. This is how his relationship with history ended.

Or was it how it began in earnest? I do not know which expresses the more strongly the threatening might of history, *Taras Bulba* or *The Overcoat*[1]?

Films which you work on are not bread rings to be baked and hung on a string; one a parcel of rolls – the next . . . And what sort of string should they be tied with?

There was a lot of talk about the use, the utility, but not very much later it was discovered that everything which belonged to that time had no possibility of being adapted for use in everyday life, but possessed just that 'unclear and suspect' quality which artists attacked in their manifestos: the beginnings of new movements in art and their link with the past.

There was a fight with literature on film and the productions of Gogol, Cervantes, Shakespeare, the gay side-show and the growing feeling of the tragic, the eccentricity of the agit-sketches and the ever-deepening link with Russian culture. Each member of the generation of film makers in the twenties went through all this.

[1] The film Kozintsev and Trauberg made of Gogol's story is usually called *The Cloak* in English [trans.].

Chapter Nineteen

GLOUCESTER'S ESTATE WAS left behind Lear's back. He was walking along the road, then over the fields. Was he turned out of the house? No, no one showed him the door. His elder daughters refused to keep his train, and harsh words were exchanged between them and their father. The cowardly and indifferent who witnessed this kept silent. No one spoke a word in his defence. He was alone. What else could he do? He walked out – of his own accord.

A walk-out . . . or perhaps an 'outcome'? A coming out of his loneliness?

Yet another theme, a new turning point in the relationship between the proportions of the single unit and the large numbers.

The word 'typical' does not seem to apply to these events. What can be typical about all this? To divide up the kingdom in one go, to curse your favourite daughter, to renounce all your power in the heat of the moment . . . Do such occasions happen in real life, do they have a place in the history of States? No, such things have never happened, they can have no place in history. So is *Lear* a fairy story, a legend? . . .

But doesn't it happen in time of revolutions, *coup d'états*, and wars, that those who held power find themselves behind barbed wire, find their nearest and dearest with nooses round their necks as well, and themselves a hair's breadth from execution?

We can bear witness: this has happened more than once in this century to many thousands, whole nations, the whole world has seen enough of it. So is *Lear* reality?

It is both. When the King thought that he was the one chosen among many, he was living not in a real world (which he did not know), but in a fictitious world (which he imagined to be reality). Leaving the boundary of the estate where Goneril and Regan now reigned, he went beyond the bounds of the fictitious (what he thought was true); and now he was walking in the world. The bolts had clanged shut by order of the new rulers. It was possible to leave a world in which he had lived for eighty years; but there was already no turning back. Lear was pushed out not into a new life, but beyond the boundaries of life. There was not even a bush to shelter under. Even the wild animals had crawled into their dens. No one and nothing. The black hole of night. And this was reality. The reality of emptiness.

But beyond the boundary of life there appeared a shadow of life, a spectre of existence. What miracle had saved these pathetic rods from being swept away by the storm? A shadow of a dwelling; here the shadow of a man was hiding. Edgar, the heir to the title and possessions of the Earl of Gloucester, was no longer, he did not exist: he had been taken away from the world and his shadow remained – poor Tom, a beggared half-wit, a nobody; hunted like a wild animal, he had hidden in the wet straw. The human features had disappeared. But this had happened to others as well: there were other people here. People like him, faceless shadows of people. People who had been flung out of life, had ceased to be human. And this was reality.

Lear arrived. Kent had led him here to shelter.

What sort of place was this? The stage direction calls it a hovel; this would hardly bear any relationship to Shakespearean theatre: plays were put on in full daylight on an open platform without scenery. However it is not the décor but reality itself; the conditions of life are shown quite clearly, and are linked with other places and events. The King spent the night on rotten straw with outcasts, rogues and swine – Cordelia wept when she recounted this.

These directions are not paid any attention in the theatre. What purpose do they serve? Should one drive a herd of swine across the stage? As far as the rogue is concerned, Poor Tom could go and fetch him (it is true that the text uses the plural) . . . Would such a description help us? Would there be any point in bringing pigs to the film studio (there was enough dirt without them)?

Their participation is of course not essential. Cordelia could also have been mistaken: she was telling the story second-hand. Pigs are not the main concern. After all they could also be a metaphor: men had been debased until they were indistinguishable from beasts. The essence is not the pigs but the night spent outside the boundaries of life – that is what is important; the very lowest rung of nature, a spark of animal warmth, almost dying in the icy darkness of the universe. As far as I see it, it is here that the highest point, the climax of the storm takes place; the climax is in the dirty bodies, lying about in the rotten straw, not in the flashing of studio lightning and the deluge produced by the firemen's technical expertise.

Tragedy forced Lear to come to this place. He had taken a long time reaching it; he had walked in circles, at first huge ones which then decreased in diameter as the world contracted. This was his journey: fortresses, palaces, castles, estates, and finally a pigs' hovel. It is not a succession of scene changes, arranged in order on a circular stage but a conflict of existences, of worlds which are incompatible both with history and with man's soul. People in the spaciousness of enormous well-heated houses, solid ancestral or state buildings, their walls built so that they should not be taken by storm or penetrated by cannon-balls – and in contrast a complete lack of space: only bodies one against the other, their only defence a few rods hurriedly knocked together; an island in the midst of the fury of the elements.

Medusa's plot? . . . Or one of the scenes depicted by Dante? After all the path Lear's wanderings takes is the same as Dante's hero: first he comes to Hell, and it is only later that he reaches Purgatory (the meeting with Cordelia).

It is easy to say, 'Let us shoot Hell'. Perhaps we should set up a canvas by Hieronymus Bosch or Pieter Breughel on the screen? But Shakespeare's nether regions have a different structure. The devilry of the Flemish School looks like child's play in comparison to it. Here there are no instruments of torture, of cunning torment; everything looks perfectly simple and ordinary. And if we must have a guide, let one of the people holding a lantern (life would be darker without them) show us once again:

> Imagine a room about twelve paces long . . . there are perhaps as many as a hundred people crammed in it . . . the soot, dirt and cramped bodies are such that there isn't even room for one's feet . . . it is dark and dirty . . . a sticky dampness . . . there wasn't even the space of a man's hand which was not occupied by a cramped prisoner . . . People wanting to walk through got tangled up in other people's chains and knocked the heads of those who were sitting underneath . . . swearing, cramp, a whole rubbish tip . . . bent backs, shaven heads, twisted arms, legs. (*Notes from House of the Dead*, Dostoyevsky)

The hovel is even smaller than the hut in the penal settlement; not only is it not hot, but on the contrary, very cold, and probably not more than about a dozen people are inside; there are no chains to be seen, but all the same the image is somehow similar: the King of Britain has landed up in a hut on a penal settlement. It is a picture which one would only see in a feverish delirium, but this fever is reality. Dostoyevsky concludes, 'If we all land up in Hell one day, it will be very like this place.'

The penal settlement wash-house is a model of life itself. It is the fate of those whom life has banished from its systems, and has forcibly driven together; has herded them into a confined space from which there is no exit, has mangled them with injustice and twisted them with want.

Dostoyevsky's image was only beginning to gather strength. In his *Winter Notes on Summer Impressions* he describes industrial towns, the enormous centres of Europe, and the model is the same; the horror of over population, destitution, deformity, crowds, crammed with areas of poverty; there are no chains to be seen but here everything is chained even more tightly – and there is no way out of the injustice; the drug of alcoholism, despair, madness, the penal steam cell has appeared in the multi-storeyed houses, an accumulation of grief and degradation. The details are different from the prisoners' wash-house, but the essence of the relationship – between man and man, men and life, people and space – is the same as in the penal wash-house! Numbers are inflated from the horror of it all, noughts are added to noughts: according to Dostoyevsky, prostitutes in their thousands walk the pavements of London. In their poverty, their rags show the trace of the whip, the brand, sores . . . which are rogues and which are animals . . . ? What is this, diseased hair or a bundle of straw? . . .

'Everyone was shouting and laughing . . . falling over, swearing and pulling those who were fully dressed down with them . . . in a spirit of some sort of excitement . . . squeals and cries . . .' Where does all this take place: in the penal wash-house in Siberia or on the outskirts of large towns? 'Cursing, crowding . . . heaps . . . bodies . . . seemed even more disgusting . . . weals from recent whippings . . . backs which seemed to have been wounded yet again . . . someone shouted an aria in a hoarse and mad voice "La-la-la-la-la!" ' (*Notes from House of the Dead*).

Poor Tom cries out fragments of curses, in his hoarse mad voice, and wails songs; he has scratched himself, has torn his skin with thorns; he has adopted the habits of animals in order to look like those who are unlike people; they will not seek him out or recognize him from the flock.

Where did this penal wash-house appear from? How did the minority manage to herd the majority into it . . . Shakespeare reveals the beginnings and foretells the ends. The links are obvious: the rhetoric at palace receptions, the worshipping of tyranny, the sacredness of the hierarchy of rank and place, the servile dumbness – if all this is evident it means that there are no longer any human faces, man has lost his image, the relationship between people has been distorted and has become rotten through and through. The higher the rhetoric, the baser the deeds; fierceness, grasping for power, selling one's soul for a tip, cruelty, lust . . . And already in the black emptiness of night you can hear the chopping of the axes; the penal wash-houses are indispensable; their turn inevitably comes. And if Edmund shows that the only god is nature, and that there is no limit to man's free will, then later those who have been branded and flogged will inevitably be hounded, will be crammed together into a hut so that they can hardly breathe.

Everything began, if you like, with the law of supply and demand. There was a demand for the word and the word was supplied. At first they were the most eloquent words: Goneril so loved the King her father that he was dearer to her than eyesight, more treasured than 'what can be valued rich or rare', dearer than 'life' . . . these words were readily pronounced and readily listened to. But then followed different words that were rough, malicious, absurd – grumbling and ambiguity: the dark devilry of the beggar, the howl of proverbs, obscene jokes. Words alone weaned them from other people. They were cured of their dreams by their delirious state.

In the hovel Lear throws off his clothes – all that was false! His clothes are his robe, his train. The King's robe was also woven with words. The robe is a cover, the gilded chasuble of civilization. But beneath are the sores and scabs, the down-trodden souls.

Lear was alone among men, sat apart from the rest. Then he became the same as everyone else, indistinguishable from the others; grief has but one face. War drove people from their houses, towns went up in flames, the roads were full of refugees. Among the victims of the fire were an old man and his youngest daughter – misfortune brought all people together.

Why did Cordelia's soldiers (young, clever people) not find her father immediately? The place where he was seen was well-known, he did not have the strength to run far. He could, of course, have hidden in the high stacks of hay (Cordelia talks about this), or he could have crawled into a ditch. Speaking in theatrical terms this is easy to explain. To explain Shakespeare? I do not like this sort of phrase (and you often hear it); you do not have to explain Shakespeare with everyday logic; it is better to try to understand the development of his poetic thought.

Here is one hypothesis: the difficulty was not in finding Lear but in recognizing him. He had become indistinguishable from other men. Just like everyone else. Were there so few white-haired tramps wandering about?

Let us look at Shakespeare's moves: the great and the insignificant; the distance between the exclusive and the ordinary is by no means constantly great, it is even inconstant. Lear is sometimes distanced from life, sometimes brought right close to it. And it is at these very moments when he merges with life that he rises above it. Dressed in his robes he is, figuratively speaking, a character from an ordinary play (or from royal life if there is such a thing); dressed in a smock, he is the hero of a tragedy. When he is elevated above everyone else, he is ordinary; there is nothing extraordinary about him. After all there is no scarcity of cases of tyrants making scenes in the history of States. There was nothing they didn't do with the general indulgence accorded to them by their subjects. But he had only to take off his robes and become just like everyone else, and he became the only one, the exception to all rules. Why? Because there had not yet been any despots who were capable of understanding the criminality of despotism, the absurdity of their own deification.

Lear understood all this. And he proclaimed it out loud – first to himself, then to Gloucester, and mankind listened to him because he was speaking in the name of the majority.

The hovel is the point at which the paths of the first man of the Kingdom and the very last (not only a beggar but a mad one) met. They were no longer distinguishable one from the other. Who brought them to this?

The court session begins. The King calls the outcasts and halfwits to act as jury. The penal wash-house has become a royal tribunal. It is not only ungrateful daughters who are called to answer for themselves, but in this case the whole of society is judged with its system of inequality, hypocrisy and callousness.

In the play the court scene does not take place in the hovel; Gloucester has brought Lear to an empty farmhouse. But Lear has not come alone; he refused to leave the mad beggar (now he calls him 'Athenian', 'philosopher'). And Poor Tom is also not alone; the whole world accompanies him. The tragedy moves with him, but not the tragedy of buskins and make-up, but a different one – a lousy tramp with a beggar's bundle.

In *Lear* there are no changes of scenery; the space unfolds with the flow of poetry (the prose is equally rhythmic); lands swim to the surface, dwellings appear, roads disappear into the distance; everything takes shape and then immediately the features disintegrate, it all begins to totter, and then disappears completely, carried away into the void, drowned by the dumb silence.

In the hovel the space howls and cries.

Whole works have been written about the utterings of Poor Tom. The sources have been revealed and the source materials well researched. The halfwits from the Hospital of Holy Mary of Bedlam used similar lamentations in the streets of Shakespearean London; they used to knock on the doors of houses, calling out laments in order that they should be taken pity on: 'Poor Tom's a-cold! Away! the foul fiend follows me! Do poor Tom some charity! . . .'

Town life, street sounds: the stalls crying out their wares, street

7a. Act V sc. iii : 'Come, let's away to prison
We two alone will sing like birds i' the cage.'

7b. Act V sc. iii : 'Cordelia, Cordelia! stay a little. Ha!
What is't thou say'st?'

5a. Act V: The people fleeing from the fighting.

6. [*overleaf*] Act V sc. iii: The duel between Edmund (Regimastas Adomaitis) and Edgar.

5b. Act IV sc. vii: 'Do not laugh at me,/For as I am a man, I think this lady/To be my child Cordelia'.

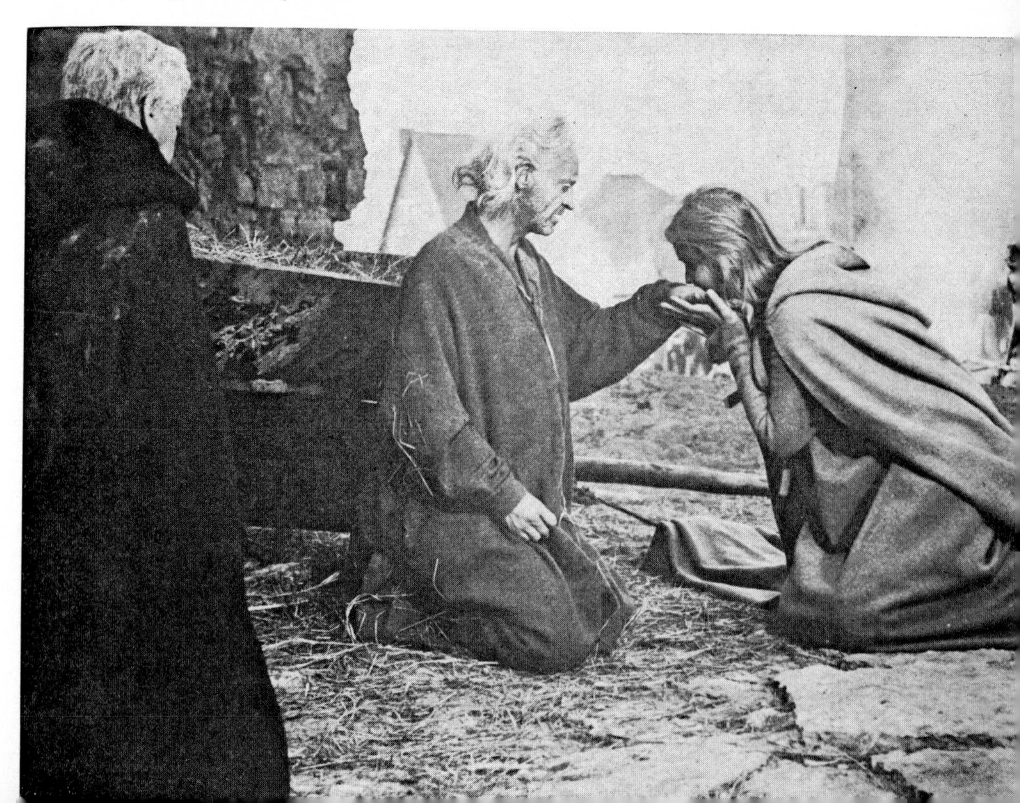

cries from wandering merchants, beggars. Something like the Russian equivalent: 'tin, soldering . . . overalls, overalls, Kazan soap . . . give a poor orphan some money for food.'

Yes, it is similar but at the same time quite different. Edgar/Tom shakes off his pursuers. However Edgar is not just pretending; suffering has already confused his reason; his thoughts are fragmented and muddled, but the life of the rich man, Edgar, penetrates through the beggar Tom's incomprehensible rambling – Tom himself judges it; suffering brings enlightenment, it is his confession. There are many different shades of meaning, and above all this, only one interpretation. Many voices have merged into one voice; Poor Tom is the leader of the chorus. The poverty-stricken hovels groan, the unharvested fields lament, the great highways beg for alms, the homeless and outcasts tramp along them – where can they shelter, who can feed them? It is not only people who are 'poor, bare, forked animals', but the land itself which lies bare, defenceless and with lost reason.

It is not just the place of action of the tragedy that is revealed in the concrete details of these images (all in Tom's speeches) but the causes of the tragedy as well.

The space of the tragedy is a penal wash-house. Yes, this is part of its space.

Are these figurative situations? The basis of the structure, the nature of the chiaroscuro, is the rhythm. This is the most important factor which I feel with an almost tangible clarity: everything is moved forward, pressed together in a large human world, amidst the bustle of life, so that one is stifled by the inequality, the tyranny and the fear; they are ordinary wanderings and ordinary sorrows in an ordinary, terrifying world.

There is nothing special or peculiar. Everything is linked together and confused. The screen reveals the links by the reality of the action, and the links go beyond the screen into the reality of time.

ONE'S MEMORY WORKS in a strange way. Much that happened a comparatively short time ago has lost its clarity, but I remember a typhus epidemic from my earliest childhood. I can distinctly remember the tone, the colours: the soldiers' greatcoats, the station platforms, littered with the shells of sunflower seeds, screwed up bundles of newspaper and pieces of paper, dirty discarded bandages, calico drawers, dented tin pans with burn marks still on them.

Chapter Twenty

THE CHORUS MUST be audible and then visible from the very beginning of the action. Or rather before the beginning of the action. The great stage is still empty: the principal actors have not made their entrance, nor have those who accompany them. Nothing has happened yet, but a mournful sound is already audible in the distance: the 'Poor naked wretches' are walking along the paths, away from the main highways and the castles, set apart from the main events. What common link can there be between the outcasts and those who divide the kingdom?

People in robes are deaf: not one of them hears the hoarse sound of the horn. But the call refers to them as well.

The sound of the horn, which a hundred years earlier was the whistle of the pipe, is also a summons, a call. I could hear an echo of the more ancient version in its long drawn out note. *Lear*'s structure (with its depth of inter-linking poetical ideas) reminds me of my favourite medieval allegory: the skeleton's bony fingers raise a pipe to its jaw; the dance begins; a pigtailed old woman without a nose drags kings, bishops, beautiful women and soldiers into the circle. There is a dance in *Lear* as well, only not a dance of death, but of life, a life that is worse than death.

This movement in the film will not be in a circle, it is true, but a straight line. The chain stretches out along the path – the outcasts of the earth are travelling, the horn sounds, foretelling disaster: for us! for the numbers which are numberless. How can one measure sorrow on earth? And one after another, men join the travellers, coming into the end of the line; first Edgar, then Gloucester; father and son, the blind man and his guide set out on their journey; and then Lear, Cordelia, father and daughter . . . The horn sounds: who will be next?

The chain grows, link by link, and disappears off the film.

We began to shoot the chorus on the cliffs of Kazantip.

I SPENT THE whole day looking at each costume, or rather, each set of rags. Virsaladze was taken ill just at the very moment when he was particularly needed (though in reality I always needed him), and I was nearly the death of his assistant over his decorative patches and romantic tatters. An artist who had recently graduated from drama school, he could not understand what it was I wanted. A lifelike appearance? But look at these holes (specially cut with scissors on new material), and what do you call this if it isn't dirt (specially painted on and with traces of brush marks)? . . .

I sometimes imagine the surprise of the reader who has already seen the film: where is the result of all this effort? The reader will remember that there were beggars on the screen; well, beggars are like any other beggars, there is nothing special about them.

The difficulty in a Shakespearean production is making sure that nothing special stands out in the shots. The ordinary quality applies not only to a feeling of proportion; it is a special form of expression with its own atmosphere and character. Any inexactitude immediately hits one between the eyes. It is unpleasant to see people who are obviously well-fed performing in a film about the hungry: smooth skin, urban faces, hands which have never seen manual labour – all this shows up clearly on the screen, and traces of deprivation which have been drawn in with make-up make an insulting masquerade.

Then do beggars mean matted hair, and shapeless rags? This is just what we didn't need. The outlines had just to be restrained and harsh.

The beggar leader had traces of pockmarks on his sunburnt, weatherbeaten face. He was so thin that the expression 'skin and bones' would describe him literally. Pavel Grigoriyevich took his work seriously. He would appear on the scene of the shooting long before he was called, slowly untie his boots, take off his usual clothes and turn himself into a tramp. It was cold and we tried to persuade him not to hurry: there was plenty of time before the shooting started. Pavel Grigoriyevich took no notice; he would take up a scythe and go off somewhere nearby, walking in bare feet in order to get inside the part. He shouted at his fellow men in real life as well.

The assistants found one man in the bazaar in Narva. He had no profile, that is he had part of a nose but it turned to one side and was somehow not very noticeable. He declined official introductions and asked to be called simply 'Vanya-polbanka'.[1] I am afraid that he did not belong to a trades union. It was a pure pleasure to film him: he was completely natural and unselfconscious. Perhaps there was after all a certain distinction in his outward appearance. Unfortunately the local militia would not allow him to play his part to the end; they had some private plans for him which did not concur with ours.

[1] Vanya half-a-tin (presumably a reference to the strange shape of his face) [trans.].

I like these small bands of people within a film. Isolated worlds with their own habits and mode of behaviour. Sometimes they all come together. On one side of the Duchess of Albany's table sat people who had a long life of film-making behind them – grey-haired first lovers, neurotics and fops from ancient provincial productions, and on the other side were the heavy athletes, the boxers, there was even a champion of the samba (who played the ghost in *Hamlet* – he was the only one who was strong enough to carry the museum armour) – these were the outward characteristics of Goneril's train.

Among the knights of the train were actors whose names had once been famous (we had invited them from the home for retired stage veterans); two of them had played Lear in their day.

In the time of FEKS we turned cinema into a pantechnicon: both giants and dwarfs wandered about our screen; there were faces that one would only dream of while delirious. Our characters would probably have won a competition against Fellini's monsters from *Satyricon*.

What does *Lear* need? How is one to define its character, its quality? Perhaps by calling it a montage of attractions?[1]

WHEN THE SHOOTING is over, the camera team hand over the photograph albums to the information section: screen tests for parts and scenes, for casting. When a new film is begun, the albums are returned to the director. One of the people whom one worked with might be needed again. The albums were there for *Don Quixote*, *Hamlet*, *King Lear*. Only many photographs were missing. The relatives of the deceased often asked for these photographs.

IT ONLY NEEDS some new features of expression to be discovered, and the ensuing course of events (and thoughts) forces one to go back on what one had only just succeeded in convincing oneself was right! One has to press on, and try out new modes of expression.

In *Lear* there is not just a storm; the author's weather could be described rather as changeable. To quote one of the Japanese tankas (Eisenstein's favourite poetry): 'The hurricane has passed. The debt collector quietly arrives.' The storm tore Lear's robes and died down. The fantastic gallop of the visionary world disintegrated and collapsed. Reality stood out clearly against the cold light of day. The utter simplicity of reality: barren earth, empty sky, poverty.

[1] The terminology for the 'arrangement of music-hall turns' which Eisenstein devised [trans.].

This is the reality of any epoch. And this is the bareness of the saying. The shots should be elemental, like the phrases of proverbs: the king became a poor man, lived with poor men, and was indistinguishable from them.

There were not many tramps, the camp was comparatively small, but the scene of the action was enormous, and its sweep unfolded with the action. Beyond the hillocks which the beggars were walking over were barren fields, hills deprived of any living habitation, great smooth-faced rocks; the view was endless but there was nothing to look at. It was an empty stage – not just belonging to the theatre, but to life, to the world.

In the play the meeting between Gloucester, Edgar and Lear takes place in 'the country near Dover'. In the film we had the walk to Dover, the movement towards destruction, a widening of the field of action: we entered history, the age of iron. A soliloquy becomes a massed scene; villages, towns, the whole country, are caught up by the action.

It all begins with everyday details: the halting place of worn-out, hungry tramps. They have little strength left and a long way to go. Lear and Gloucester talk, as yet in the foreground – two participants (Edgar/Tom is on one side), but the horn sounds, the beggars get up – it is time to move. And the monologue continues as they walk among the other travellers. We shot Lear from a cart, our pace imperceptibly quickened and the camera overtook the group – now Lear was in front of the travellers, and if the point of the camera was lowered, Lear was taller than the rest.

We reached the 'peak' – the point of the image: people in smocks, far off barren lands, the clatter of scythes, stern, suffering faces, words of accusation. One would like the wind of ancient times to blow across the shots. Biblical prophets, and then the itinerant preachers of the middle ages, the mad heretics, the ringing bells of the Fool.

> Where the people's vision is cut short by the leader of the hungry hordes.

– the line by Mayakovsky kept coming back to me all the time we were shooting the sequences. Of course it is not a revolution; grief and wrath walk the face of the earth.

The monologue unfolds with the sequence of the shots – the hills, steppes, valleys, estuaries of dried up rivers. We shot the scene in a number of places on our expedition (from the Azov Sea to Estonia).

There is no need to invent anything. One only has to forget how the play looks on stage, how we have grown accustomed to seeing it:

the artificiality of the meeting of the three main characters, the monologue spoken on one spot. If one studies the text of the whole Act, one uncovers other places of action, a new number of participants. The short dialogues remind one of the telegrams in war plays: 'the enemy has invaded, the cavalry have charged, the drums are beating, the soldiers are on their way.'

It is no longer the horn of the tramps, but a new call: the alarm, the tocsin, panic and disaster. People are drawn into the sequence of events. Now a real chorus of a thousand voices take up Lear's words: 'We came crying hither: Thou know'st, the first time that we smell the air we wawl and cry.'

Lear's face among the multitude of faces, among the people's grief, the destruction which has befallen the country.

The irony, a parody on a sermon turns into a tragic sermon.

The shot with Lear at the head of a crowd of travellers runs through the whole film. Like a leitmotif for the action. There is continuous movement, but the dimensions are changeable.

Lear with his courtiers, train, knights.

Lear with the beggars.

Lear with the fugitives and the victims of fire.

Lear with the prisoners and captives.

And the general movement: Lear and people; if we look closely at the ranks we will see ourselves. Movement, walking. Hesitating, rejecting what he once believed in, believing it again, rejecting it once more, but all the time moving forward. Walking, marching.

Time has helped me to prepare this Shakespearean production; I was frequently sent off on 'creative expeditions'.

IT WOULD BE stupid to pretend that Virsaladze's work was confined to costumes. A costume is made up according to a pattern, torn in the right places, spattered with mud to give it a realistic look, and it is ready to be worn – the acting can begin. But this is nonsense, it is with this very aspect, the outward appearance – the shades of significance contained in the line, and the material, that the small beginnings were made. Irony and tragedy, base reality and the force of generalization – no nuances are missed by Virsaladze's art.

The cut of Lear's rags reminded one of a king's robe, but the cloth was of the coarsest kind, the train dragged along the ground, the sloping line accentuating movement; the hem was torn enough to show his bare legs. They are elements of the grotesque but at the same time of tragedy. And there was nothing contrived about the image which would draw one's attention to it.

Virsaladze's long years of working with ballet had probably taught him to see not a costume but a movement, gesture, a body imposing itself on space.

When different people's work comes together and they grasp each other's ideas as they go along without lengthy explanations, each working the idea out in his own field, then things are going well. I was full of admiration for Yarvet's way of walking. He moved forward with a sort of clumsy ceremony, with grandiose steps, slightly turning his head towards Gloucester. He was truly great in this parody of a king. Yarvet has a sinewy, wiry body, with enormous peasant's hands. He is just like everyone else, and first among other men.

From a letter to Virsaladze June 1969

Dear Suliko Bagratovich

I am very sad that we did not manage to meet. I wanted to be able to look at what we had shot in Kazantip with you and to think about the next stages. I think things have got a bit dislodged. Just a bit . . .

I have one request: please do a sketch for the horse cloths. Of course the horses' costumes are not your responsibility but what can I do? There is nothing suitable amongst the material we have (for the soldiers, or the contestants in the tournament): the bands, checks, coats of arms are all sumptuous and decorative, but what we need is the sombre face of war. It is as if the horses were wearing armour, with only their eyes squinting through the slits. The colour should be dark; I am afraid not black, though, otherwise it will look like a funeral.

I would not like to see Cordelia in men's clothes even in war: the image is a feminine one or rather a girlish one. She must of course look true to life; she is on horseback and protected from the cold. She should evidently have a cloak with a hood (of woollen material), and boots. There should be nothing royal about her; there is a war on, and order has long since broken down. She is accompanied by a few armed men (the guard). She does not look odd among the soldiers.

And there should be nothing ducal or military about the Duke of Albany; he is a civilian; he has a sword hanging from his belt and that is all.

On the other hand Edmund is a man of war. Now he is handsome, masculine; he has reached his peak. Perhaps one should add iron to his fur costume (sealskin) – pieces of armour round his neck, on his shoulders and elbows. War in its coarsest form.

In the duel scene Edgar also does not look like a knight; he has taken a dead soldier's tunic and picked up a sword and shield on the field of battle.

I wish you a good trip to England and great success with *Spartacus*.

We have all exhausted ourselves. It was a difficult expedition . . .

From a letter to Dmitri Shostakovich

I would like to ask you to compose a few simple tunes: snatches of songs which Edgar hums when he is pretending to be mad. They should be like English folksongs in character, and unaccompanied. But these are not even musical numbers but rather part of Poor Tom's vocabulary – one moment he is humming, the next muttering and then he wails. I would not have bothered you but the English editions of the play do not include music and it is essential that these words should be sung . . .

From a letter from Dmitri Shostakovich

Dear Grigori Mikhailovich

I am sending you Poor Tom's songs. I have marked the approximate metronome speed against each one. One could of course sing them a bit faster or slower. However they need to be sung a little sorrowfully . . .

From a letter to Dmitri Shostakovich July 1969

Yesterday Leonard Merzin (Edgar) sang me the songs you sent me. I like them very much. They are exactly what I wanted to hear with a wailing, folk-like quality. I want if possible to avoid anything at all loud, solemn and pathetic. We must try to find a tone which is rather sorrowful, mournfully human.

I had the idea that perhaps we should start the film with one of these songs – with a sad voice, barely audible . . . I now understand what Pasternak felt when he wrote that *Lear* is interpreted 'too noisily'.

The work has already turned out to be horribly difficult. *Hamlet* was clearer in both subject matter and in methods of interpretation.

We will be another two and a half months in Narva . . .

Chapter Twenty-one

THE TOWN OF Narva (on the frontier with Estonia) is divided by a river; the ruins of a castle of the Livonian Order are on the left bank, and a fifteenth-century Russian fortress on the right. This was our new location. In our young days we always used to acknowledge the architect without giving the matter very much thought: A. Montferand appeared in the credits for *The Adventures of Oktyabrina.* The girl komsomol, Oktyabrina, a model collective farm leader, and Auguste Richard de Montferand made a beautiful combination of names but we did nevertheless have a certain justification in including a representative of neo-classicism in the FEKS production; we set up our film studio on the top of St Isaac's Cathedral; the Nepman[1] in boater and fashionable checked suit picked his way along a tightrope to Montferand's dome; the shark of capitalism in top hat and with a 'ribbon' of decoration across his shoulder drew up a safe from the State Bank with an enormous magnet and the steel cabinet flew through the air (using film in reverse) just missing the columns, *bas reliefs*, statues, right up to the top platform from which you could see a panorama of the whole town.

I am often asked what exactly was FEKS ('this mysterious FEKS' as I recently saw it called in an English cinema periodical)? If one were to start with the first cinematic steps it would probably become evident that they were made here, on the dome of St Isaac's Cathedral – the masks of the agit-carnival, wandering about the classical architecture at the same height as birds' flight; this was the sphere of eccentric comedy, the sphere of the gag.

Perhaps it was not only mischievousness that made us mention Montferand's name but a sort of aesthetic concept as well. Following the same tradition we should now be including Tsar Ivan III in our team – it was on his orders that the artisans from Pskov built the fortress on the banks of the Narva. The Russians and Swedes fought over it for centuries; the fortress fell into ruins, was rebuilt; and again nothing but a pile of ruins was left. Eventually it was bombed by the German airforce. The place had a lived-in air about it. Every

[1] Representative of the Nep period, when Lenin deliberately encouraged private enterprise in order to stimulate Russia's economy, shattered by the civil war and wars of intervention. Kozintsev and Trauberg were satirizing the typical business man in their film [trans.].

stone had a story to tell. There was a natural transition from the boulders of Kazantip to Ivan's town, from nature to history; the cracks in the ancient walls reminded one of the wrinkles on Lear's face.

We felt at home here. Every corner was adapted to the purposes of the shooting, the inner courtyards were turned into Goneril's castle and Gloucester's house[1] with the help of a few additional constructions; the stables were occupied by the short-legged, stocky Taurian horses specially brought for the film; I had turned down the elegant thoroughbred steeplechasers.

And in the back yard the eagles and falcons lived in their cages. Estonian horsemen schooled the King's four. The fire specialists built up their stores in the basement and there also was the bus with the sound-recording equipment.

When the weather got cold we used to take it in turns to climb, even if only for a few minutes, into the cabin in order to warm up (there was no air to breathe, the sound-recording men, as if to spite us, smoked), the remaining parts of the fortress (including the outbuildings) had already been burnt down.

The place was excellent: the simplicity of line and form, the absence of any architectural style – all this matched the outward appearance of the people and their faces. There was only one factor by which one could date the building – the year when it was destroyed. A time of murder and destruction – that meant that it was suitable for this tragedy.

The long-shot of the castle gave us the most trouble. From far away the fortress looked imposing but it did not look like Lear's castle. I do not think such a castle exists anywhere: the work itself did not allow the possibility of defining its shape. Any real building would have looked 'unsuitable'.

We discovered the reality (not of the overall view but of the separate living quarters, fragments of the building) later, during the action, but at that one moment I wanted to show not the castle but a hazy impression of it: this is how it would have looked to people approaching it from afar, hoping to find out how their fate had been decided. We had not so much to film the real object (the fortress) as to transform it (and fundamentally) by means of photography.

We chose weather in which cameramen are usually given the day off: the sun would come out only for a moment, the light was constantly changing – conditions which are generally unfavourable for shooting. But all the same Gritsus caught the precious few

[1] Although Shakespeare gives Gloucester a 'castle', Kozintsev sees it as a sort of country estate from a Turgenev novel – see pp. 55–6.

seconds; the crowd of people gathered together on a hill were covered in mist and far away where everyone was gazing, flickering spots of light filtered through on to the fortress walls.

WE REACHED THE shooting of the battle scenes, as they are usually called, and actually a war is being waged in these episodes and there is talk of fighting. But a battle is just what one does not want to see on the screen. The inner action – fate, feelings, thoughts – is easily obscured by the outer spectacle. Clausewitz says that war is a continuation of politics but by different methods. The politics in *Lear* are falsehood, hypocrisy and madness. Therefore this is what has to be continued, carried to a greater degree. In the play the battle action takes place offstage and is talked about in the barest dialogue – how does one show battles on stage? In cinema it is not difficult to show them and still easier to obscure the fates of the main characters by the massed action, and to substitute the genre of battle for philosophical poetry.

In *Lear* it is not the panoramic events which are important – the movement of battalions, advances, attacks – but faces and eyes: if you look deeper into them you can see (in their eyes alone!) the fields of battle, the defence of fortresses and the piles of bodies.

Shakespeare does not work on the screen through naturalism – I often come back to this idea; 'real' war contributes little to his poetry. And what is more, in this instance the conventionalities of the theatre are even more convincing. For the battle scenes in *Coriolanus* the Berliner Ensemble used traditional Chinese and Japanese methods of production, the alternation of dynamic movement and complete immobility. On stage the succession of groups of immobile soldiers, as if the culmination of hate and fury, seemed to have more force and tragedy than the cinema crowds of extras, herds of horses and pools of blood (as in real life!). The bazaar-like curiosities of severed hands and heads bring Shakespeare closer not to contemporary life but to the box office: a certain part of the audience will pay in order to be frightened; they will go into ecstasies simply to have been scared out of their wits during the course of the film.

On colour film blood does not look like real blood; it reminds one of ketchup. And now they have added kitsch to the ketchup: knights in full armour trip each other up with their heels, butt each other with their shields, kick each other's armour with their feet; they are of course furious fights. But when one hefty fellow all arrayed in armour turns down another thug's visor and the other gives him an 'oecumenical pasting' with his iron sleeve, it is evident that the armour is all show: it is difficult to walk even a few steps in real armour, so therefore they are idiots fooling around on the screen; they smear the tin plate with ketchup.

Small boys like playing a simple game; they tie an empty tin to a dog's tail and what fun they have! The maddened dog rushes about; something is making a noise and frightening it to death – the empty tin rattles over the cobbles.

But we are not concerned with cruelty. When Toshiro Mifune, the Japanese Macbeth, is pierced with arrows from all sides and with the arrows in his body is transformed before one's eyes from a man to a monstrous wild beast, and when finally the last arrow penetrates his neck and pierces his carotid artery – the picture of death horrifies one but not at all because it is a naturalistic imitation; revenge is turned into ritual and Kurosawa presents it with such accomplished rhythm and plastic form that it takes one's breath away (*The Throne of Blood*). Kitsch with ketchup looks like a feeble diversion if you remember the hair waving on the corpse of the woman shot on the bridge; the corpse rising up with the drawbridge and the horse which was also killed in the same place, harnessed to a cab, being lifted up towards the sky, and then the harness breaking – and the dead horse plunging from an enormous height to the abyss of the river (*October*)[1].

The war in *Lear* is greater, broader than the most imposing panoramas: it is not only the State which perishes, but all the spiritual treasures created by man; the real culmination of the storm – here in these scenes of destruction, the epidemic which has seized hold of the times; and neither the sword nor fire will cure it.

And at the same time this war is the fever of a real illness: dying Lear. Cordelia's soldiers carry him on a stretcher, he is delirious – the stretcher moves with the army, fighting continues all round.

On the screen only the face of the sick man should be clearly visible (in close up); the camera moves through the flames, through the war, and what appears and disappears in the distance – armed men caught up in the thirst for murder and destruction – is born of his delirium, ghostly visions of hatred and fury.

The chain begins to form: disease – delirium – war.

One more point of interpretation: the King is being carried in the present, but in his delirium he is travelling through his past; he builds his kingdom once again by fire and the sword ('I have seen the day, with my good biting falchion,/I would have made them skip') what is being destroyed now, his past, must be burnt in the fire – and when he is kneeling before Cordelia he becomes a different man; fire purges.

[1] Directed by Eisenstein, 1928 [trans.].

The bare-faced fate of Edmund celebrates the victories of battle in the midst of grief and tears. The hero of the age is moving towards ultimate power; he fights for power and kills for power. The bastard son with no common rights has become a general; one more minute and he will have won the kingdom.

I have never seen his rise to power in the theatre. On the screen one must hold back and show his warlike triumphs slowly. This perhaps is the one place where flags and triumphant shouts would not interfere. He has risen to the highest rung and immediately calls the executioner; he needs a rope and a piece of soap – he is afraid of Cordelia.

It is a pity that there was no time to shoot the moment of triumph when he tossed a coin: heads or tails? Goneril or Regan? Which of the two old women should he choose?

There are a lot of knights prancing around and flags showing coats of arms unfurling in the wind! . . . Two middle-aged women, crazed with desire, wild with jealousy, enter the scene of action, the zone of contamination (which they themselves initiated), searching for their lover; each sister watches the other in case she has stolen her lover from the other, or is rolling around with him here, among the corpses and the carrion.

This is how Shakespeare's war is described. One has not only to listen to the dialogue but also to look closely at the different fates: they are all exactly the same; they are all heading towards madness and eternal damnation.

To the same damnation?

Chapter Twenty-two

THE MUSE, THE ANGEL AND THE DEVIL

I SHALL HAVE once more to return to the history of contemporary theatre and its complex development in this century. The central movement is inseparable from the names of Stanislavsky, Craig, Meyerhold and Brecht. There are of course other important directors in the flow of this movement. But by some strange counterpoint the names of completely different artists arise outside the general development. At first they are linked by something that is wild and hideous: a short-lived memory of scandals rather than productions; their names disappear, are forgotten for years (contemporary opinion thinks forever), but then after not so very much time has elapsed, they are remembered once again. Forgotten productions which were seen by ridiculously small audiences, put on in a hurry, clumsy and unpolished, suddenly occupy the centre of attention; names which faded long ago, all of a sudden become great; names turn into banners – whole movements are called after them.

The *avant garde* is in favour at the moment: their manifestos are re-read, and the hurriedly reported exchanges spoken in the heat of the argument are learnt by heart; philosophers and psychoanalysts find the keys – even the craziest contrivances are deciphered: everything is rearranged and becomes a miracle of harmony; there are no artists – only thinkers. And meanwhile one forgets what real life is like – only aesthetic systems are discussed.

Nowadays, we begin counting the new age of the theatre from 10 December 1896; the curtain of the Théâtre de L'Oeuvre went up (or parted), Ubu Roi, the hero of Alfred Jarry's play approached the footlights and said, 'Merde!' (It sounds stronger in the original.[1]) A grotesque farce – the boisterous muddling of all planes, a fantastic debaucherie – occupied the stage. The 'Theatre of Protest and Paradox' was born (as it was called in some American article).

It is not easy to judge such productions; they belong to their own times and in order to understand them, one should direct one's gaze not only from the stalls on to the stage but also from the stage to the audience and beyond the limits of the theatre. The legends which follow tend to form layers on top of reality until no trace of

[1] The Russian word used by the author was 'Dermo' [trans.].

what really happened is left. The destinies and biographies remain and they give one plenty to think about. Why for instance was the part of King Ubu played and with such success, by Firmin Gemier – a pupil of Antoine,[1] who spent his whole life fighting for a national theatre? . . .

Now everything has become confused: the conflict of ideas, the fantastic figures of the bohemians, feelings which never turned into thoughts, thoughts which had nothing to do with the business, the exotic details of the *Paris of Guillaume Apollinaire*, quotes from Nietsche and Gousserles, memories of fashions in the occult sciences . . . And now there is an abundance of academic research papers which (either upholding or refuting) treat farce as a philosophical treatise, mystification as mysticism.

It is of course expressive material. What will they think of next to surpass it in importance?

It would be hard to find anything more important but for some reason I am reminded of the sad words in Gogol: 'And what about Kasyan? What about Borodavka? Kolopyer? Pidsytok?' And heard only in answer that Borodavka was hanged in Tolopan, that Kolopyer was skinned alive at Kizikirman, and that Pidsytok's head was preserved in a barrel and sent to Tsargrad itself. Old Bulba hung his head and said thoughtfully: 'They were brave Cossacks!'[2]

When he was young Antonin Artaud, the poet, director and theatre critic, was startlingly handsome. In the early twenties Autant-Lara asked him to take the part of the 'gentle angel',[3] and even his death on the screen was angelic (shot in slow motion); then came René Clair's light-hearted *Entr'acte*; next he was the monk shown the true faith by Jeanne d'Arc in Carl Dreyer's film; Marat in Abel Gance's *Napoléon*. 'He was marvellous', wrote a contemporary, 'his deep-set eyes showed up on film like light shining from a cave . . .'

When he was discharged from hospital in May 1946 he could have been taken for a very old man, a human wreck: he was unnaturally thin with a pale emaciated face and sunken cheeks. His epic poems, his articles and manifestos had already become indistinguishable from his life; both his own words which he despised and no longer believed and his erstwhile teachers, the 'accursed poets' Baudelaire, Rimbaud, Lautréamont, showed him their strength and became a reality. He cursed reason and spent nine years in mental hospitals, moving from one to another; in his biography their names

[1] Theatre director (1858–1943) [trans.].

[2] A quotation from *Taras Bulba*, Gogol's heroic novel about Cossack life [trans.].

[3] Claude Autant-Lara's film, *Fait-Divers*, appeared in 1922 [trans.].

sound like the ringing of bells: Scotteville-lès-Rouen, Sainte-Anne, Ville-Evrard, Rodez.

The points of departure for his theatrical ideas were not new: according to him contemporary theatre was dead, the play was a pitiful slave, taking up its unseemly place on the stage; complete power should be given to the director – like a magician, he can create miracles which are above the words, by movement, masks, light, sound – you can read all this in Gordon Craig or Meyerhold. But then his own ideas begin: the theatre is destined to wipe away the rotten filth of European culture, the pitiful rationalism; its influence, like a plague epidemic, brought about a return to the force of the ancient powers of darkness; during a plague epidemic there are no restrictions; in towns, which have gone mad from the horror, a frenzied carnaval begins amongst the bonfires on which the dead bodies are burned; those who are still alive dress up in wild costumes, and stick masks to their faces; they seek freedom from everything which civilization has suppressed – and perhaps these people will conquer the epidemic, and will stay alive.

Theatre should shake up its audience, it should act by shock treatment.

Artaud's teeth had fallen out and his hair had grown thin from electric shock treatment: 'this is a spiritual and physical death', he wrote from the hospital. He was famous for his hallucinations and visions induced by drugs. But in real life the strongest doses of drugs did not take away the pain; the doctors could no longer contain him; his suffering was unbearable. The theatre of cruelty (cruelty as a component of energy), which he wanted to create, was to have touched on the priceless secrets of existence; he studied the mystics, Cabbala, alchemism; he lived with a Mexican tribe which had still kept their ancient culture. The discovery of secrets, a dawning, revelation . . . A haemorrhage began from the rectum. The diagnosis was cancer, and inoperable.

The Theatre and its Double (1938), a collection of articles by Artaud, 'is the most significant and important book on the theatre written in the twentieth century', wrote Jean-Louis Barrault. 'It should be read over and over again.'

IT IS A difficult subject – the conflict of certain fundamental elements. An ancient contradiction which has not yet been solved.

In his last lecture, Federico García Lorca said that every artist has his own muse and his own angel: the muse awakens reason, the angel leads and illumines, and with their help the artist can talk of love or dance; but verse which has been dictated by the muse and lit up by the angel, is 'gilded gingerbread', it has the 'false taste of the monastery'. The angel and the muse live somewhere up above; they float over the artist. But there is a force within the artist himself which the artist has no need to turn to: the demon slumbers in the innermost recesses of his blood, all he has to do is to wake him.

What happens when he wakes up? . . .

Lorca told a story about the famous Andalusian singer, Pastora Pavan (nicknamed the girl with the combs); once she took it into her head to perform in a simple inn in Cadiz; that evening she sang particularly well, her voice was marvellous, 'flowing like molten pewter, as soft as if drowning in fur, she let it die in the locks of her hair . . . sent it away to far off thickets'.

This wonder did not make any impression at all in the inn. The great singer was a flop; she ended her performance in complete silence, no one applauded, not even out of politeness. There was an ironical remark from the back, everyone laughed. They didn't care tuppence for the muse and the angel, 'these people were not interested in talent, technique or mastery, they needed something else.'

And what was this 'something else'?

'Then the girl with the combs jumped up in fury, her hair in disorder like a medieval mourner, she drank down a glass of fiery casal in one gulp and began to sing again, with no voice, no breath, no subtleties, but with her fiery throat. She succeeded in eliminating all the ornaments in the songs in order to leave the way clear for the furious fire-eating demon, the brother of the sandstorms, which made the audience tear at their clothes, almost like Antillean-Negro sectarians when jostling in front of the statue of Santa Barbara.'

The burning throat set fire to their hearts.

You would have had to destroy her voice in order to tear yourself out of earshot of her singing, beyond the boundaries of time, and then the ancient frenzy took hold of the inn: 'Her voice was like a flow of blood . . . in its true torment it stretched out, as the hand with ten fingers in Juan Juni's scuplture stretches out towards Jesus' feet, nailed but full of passion.'

The ecstasy of baroque art seems a little theatrical to us now; perhaps the comparison of a singer's voice to a flow of blood is exaggerated as well? But cruelty, suffering and death are in the ancient roots of Spanish art; this is the natural answer in defending the poet's metaphor.

But there are other answers. When the Falangists ordered Lorca to be shot, Spanish symbolism was not taken into consideration. The voice and a flow of blood; art is like torture – great poets do not make literary comparisons but have visions of their fate. Versifiers throw words to the wind but real poets pay the highest price for them. The firing squad aims of course not at the poetry but at the poet, but the poetry, paid for by the bullet, returns to life as a reality. It can happen that literary criticism also takes on a particular form: a bonfire. Books which set people's hearts on fire are burnt on bonfires. This is nothing to do with the Baroque.

Literary trends are not demarcated by the words of manifestos. Sometimes what divides them also barricades a street. Then it is clear that the struggle is not between the *avant garde* and the academicians. Marinetti[1] wrote of the 'teatro di varietà' – a few years later he had sided with those who killed Lorca; Eisenstein invented the theory of the 'montage of attractions' – *Battleship Potemkin* helped to eliminate Lorca's murderers.

After the First World War European art became even more uneasy. Nothing happened normally and the concept of 'normality' seemed an insult. As a matter of habit people talked about progress and the wonders of civilization; even in the preceding century Dostoyevsky had angrily written about 'crystal palaces': if the price for the right to live in them was general heartlessness because the majority would be driven off to the 'penal wash-houses', then it would be better to stick one's tongue out and make a face at these palaces. Tragedy in Dostoyevsky often turned into grotesque scandal: people grimaced and stuck out their tongues – such was the indecency that upstanding people blushed from shame. And it was just this sense of decency, belonging to the bourgeois (a mask of respectability), which Dostoyevsky hated with all his heart.

Artists, who to their own misfortune, did not have elephant's hide, hated the 'healthy theatre': where the actors had rosy cheeks and amused their audiences with bedroom romances – just like life, but with an elevated style. They felt what was in the air. A fragmented world deprived of human form appeared on the canvases of the cubists. Our art began to talk of revolution without conventional embellishment and sweet sounds. The threatening needs threatening sounds. In his first film Eisenstein used an abattoir as a metaphor for the dispersal of a workers' demonstration (*Strike*); the camera was set up inside the abattoir: a black stream splashed on to the screen. In the meat which was given to the sailors (*Battleship Potemkin*) there was a seething mass of maggots shot in close up. The sweep of a Cossack sabre – a broken pince-nez; a bloody eye. The baby in the pram rocked through blood, death and hell. This is what the national tragedy looked like on screen.

[1] Filippo Tommaso Marinetti (1876–1944) [trans.].

In *Nature is not Indifferent*[1] Eisenstein studied the structure of pathos, going beyond its limits to the uttermost degree of its influence. Eisenstein understood perfectly both the laws of pathetic composition and the price which has to be paid for it. Choosing a detail from an El Greco painting (only a detail), a stormy landscape in Toledo, he wrote: the colours 'shimmer . . . with no less animation of holy excitement than as if the blood-stained artist had been alive, crucified on one of the crosses'.

In his art Eisenstein called neither the muse nor the angel to his aid. I don't think that the demon in the innermost recesses of his blood ever managed to get enough sleep.

One thing our art did was to awaken this demon. It was not the angel who advised Meyerhold to direct a burst of gunfire into the auditorium (*The Final and Decisive*[2]), nor the muse which created the mad cacophony at the end of *The Government Inspector*: the mayor leaping about in his waistcoat, the ear-splitting bells and whistles (how many years was it before this kind of expression became the universal rage!).

Antonin Artaud also studied under Meyerhold; he played one of the mystics in the Paris production of *The Fairground Booth*; Georges Pitoyeff produced Blok's play (before that he was a member of Komisarzhevskaya's company, where Meyerhold's production was still in the repertoire). There was probably another influence; Guillaume Apollinaire translated the play; in 1913 Meyerhold went to Paris; they met frequently and became friends.

Blok and Meyerhold made fun of the 'mystics'; I do not know whether Pitoyeff retained one detail from the earlier production: the heads of the mystics disappeared into their collars looking as if there were no people, only highly respectable jackets and shirtfronts painted on cardboard. It was a fantastic combination – Blok's whirlwind over the whole universe and Apollinaire's sun 'with its throat cut'.

They were dissimilar roads, paths going in different directions, and then suddenly there would be an unexpected point of intersection, a meeting, and then an immediate movement in yet another quite different direction, towards a different goal. They were meetings not just of artists but of artists and history: Baudelaire on the barricades of 1848, Rimbaud amongst the *communards* in 1871. What Western

[1] The title of one of his unfinished books, written between 1945–47 [trans.].

[2] By Vsevolod Vishnevsky. Produced in 1931. The title is taken from the Russian words to the Internationale, 'It is our final and decisive battle' [trans.].

artists did not come into contact with the art of the first years of our revolution?

Artaud produced a play based on Pudovkin's film *Mother*; he was also planning to make a film of the play, *The Dybbuk*.[1] I remember Vakhtangov's production: the sloping surface of the floor, a girl in a white dress staggering back in horror, the evil figures of the beggars (and this was long before Brecht) . . .

Pushkin thought that one of the main streams of imagination which the theatre activated was horror (the other two were laughter and pity). He made a sketch for one of the scenes in the Pugachev rebellion: a raft is moving down the river. On it are gallows, and corpses swing from the nooses.

Russian art has not been afraid of the most extreme forms of expression. There have been influences which have been almost unbearable, like the unbearable description of Raskolnikov's dream when a horse which has fallen is killed, beaten with fists and kicked with boots and then whipped, six lashes in its eyes. Six lashes at one's heart. This is how elegant Russian literacy wrote of injustice, heartlessness and inhumanity.

Soon after Artaud's death, Maurice Saillet wrote: 'Antonin Artaud died March 4 1948 at the age of fifty-two. This date should be remembered as that of a new and terrible birth: the moment this body and this mind, riveted together by long agony, parted company, Artaud's real life began. The hailstorm of his thoughts now batters our own.'[2]

'He was not understood during his life-time.' Naomi Greene writes in her book about him, 'but he was later proclaimed as a prophet.' These words are no exaggeration: academic papers are now published on Artaud and his name is never absent from the Greenwich Village newspapers; many theatre productions in Europe and America have shown his influence, and the bloody nightmares which stifled him haunt the screens of the 'underground cinema'. Even his astrological prophecies have been realized on the screen (Kenneth Anger's *Scorpio Rising*).

Theatrical journals devote whole numbers to him: among those who have contributed research are Jerzy Grotowsky (in the Polish *Theatre Laboratory*), *Living Theatre* (USA), Peter Hall, Charles Marowitz, Peter Brook. There are too many to name them all.

[1] By Solomon Ansky (1863–1920), produced by Vakhtangov at the Habima Theatre [trans.].

[2] 'In Memoriam: Antonin Artaud' by Maurice Saillet, trans. Richard Howard, in Artaud, *The Theater and its Double*, Grove Press 1958, p. 147 [trans.].

Grotowsky even writes that in many contemporary productions he thinks that the 'cruelty' above all shows the influence of Artaud's ideas.

The production which was put on in chaos, without a company, without money, or a theatre, ending its brief existence with a single performance of *The Cenci* (the Stendhal adaptation of Shelley's play) at the Folies Wagram (1935) still occupies the centre of attention. The agonized face with an enormous forehead and a cigarette drooping from the corner of his dissolute mouth, like the face of a teacher, appears with more and more frequency. His photograph was even printed a few years ago on the programme of the Royal (Artaud and royalty!) Shakespeare Theatre Company's Workshop.

I went to one of the Workshop's rehearsals. Many places in Jean Genet's *The Screens* were acted with truly scorched throats. Frenzy, hoarse shouts, furious gabbling, bursts of complete incomprehensibility, howls, and now and then a sort of hoarse barking; hysteria and the grotesque; the actors themselves painted red spots (fire? blood?) on the white screens; fantastic stuffed birds, ritual rhythms, masks. It was not difficult to distinguish Artaud's ideas.

It is interesting to watch Peter Brook at work: the yellow hawk-like eyes watch the action unceasingly: at the slightest inaccuracy he signals to his assistant who makes a note in the book; at the sound-effects panel the smallest noise is adjusted (the sounds are reminiscent of the Noh and Kabuki theatres), each coming in at the correct second, wound up for the correct number of revolutions, set in motion, combined with others and off it all goes; rhythm is the basis of everything.

The history of the theatre does not wish to doze quietly and peacefully in the back rows of academic courses; some of the chapters drag out a lazy existence until the exams approach, when the students, cursing, have to mug up names and formulas which mean nothing to them; others suddenly get younger and burst in on contemporary theatre as innovators. This is how the Noh and Kabuki theatres and the medieval parables and moralists gathered their strength. In explaining his formula for pathos, Eisenstein mentioned Ben Jonson with enthusiasm: the construction of the character of the hero by a salient feature which was carried to a manic extent, to deformed grotesque, 'to pathetic effects by means of forcing an ecstatic state which tore out of each man elements of an ever-increasing intensity'.

Peter Brook is also seeking the breaking-point, an escape beyond the limits of the theatre, beyond the boundaries of theatrical aesthetics. It does not matter what it is – the theatre of cruelty, collage, Zen, a happening – as long as it tears apart the net of the commercial theatre, the imperturbable stifling atmosphere, the pointlessness. He tests the limits of the register, different forms of expression. He can't stay in one place. He appears on the horizon like a meteor in a number of countries: photographs of his *Tempest* have just arrived here – an enormous empty rectangle, the national furniture museum in Paris. Steel constructions are erected like scaffolding, only on wheels; Ariel flies in, almost in the air – the Japanese actor from the Noh theatre. Again the Stratford production of *A Midsummer Night's Dream*, like a circus parade: elegant celebrities in ballet shoes, a white area shining under an electric sun. He abandons England and together with his young company opens the 'International Centre of Theatre Research' in Paris; in Iran they act in some old ruins the myth which represents the story of mankind; the actual setting and the rising of the sun enter into the director's scheme. In his last letter, he writes that he is preparing for an expedition to Africa, where the actors will put on plays in the villages, trying to communicate to the audience directly, by breaking down the barriers of civilization. He ends his book by saying that by the time it is printed he will probably have already changed his mind about a lot of things.

Peter Brook loves Shakespeare; Artaud preferred John Webster, the repertory for the theatre of cruelty must have been started with him. In *The Duchess of Malfi* there are plenty of black diversions even by contemporary standards: there is an execution on stage, the audience is startled by horrifying wax dolls, severed hands are offered to be shaken, and there is a chorus of madmen. The general view of life in the play looks like this:

> O, this gloomy world!
> In what a shadow, or deep pit of darkness
> Doth womanish and fearful mankind live![1]

Edgar Allan Poe was an avid reader of Webster. One can guess that Artaud did not discover his carnival in time of the plague either in the ancient chronicles or invent it himself. In Poe's story, 'The Mask of the Red Death' the characters locked themselves up in a castle from the plague and held a fancy dress ball; the jollities are interrupted by an unbidden guest wearing the mask of the plague; when the mask is torn from his face, there is no face beneath: death and destruction have come to the castle. The meeting with the plague, and the attempt to resist it, is an enormous theme in art. The edge of the age, the eternal darkness of history – this is how Pushkin treated the plague with the fearlessness of poetry (the weak English play *The City of the Plague* was only a starting point for him). It is not the fantastic

[1] Act V, scene v [trans.].

changes of style which makes one think about this element of poetry which is not afraid of looking down into the abyss, but sharp turning points in history. The plague often stands at the threshhold.

WEIMAR IN THE last century.

'Today with Goethe at dinner conversation soon turned again to the demoniacal' Eckerman carefully noted down in his diary. They discuss this subject 'at dinner', in 'conversation'. Goethe said in clarification, 'The demoniacal is that which is not to be solved by means of the understanding and reason.'

'Does not also,' said I, 'the demoniacal appear in occurrences?'

'Quite specially,' said Goethe, 'and indeed in all which we are unable to solve by means of the understanding and reason . . . it is manifested in the most different way in the whole of nature . . . Many creatures are of an entirely demoniacal sort . . . With Paganini it is shown in the highest degree with which there also he produces such great effects.'

'We were taken up in continuous talk about the demoniacal . . . So too the demoniacal throws itself on important individuals, especially if they have an exalted position as had Frederick and Peter the Great.'

A quiet conversation, low voices – 'Would you like some more soup? – Thank you. Would you be so good as to pass the salt . . .'

'In poetry,' said Goethe, 'there is something thoroughly demoniacal and indeed principally in the unconscious . . . and therefore it also has effects beyond all comprehension' . . .

'The effective power, which we call demoniacal, does not appear', said I tentatively, 'to enter into the idea of the Godlike.'

'Dear child,' said Goethe, 'What then do we know of the Godlike?'[1]

The house in which these words were spoken is still standing. Goethe built it in 1709. The rooms are small with stucco mouldings: there are ancient masks, Zeus on his throne, Moses, collections of crystals, of Italian majolicas, herbariums, a library. It all makes cosy surroundings in which to discuss the verse of Apollo and Dionysus. There is a small walled garden.

For generations people have remembered the words of Goethe while reading Shakespeare: Hamlet is an oak tree planted in a flower pot. Is this true of the Prince of Denmark? . . . But perhaps true of the privy councillor of the Weimar Republic himself – here in the house with the tiny walled garden.

[1] Eckermann's conversations with Goethe, trans. R. O. Moon, Morgan Laird & Co., pp. 368, 370–1 [trans.].

Or perhaps it is true of every artist who feels the impossibility of giving expression to a time of tragedy within the outlines of the circle of art.

In 1945 Goethe's house on the Frauenplatz was hit by several bombs. Later it was rebuilt and all the belongings were restored to their rightful places.

Not far from Weimar, from the house where Goethe lived and the house where Schiller lived, both now museums, is Buchenwald, the museum of the concentration camps of death. Time changes the rhythms of art, the character itself of the artists' spiritual life becomes different from preceding centuries.

Sometimes it is not a firmly built bridge which spans the past and the present, but unstable planks and branches, badly pieced together; you would have to be at gun-point to cross by them. Art goes through fire.

The sleekness and elegance of art form sometimes becomes hateful. At the beginning of the Revolution Meyerhold's most abusive word was 'corpulence'. According to his demands, the play had to be cleansed of fat literary qualities and transformed into a script, into a 'lean body'.

What was to give this body live movement, to fill it with passion? 'The comedian's nerve,' Meyerhold replied. The 'slackening of the muscles which comes on after a bath', attributed to psychological naturalism, was exchanged for energy and nervous tension. Meyerhold found the trends for all this in the tradition of folk theatre.

The wandering comedians, the lawless defenders of freedom summoned their audience from all four corners of the earth to their stage on the market squares; the power of the emotional message had to be such that echoes of the alarum bell could be heard in the sound of the fool's bells. The buffoons belonged to the race of the cursed tribe of devils, and it is not surprising that they were not allowed to be buried in the city burial grounds.

The black leather mask which Harlequin wore did not look like the face of a just man. In all history the priest and the comedian have never stood side by side, they have always been enemies. Harlequin himself was a magician. He worked miracles; but these miracles disturbed the peace and sowed seeds of rebellion. The comedian worked miracles and then laughed at them.

This is why he needed this resounding 'nerve'.

Following Meyerhold's example (through the influence of Brecht), Brook strengthened these qualities still further, drawing the 'nerve' even tighter. He became interested in a particular scale: singing with one's throat on fire. This is why this 'nerve' was so important to him – the activity, the passionate nature of the relationship towards the phenomena of reality. A new internal technique was developed, perfect in its own way. Brook's actors can wake the demon in their blood even twice a day (when there is a matinée).

It had important results: the young company of actors learnt how to breathe freely in the fantastic world of the grotesque. The uplifted leg of the clown could be suspended over an abyss.

In Brook's productions, the 'comedian's nerve' – like a taut string, a coiled spring of energy – is not at all an abstract quality of temperament, but a way of relating to the tragedy in the world, to the grotesque in life. It is the link the director holds with particular phenomena of life by means of a multitude of thoughts and feelings, such as anger and pain.

Now many others have assimilated these experiments. And what lived in Brook's productions by its passions, wrath and alarm has now been turned into a 'style'. In the West they now say that the nineteenth century was characterized by Romanticism and Sentimentality; the twentieth by black Shakespeare and the theatre of cruelty.

IN THE *Cenci*, Artaud's only production, the father, a monster of depravity, tried to rape his daughter; while he is asleep, his children strike one nail into his eye, and another into his throat; they are executed.

Shelley found this story in some old Italian chronicles. What terrible deeds are written in the chronicles of our time: gas-chambers, massed murders, the atom bomb . . . It is no wonder that the artists of the age of cruelty remembered the theatre of cruelty. They read Shakespeare – and next to the ghosts of those murdered by Macbeth they see the ghosts of those who died in the gas chambers. In Victorian illustrated presentation editions Hamlet is portrayed as a gentle youth. 'I must be cruel' – thus speaks not an anti-hero of an anti-play, but the Prince of Denmark; this is how he behaves not only towards King Claudius, but also towards his Mother and the girl he loves.

I said that you can only see a Shakespearean war through the eyes of the main characters. You can also see it through the holes which are in place of their eyes. In the Stratford production of *Lear* there was no hint of battle on the stage; Brook gave it shape and solved its formula by sound alone. Gloucester sat on the floor on an empty stage which was uniformly lit; Edgar had left his father there and had gone off to fight. You could hear the rumbling and clashing of steel, the face of the blind man was turned towards the audience, he sat absolutely still, like an enormous, clumsy doll, a mannequin, and for an unbearable length of time (in stage terms) the empty eyeholes looked at us, through us. It was impossible to perceive the moment of death, and the steel went on clashing and banging just as loudly.

The strength of this image shook me to the roots. But I was sorry that the director cut the tree down.[1]

WHEN A FILM is made for the wide screen, a copy is often taken for the small screen, the normal size. When this is done, often a part of the landscape or sometimes even a character is cut off; from the side of the finished shot only an ear or a nose sticks out. This is how we behave when we make a production of a Shakespeare play. And we even boast that we have succeeded in purging the Elizabethan original of nineteenth-century additions. The poor nineteenth century! How much have we blamed it for! And it is true that in taking away layer after layer of what we think of as Romanticism, Sentimentalism, pathos, we eventually reach some sort of pure mirror-like surface. This is the mirror in which we see our own confusions, pain and anger . . . After cleansing it of the nineteenth century we uncover not the sixteenth but the twentieth or rather ourselves in the twentieth century. We cannot do otherwise. Let us stop thinking that someone may be capable of producing 'real' Shakespeare, an irrefutably correct production (or film) – the man whom the author himself dreamed of. One cannot do this. Neither Stanislavsky, Craig, nor any other theatrical genius could have done it, because the production of a Shakespeare play is the reflection of his poetry in the moving space of time.

But the poetry itself is stronger than time, and it is only in comparison with it that our 'editions' can be judged. The poetry is a reality which existed before us and will continue the same after we are gone; it exists outside us, as the objective reality of an irrefutable arrangement of words and rhythms – an animated dimension which is full of life. This unity of poetic material is endlessly varied (just as any living being is). The texture of Webster's art seems elementary in comparison, not because there is less horror and darkness in Shakespeare's world (sometimes the darkness is even more hell-like than in *The Duchess of Malfi*), but because in this dimension, saturated with movement, nothing perishes without trace, and death is answered by birth, and when the darkness reaches its utmost limits, an almost invisible spark already begins to burn, and the darkness loses its power in comparison with this tiny fragment of light.

It is getting light. Edgar follows the road, leading his blind father.

[1] In the play, Gloucester dies in the shade of a tree [trans.].

The far distant horizon is visible, the light begins to be felt and it is warm. The son begs in order to feed his father. It is a hot day. There is a tree and the tree has shade. The son sits his father down in the shade.

How have I the audacity to describe the scene in such detail? All this is in the poetry: the tree, the tree's shade. It is all poetry.

I want to 'print' the shade from the tree only it must be this particular shade. It is not difficult to film a tree in the sun so that it throws a shadow on the ground, but this would not be Shakespearean poetry. The sun, the shadow, and the resting in the shade – all this springs from the one source: the reflection of love and compassion. These are not just the spiritual qualities of a man called Edgar, but the quality of the poetic material, brought to life by a man called Shakespeare: he singles out such moments even in darkness.

I am thinking not of particular fragments of Edgar's monologue (the description of his father's death), but the fullness of the movement of life, which continues and will keep on going – the race of mankind does not hand down the genus of cruelty alone. At the heart of the structure, at the foundations of the rhythm, are continual outbreaks of light: Gloucester recognizes his son; and then the second, stronger outbreak – Lear finds Cordelia a few moments before darkness and death. The two moments of happiness are so powerful that they are unbearable.

The poet pushes Lear with his hands, the father's fingers touch his daughter's cheeks, there is moisture on the ends of his fingers – 'Be your tears wet? Yes, faith.'

And then the devil receives his compensation from the poet. It is the devil's hour of death, and perhaps even a whole day's holiday. He can snore in the poet's blood with the sleep of the dead. He has grown bored of the poet and begun to hate him: how many times has his fool's tail and absurd horns flashed in life, in history, so may he sleep as long as possible in the blood of art.

Wise and sad, the muse and the angel fly to the poet with scorched wings. They give the poet a present of golden butterflies: Lear talks of them to Cordelia when they are led off to prison. The theatre of compassion lights its lamps, the curtain falls on the theatre of cruelty; now there is nothing for it to play.

The father tells his daughter that they have found each other and that there is no power which would be capable of separating them: they will be happy in the prison cell, they will still have songs, fairy tales, the right to forgive one another.

Perhaps these are the foolish words of an old man who has reverted to second childhood? It can seem like this if you see two people on an empty stage, and besides them, a few figures dressed in the conventional costumes of soldiers. But if you see the whole reality, the whole dimension? Then it is no longer a monologue, but the scene of battle, the climax of the conflict: the action includes a whole army, a younger general, the full strength of the conquerors, and two weaponless and weak people: an old man and a young woman. And then the featherweight words gather strength and the two powerless prisoners become the conquerors.

The words are addressed not only to the daughter, but to the steel, the cruelty and the violence.

Edmund hurriedly orders the prisoners to be secretly executed. Why does he have to eliminate them so urgently, as quickly as possible? Because people are afraid of them, they inspire fear. Edmund declares: 'Men are as time is' (in the original: people are like the times they live in[1]); if you submit to the times, you will rise high in the world.

But time is powerless before the fearlessness of father and daughter who have found each other. They can be killed but no one can take away from them that moment of happiness – like a blinding flash of light – not even the whole army has the strength to do that. The same army, which has achieved its aim, and which for some reason (history knows why) in a short space of time disappears without trace, leaves not one single soldier behind, not one loyal soldier who will defend his general. What then is the true reality?

Of course in a moment a noose will be thrown round Cordelia's neck (what could be simpler), and Lear will follow her. But surely they are the heroes of the tragedy, not living people. They are more real than living mortal people, the heroes of tragedy do not die, they come to life again with each new generation and again accompany them along the same path, repeating the same words, the answer to the new Edmund. The rebuff of darkness. The repulse of the plague.

NOT FAR FROM my old school in Kiev is the Kievo-Pechersky Monastery. During the first years of the Revolution we used to play truant from lessons and go down to the caves where the relics of the hermits lay. We would have to climb down narrow steps, squeeze through small passages and under low ceilings. The burial chambers were dark; the dim flames of slender wax candles lit up the niches where the remains lay in open coffins. Old women wailed in the damp gloom and one could hear the mutterings of prayers and someone

[1] Pasternak's Russian translation can be translated literally as 'Man must accommodate himself to the bending of the age' [trans.].

sobbing. I pretended to be brave and did not let my school-friends see that I was frightened; because it was dark, and one had to find one's way bent double, and because of the decaying cassocks, the shrivelled bodies in the coffins, the wailing, I felt oppressed and could not think of anything else but getting out as quickly as possible into the fresh air, the light, and being able to stand up straight.

A few years ago I went back to Kiev. I had difficulty in finding the house in which I had spent my childhood: there were new buildings and a completely different, strange street. Nor could I find the place where the school had been. But the entrance to the Monastery caves was just the same, and I climbed down into the burial chambers once again. Exactly the same feeling came over me as I walked, bent double. I could not wait for the moment of emerging into the light and straightening up.

There was the same dark oppressiveness as there had been for decades, for thousands of years. The constricted, confined space was no space; there was nothing human, it was impossible to stand upright...

It is impossible to imagine. Total darkness. All light has gone from people's faces. A wailing, but not one articulate sound. Bands of the Black Hundreds, embroidered miniature portraits of the Tsar and Tsarina on shrouds, no foreheads, no eyes, only black holes for mouths gaping wide in a scream . . . maddened punitive detachments of White Guards, followers of Petlura in clumsy jackets and fancy Caucasian hats, whistles, halloos, whoops, shots fired into the night. Night. Shattered street lamps, windows without lights. People are afraid of the light. Light means death. It is all delirious raving, a caricature, the only reality is not being able to stand upright; the threat of death – this is the only thing which is like real life.

People are afraid of noises, of words, they are afraid of their own thoughts.

This is my idea of the black death. I saw more than enough of this sort of darkness or black death in my early childhood.

IN ORDER TO reach the isolated spot in the mountains of the Altai we had to ride a long way along narrow paths. In 1930 we made the film *Alone.* It was then that I met Kondraty Tanashev. He was a professional shaman and knew his business. He worked on real fuel, never free-wheeling: an epileptic, he knew the signs, how to take advantage of an oncoming fit. Besides that, he was an inveterate drunkard.

He used to heal sick children before my very eyes in the dark, smokey yurt.[1] He would strike his tambourines with a stick, wail,

[1] A nomad's tent [trans.].

intone some sort of incantation in a husky voice and then leap up, twirl round and round, stamping his boots. He had a good sense of rhythm. Accelerandos, unexpected pauses, syncopation – he knew how to use them all. The big tambourine was made after the ancient models; inside the rim on the cross-piece was carved the dark wooden head of the god Ulgen with iron eyebrows and nose and copper bells. Tanashev alternated between striking the leather, tightly stretched over the rim, with sharp taps, and shaking the tambourine so that the bells rang. He wore long narrow rags sewn to his body with some shrivelled rubbish (frogs or tiny creatures) on the ends. When he spun round, the ribbons unwound, the hearth flared up from the movement, the yurt filled with smoke, it became difficult to breathe, one's eyes smarted, but the shaman speeded up the rhythm of his movements, struck the tambourine more frequently, everything clanged, jingled, and you could hear hoarse cries. And suddenly Tanashev would fall to the ground, as if mown down, his body would writhe in the throes of a fit (real or simulated), his eyes would protrude and his mouth froth.

We had come to laugh at his performance. However we were in no mood for laughing.

We took Tanashev to Leningrad to film him in the studio. He obligingly repeated (several times) the whole gamut of his incantations. Nothing of their power came over on the screen. There was nothing for it but to ride for five days, to catch sight of the decaying horse-hide on the pole at the entrance to the yurt (knowing that it had been skinned from a live horse), to sit with smarting eyes, with a sick child lying on a rag, the eyes of its mother watching the epileptic drunkard with alarm and hope.

The horror did not at all lie in the ritualistic rhythms and the magic incantations.

Tanashev's adaption to civilization was sad: he became a complete alcoholic and I do not think he ever successfully carried out his work again on returning home.

SHAKESPEARE SAW A black cloud encroaching on history, a black death threatening to annihilate history, to return it to primeval horror. And he expressed it with all the demonic power of tragedy. But he also wrote of how Cordelia found within herself the strength to say 'no', and of Edgar's brave behaviour, and, first and foremost, of the fearlessness of Lear's thoughts. 'I must be cruel' said Hamlet, however this is only the beginning of the sentence. 'I must be cruel only to be kind.'

Chapter Twenty-three

A YOUNG ENGLISHMAN came to watch the shooting and made me a present of a small volume, bound in red leather, an ancient edition of *Lear*. I thumbed through the first pages and was immediately held by the famous quotation from Charles Lamb which is used as the epigraph. Now I remembered these words once again: 'But the Lear of Shakespeare cannot be acted,' Lamb maintained. 'The contemptible machinery by which they mimic the storm which he goes out in, is not more inadequate to represent the horrors of the real elements, than any actor can be to represent Lear.'[1]

Thank you. The gift came just in time for Easter; before filming the same storm which is beyond the powers of a director to portray. Nevertheless Lamb was referring to the stage; the cinema of course presents other possibilities. What exactly? Well, technical ones at least: the technicians (provided they are amenable) can indeed produce such buckets from the fire brigade and run the wind machines with such force that it is difficult to stand upright. So does the superiority of the cinema lie only in clever simulation, imitation? It is at this very point in the tragedy that both the actions and the links (very complex ones) between the characters and nature are very far from naturalistic.

On the other hand Shakespeare's world is still realistic; even the excursions beyond the boundaries of the living are materialistic: the ghost of Hamlet's Father feels the cold of the morning air, sees the lights of the glow-worms going out, dawn is approaching just as it does on our earth; the colour of the sky changes in the same way, as does the outline of the earth. In essence this world is utterly indistinguishable from our own. If I had thought otherwise I would never have had the courage to make films of Shakespeare – I understand very little about ancient Britain or Celtic legends. In order to create poetry on screen you must first of all discover the prose in it.

It would seem to be a perfectly clear situation but unfortunately not only did it not lighten the burden of the director's task, on the contrary, it made him increasingly conscious of the limitations of cinematic convention. The unfortunate truth is that we often

[1] Charles Lamb 'On the Tragedies of Shakespeare' in *Essays*, Folio Society 1963, p. 32 [trans.].

interpret both prose and poetry too directly. Marina Tsvetayeva wrote, 'I will never believe in prose, it doesn't exist, I have never once met it in my whole life, not even the tip of its tail.' (Her poetry is perhaps an example of the close connection between poetry and prose). 'When beneath everything, behind and above everything there are gods, disasters, spirits, fates, wings, tails – what sort of "prose" can you possibly have? When everything is a revolving globe with an inside of fire!'

I don't think I have ever read a better or more accurate description of *Lear* itself. It is as if Tsvetayeva had this very play in mind and was trying to convey with complete accuracy what takes place and how it takes place. Of course there is one reservation, the words in inverted commas, 'prose'. Does that mean that there is another sort of prose, without inverted commas? Perhaps you can also catch the tip of its tail? Of course everything – on the revolving globe and within it – is fire, but the outside, what is in front of us and what we are used to seeing, is earth. It is a moving substance whose quality we are capable of grasping. And even if the properties change in this movement, so that new things appear before us, this is also reality.

The flashing of lightning and torrents of water are very insignificant manifestations; 'the storm' is a different reality into which the heroes have been flung together with the landscape which has been discovered, beyond the boundaries of the world in which they lived. They have been buffetted, blown out of life. In bad weather? Is this really the essence of the scene? The more exactly the bad weather is reproduced, the more 'prosaic' will it appear. This night is not fixed by the movement of the barometer's hand from right to left ('rain', 'wind and rain', 'storm') but by an upheaval, a distortion of relationships, a break with the normal state of affairs. This means all relationships including the relationship between man and space.

Stanislavsky taught that if you are playing a miser, you must look for the times when he is generous, and, having mastered the evil side, uncover a moment of kindness in him, otherwise the part will be a conventional stereotype. Every shot of the storm where there is no storm (rain and wind) is precious to me.

In his plans Gordon Craig violated proportions, lengthened verticals and sent his heroes away into an infinite distance. He understood the visual aspect of Shakespearean catastrophe, the confusion of perspectives, the threat of emptiness. In his sketch of the 'storm' almost the whole sheet of paper was taken up by a weaving together of willow branches (the motif of the hovel) – a gigantic basket trap? the labyrinth of a spider's web – and only in the furthest depths (accentuated by the movement of lines going into the distance) are three tiny silhouetted figures: Lear, Edgar and the Fool.

The linking of visual portrayal with sound is not easy. Sound travels over space and changes its shape. No-one is surprised by the epithet 'silence' in describing a landscape. It can be not only silent but also dumb. Innokenty Annensky also wrote of 'dumb squares' ('the deserts of dumb squares where people were executed before dawn').

In defining his plan for the Chapel at Rondchamps, Le Corbusier described its architecture as 'a visual acoustic'.

The action in the stormiest part of Act III must unfold consecutively, even peacefully: at first it is everyday action – Lear leaves Gloucester's homely mansion; the doors close behind him, creaking on their hinges; he walks further through the back yards of the house, through 'prose'; the horses quiver, sensing the approaching storm, the servants take down the clothes which have been hanging out on a line; the guards pull the heavy gates to, behind Lear's retreating back. And then the prose changes to poetry. Man no longer walks through the rooms and lands of an estate, but through the threatening lands of tragedy. The proportions have suddenly altered, man is insignificantly small, powerless, defenceless, and the expanse is enormous and hostile.

We wanted to shoot the 'visual acoustic' in the David Garedza Desert[1] (in Georgia). The massive scale of the place bowled one over. One's eyes were confronted with infinity. There was nothing living here, only endless tiers of rocks; Leonardo da Vinci's paintings have similar landscapes, visible through the windows. The Madonna and Child warmly continuing life, and beyond the boundaries of the hovel – a distant, cold planet, eternity.

We wanted to make the transition to this landscape unnoticeable, without it being felt. Fragments of the same scenery were to link together the stone halls of the fortress of Ivangorod[2] and the Georgian desert; we had to put up a piece of gate, the boundaries round the estate (as they were in Narva) in the David Garedza Desert as well – so that the panorama turned, Lear found himself in empty space, insignificantly small amidst the enormity of distant piles of rock. It would probably have been difficult to have found a better place for the storm. But our allotted time for shooting was running out; we had no chance of making any more expeditions. We had to find 'the universe' in small, cosy Estonia, where the landscape is peaceful, the flat fields bring peace to the soul.

What could we do? . . .

[1] Named after David Garedzeli, a sixth-century Georgian philosopher. [trans.].

[2] i.e. Narva, Ivan's town [trans.].

CHILDREN ARE OFTEN asked the following riddle: how can you ferry a wolf, a goat and a cabbage in the same boat? It is a simple problem. But how do you accommodate an artistic idea with production possibilities, the programmes of several different theatres (where your actors are engaged), the weather (never what you want) and a host of other elements which do not synchronize, or harmonize but which contradict each other? . . .

The wolf when joined by the goat capsizes the boat into which the film director would have climbed, and they throw the ball of cabbage at his head so that at least he shouldn't be able to come up to the surface.

So, what can you put your trust in?

Chance.

LONG BEFORE WE arrived at Narva we could still see the smoke in the sky. The thick black columns would sometimes look like a thunder cloud. This was the Baltic GRES[1], a power station run on shale oil. Six chimneys between 150 and 180 metres high were no small hindrance in choosing our location. I looked at the smoke-filled sky trying to see whether one could take the blackness for a storm cloud. But from whatever angle you shot it, it would be evident that it was smoke. We couldn't find anything. Not far from the power station there was a high sandy embankment. Somehow on our way to the shooting, Gritsus decided that he must at all costs climb it. Of course we were hardly likely to find enough space to shoot the whole scene there, but it could be the place for a few separate perspectives: it was difficult to find a suitable location outside the boundaries of Ivangorod.

A quite unbelievable meadow stretched out before us. It was covered as far as the horizon with uniform light-grey, almost white layers, curving a little at the edges, and the rhythm of this endless repetition of curving lines was so clear that it was as if molten lava had suddenly been frozen and the waves of ash had turned to stone. It was the surface of some as yet undiscovered planet. There was nothing real about it but at the same time it was completely real. It would have been impossible to imagine anything like it and even more impossible to construct on such a large scale with such accurate form, uniform and yet breaking at the edges. Nothing like it existed on earth and yet there it was in front of us, an irrefutable reality. This scenery had been prepared for us over the decades by the outpouring of the ashes from the burnt shale.

[1] State Regional Electric Power Station [trans.].

It was a visual image which contained within it the possibilities of the most varied associations. It was something like the beds of dried-up rivers, but more lifeless, harsh. It made an ideal area for the action of a tragedy; we could not have dreamed of a better one. Here we could shoot many sequences and of course first and foremost the 'storm'. Now it was no longer only the wind machines and sheets of water which defined the image, but the very rhythm of this dead earth, in whose folds the tiny figures of people were lost, pawns in the encroaching terror of emptiness.

We commandeered the water tower; from its highest point the horizon looked bent (a distortion which the wide screen and fish-eye lens gives to a straight line); it looked as if a man was running round the earth's globe.

There is nothing better than these sudden chances; everything immediately becomes interesting and new facets of expression are discovered. We decided to substitute the camera for wind. The rails were laid and the camera like the wind chased after the Fool and Lear, lost them in the emptiness of space (the lines of the folds alone looked like rushing gusts of wind). There were no extraneous details, only the relationship between the insignificantly small figures and the vast, barren planet.

Our construction began on one part of this location; the frame for the fence by the gates of Gloucester's estate had already appeared; there was very little work left to do and we could get to work on the main scenes. Meanwhile we shot Gloucester's death and the sequences where Lear and the Fool meet in the storm. We solemnly christened this place 'Plateau Phoenix'. Not far from our area, we heard a noise, the pumps had started; a sort of grey fluid poured out of the hoses on to the ground.

'Phoenix is no longer' Shapiro, the producer, said to me in greeting, almost in tears – 'They have broken through the pipes and buried the ash.'

From a letter to Yuri Yarvet

The storm is not only the weather in which we are shooting, but also your partner. Get to know it. The closer the relationship you have with it, the more expressive it will be. Listen to its answers (thunder) look into its eyes (lightning), even if it deafens and blinds you. It is not of course an ordinary speaker but after all Lear is no ordinary man. And, the main thing is not to let your partner get the better of you; cross-question it, search for its meaning, and when you have grasped what it means (as far as you think) enter into an argument with it. Grasp the points of contact, the face-to-face fits of exultant evil. This is the dialogue, the action. The usual interpretation of this scene as representing the chaos of the hero's spiritual world through the boisterousness of the elements seems to me to be literary and static. Here the most important things are movement and conflict. The main concern is not chaos (madness), but the fight against chaos: what is the reason for breaking all links, for the inhumanness of it all? Where are the roots of evil hidden? Lear converses with the elements straight-forwardly, as an equal; he demands their sympathy and gets angry with them for being heartless. The thought broadens out into a generalization – world evil – and becomes definably concrete: in the hovel the main subject of interest turns out to be right by his side, under his nose – the naked, defenceless body of Poor Tom. And again – he turns to the world as a whole, to nature itself.

The stronger the emotion, the more restrained must be the mode of expressing it – only then will your eyes really light up. For us a sentence spoken softly is worth its weight in gold. The sharp changes, the sudden reversals of fortune – all these are already in the past, at the beginning when Lear was 'normal' (i.e. to all intents and purposes out of his mind). Here there is no spilling out of emotion, but a concentration of thought turned towards the deepest subjects, the link between different substances, the essence of life. What makes people as they are?

I think that your best scenes so far have been the shots where you show the beginnings of madness, the conversation with blind Gloucester, and the meeting with Cordelia.

We are about to tackle the most decisive scenes – the storm, captivity and death.

They are difficult scenes, the most difficult and decisive, what you might call the main ones. But are there such things as mere scenes in this play? Alas, dear Yuri Yevgeniyevich, this work has no such thing.

THEY MERGE (the storm and man) and then divide into two arguing opponents: the evil of history, and man questioning history. The argument is out in the open where man has been thrown from all directions by all his fellows and rejected by history. This is the whole essence.

Russian culture has experienced (in completely different forms of course) similar frenzied demands for a lifelike reply from abstract concepts. So Belinsky, in one of his 'extreme' periods, stamped on Hegel's 'philosophical cap' – demanding that the absolute spirit should answer for all the atrocities of the inquisition.

The beginning of the scene is utterly quiet, or rather lyrical. Lear has been abandoned by everyone. There is no-one left on earth to whom he can turn for help. Now he can converse only with the sky. Man and sky. A very old man and a primeval sky. Lear addresses the sky (the gods) and says that if they are as old as he is, they should take pity on him.

The problem becomes clearer: we must convey this folk-like

parallelism in visually concrete terms – grey (sky grey) hair, grey (like grey hair) sky with dishevelled clouds; the sky also cries – we must shoot far off rain so that the tonality of the face, the clouds and hair is one and the same.

The sky does not reply at all as man supposes it will: an enormous black wing slowly covers the world. Here man's voice is powerless, the voice of Shostakovich's music must be heard.

Day after day the sky over Narva remained clear, bright, without one single cloud. My student director, August Baltrushaitis, set off in search of sky – for the 'black wing', the 'grey-haired clouds', for the 'exultant evil' (he was also given this last task); the weather forecasters mapped out a course for him (a long way away since all the thunder-storms were in the east), and on the way he somehow had to shoot a herd of wild horses, sniffing the oncoming storm, and wild animals running into the undergrowth. The other team was already shooting the fire, the wild oxen breaking free.

We were sent some shots of wolves and bears being startled from Moscow. On the screen the wolves looked like well-groomed sheepdogs, and the bears forcibly reminded one of the picture on the sweetpaper wrapping 'Clumsy Mishka'.[1]

YARVET, A FEARLESS, masculine character, suffers from vertigo. Without knowing this I had devised the following plan: Lear stands on the very edge of the high wall of the fortress near the tower; Cordelia's hanging corpse is visible through a break in the tower. Looking down from this narrow unenclosed platform – with a sheer drop at one's feet – was unpleasant enough. Now it appeared that we would have to leave this shot out.

As it was explained later, Gritsus had nevertheless persuaded Yarvet that it was imperative to shoot him on this very wall.

Waiting for the shooting to start Yarvet stood with closed eyes, convulsively clutching on to the small column which had been placed at his back. There was a pop and the shooting began. Yarvet immediately moved away from the column; he stretched his arms out in front of him, threw his head back, and his body crumpled as if in the throes of unbearable pain. He gave a long slow groan.

As far as I was concerned it was excellent. But one of the team looked at the lens and said that a re-take was necessary. Again he stood with eyes closed and holding on to the column. A pop. And again: 'Permission to re-take – the wind changed and there was

[1] Name of a popular Russian sweet (Russian bears are traditionally called Misha) [trans.].

smoke in front of the camera.' Then the pan handle vibrated the camera and there was no option, 'We will have to do it again, I am sorry, it didn't work . . .'

I began to watch the actor. He was carried down, violently retching, and numb with cold. The fantastic blue eyes were shining.

'It is a good thing that we did shoot it there,' he had difficulty in uttering his words while he was incapable of controlling his shuddering. 'It had to be done. Of course it was a good thing . . .'

One of the greatest qualities of his gift is his spiritual grace, and, whatever he was acting, even the coarsest displays – you could always feel the true hallmark of artistry.

'It's not that he is a bad actor,' Dovzhenko said of one of the cast in a production he was doing, 'It's that he is spiritually uneducated.'

Yarvet above all is spiritually educated. It is not only a question of the number of books he has read; this is not everything; even a man who cannot read or write can possess this quality. A degree on finishing a course at an establishment of higher education does not insure one against emotional ignorance or spiritual coarseness. These are the innate, organic qualities of talent; they can be developed but they are not for hire.

It is not only the roles which an actor has already played which are important to his fate but there are also some roles which it is important that he should not have played. Yarvet was not counting on making an easy hit. He did not make up with the puny beard of an endearing but capricious old man – the combination of foolery and sentimentality is alien to his art; he had not learnt to pronounce empty words importantly, between deeply significant draws on a cigarette – he was not master of the art of diluting the plot.

When work was going well, happiness lit up his face and his eyes shone. But there was no self-satisfaction in the emotion he was feeling, it was just good that things were going well; such work had to be done as well as possible. He was a tireless worker. He rehearsed only at full strength. He never saved his resources, or spared himself. He was goodnatured towards his opposites even when he was having to act opposite a stereotype who was incapable of stringing two words together.

IT SEEMED THAT the geography of the film was beginning to take shape. There were practically no more white spots on the map. This was the route for the journey from one end of the kingdom to the other: the palace – castles – estates – fields – roads – cliffs, a sharp precipice – the sea. There the road ended. This was the end of it all. But the important thing is that this journey happens twice. The fortunes of war are unstable: at first the opponent penetrates to the very heart of the country, then he is cast out of his position of power. And the main characters follow the course of the war, back along the same road, only proceeding from the other direction. The roads are the same but now they pass by ruins and ashes. And finally they come to the place where they began: this is where it all started, here are the charred stairs by the ruined tower – these are the steps up which the King climbed towards the sky itself; here he cursed his daughter, and when the people, far below, fell on their knees before him, as if before a god, he did not give them so much as a glance.

The characters return to the source of their destinies. Here two brothers joked with each other before the beginning of the palace ceremony. Now they meet again in order to fight to the death. The illegitimate Edmund has achieved everything he wanted; now he is Earl of Gloucester, while the rightful heir has become a nonentity – Poor Tom. Edgar took the shirt off the back of a dead soldier, and picked up a sword from the field of battle, now he had a covering for his nakedness and something to kill with. His face is shielded by a soldier's helmet. Retribution has no face.

THE DUELS IN *Hamlet* and *Lear* are very different. In Elsinore it is a sport, a game; umpires make sure the rules are observed, keep time with their watches so that the sportsmen should not wear themselves out, and award points. There are not many fans: the King and Queen and a few courtiers. It is in one of the castle halls; there are ingratiating faces and elegant clothes. An insignificant detail destroys the game – a drop of poison on the sharpened tip of a rapier. There is another poison which Claudius puts into the chalice. What does the poison look like? Like a pearl which seven Princes of Denmark have boasted of. This is how people are killed.

The duel between Edgar and Edmund is fierce and brutal. There is no umpire and no rules. There is a challenge to fight, an accusation of betrayal and treason, and an insult. Each opponent has one desire: to finish the whole accursed business and to kill. What sort of surroundings can this duel have? It is a town after an invasion, dead bodies lie about, the fires are not yet put out. The soldiers mark out the area of the fight with lances. An arena? A ring? The crowd presses against the fencing, a roar accompanies each blow. This is the sort of tournament it is.

I asked Ivan Koch – he produced the duels for all my productions and films – to concentrate not on the effectiveness of the fight (I would like it not to be at all effective), but on the psychology of the fighters. Edgar has come not to show off his fencing but to execute his opponent. He is biding his time, waiting for the moment to make one stroke only, the kill. Edmund is stronger and more skilful; he rushes into the attack, brings down a rain of strokes, intimidates his opponent, trying to throw him into confusion. But the fighter with the closed visor deflects the blows and waits. The man of iron will and action makes a dash for a still stronger freedom. This retaliation comes not from a single opponent but from other people, the expressions of whose eyes has shaken him.

Edmund is defeated even before the fight begins. Suddenly time has deserted him, the pace of time has changed. Why were Lear and Cordelia so fearless? Why did the weak Duke of Albany come out from under his wife's heel and destroy her plans? Where did this faceless man come from who was deflecting his blows? Why was he so assured? How many more were there like him? And what linked them together?

In order to overcome his fear (was it death he was afraid of?), Edmund tore the helmet from the other's head: who was it, who capable of frightening him? And he was overwhelmed by a greater fear. And then what? There is no need to look further: Edgar finally struck him, or Edmund purposely impaled himself on Edgar's sword.

It is all shrouded in a leaden grey mist, smoke, and soot. The hour of judgement.

THE COLD WEATHER hit Narva unexpectedly making our breath steam. It had been snowing all day. We swept the snow away from the foreground but white spots were clearly visible in the distance on the black ruins. It was already getting dark earlier; the day's shooting was becoming very short. We would not finish it in time. We hurried, shooting without a break; after finishing the day shift we would immediately start shooting the night scenes. No one had had any days off for a long time. If only we could finish it. It is the heart-breaking norm of how things turn out in art. The location reminded one of the hive of activity in our films on food production: the wind tore down the foundations (the remains of the sets), one moment it would be raining, the next snowing, everyone was wearing quilted jackets, covered in mud, frozen, voices hoarse from shouting and with inflamed eyes. Hurry. Let's get on! We were behind schedule. No, we would not finish. Snow was forecast for the next day. Again we hurried, some one went off somewhere for something which was missing – of course the most vital object. But where was a car?

There was no car. In the office they tore their hair – the master plan was going up in smoke!

It was a terrible situation. The only consolation was that Shakespeare wrote his plays more or less under the same conditions (I am deeply convinced of this); he had a deadline, had to hurry, finishing the dialogues on the day of the première.

SHAPIRO, THE PRODUCER, was not on location. He was never late. When we had finished shooting I went to the hospital. A man who never for one moment stood still while he was working lay motionless; a thin rubber tube was attached to his bandaged arm: drops of glucose were being let into his veins; there was another tube with oxygen in his nostrils. The condition of the patient according to the doctor was 'of average gravity'.

I went away to prepare for the next day's shooting.

What sort of ending does the play have – noble grief which purges the soul, a paying of last rites before the final curtain. There is nothing like that in *Lear*: neither reconciliation nor edification. In describing this tragedy, Alexander Blok consistently repeated two words over and over again: 'dry and bitter'.

And dry and bitter means empty and gloomy; the charred stumps of trees stand out in the darkness, there is blood and dirt. National grief, black days.

In *Hamlet* I did not want to film a magnificent funeral at all; I do not like ceremonious shots. But I could not think up any alternative and the point of such a departure for the main characters was clear to me. It was Shakespeare, not Fortinbras, who ordered that there should be music, gunshots, 'all the rites of war'. Why was this necessary? The troops gave the salute, and the nation's flags unfurled over the body of the dead student.

There is nothing like this in *Lear*. There is no time for paying homage to the dead; life must be given to the living, they must be fed. Tears are not what is needed, but to carry the 'weight of this sad time'. The dead bodies are carried through the town which has been captured after a siege. What can be left? A heap of ashes, man's grief. I try to visualize the scene in all its reality. There is nothing. And there aren't any stretchers either (what sort of Red Cross would they have?). Let them adapt whatever comes to hand: boards are knocked together, the burnt ones being shorter than the others. The door from a ruined house? It will do. There is hurrying and a general confusion. But one must be able to see the faces, the masques of death, they are all different: death struck Goneril and Regan in a moment of fury, hatred – the expressions of fury and hate have frozen into grimaces; the faces of Lear and Cordelia are calm; let us pay them the honour they deserve and let them be carried on the same stretcher.

In the whole scene there are probably only two peaceful faces: the father and his youngest daughter.

In planning this I wanted to achieve at the same time complete reality and also an element of folklore, imperceptibly showing through the reality. The end echoes the beginning: the King and his three daughters are carried through the ruins of the kingdom. The Fool who amused the King at the beginning – the boy in the dog's coat, put on inside out – turned out to be both the last man to stay by him and the only one to mourn him.

I couldn't bear to lose the Fool half-way through the play. Oleg Dal helped me to grow even fonder of this character. A tortured boy, taken from among the servants, clever, talented – the voice of truth, the voice of the poor; art driven into a dog's kennel with a dog's collar round its neck. Let one of the soldiers carrying the bodies finally aim a kick at his neck with his boot, to get him out of the way! But his voice, the voice of the home-made pipe, begins and ends this story; the sad, human voice of art.

Such a shot could probably end it but Shakespeare ends the story with Edgar.[1] We rehearsed the final words with Leonard Merzin.

From a Letter to Boris Slutsky

I am writing to you to ask you to edit Edgar's last lines. The thought in the original is deeper than in all the translations. I will give you an example:

> The weight of this sad time we must obey;
> Speak what we feel, not what we ought to say.
> The oldest hath borne most: we that are young
> Shall never see so much nor live so long.

The measure of an actor's talent has always seemed to me to be his eyes, not the way he reads lines. At today's shooting Leonard Merzin tried acting the whole speech without uttering a word. And I recognized Shakespeare's thought in his eyes. Perhaps the audience would also read these lines in the look he directed at them? . . .

From a letter to I. S. Shapiro *October 1969, Leningrad*

At last I have arrived home and can write to you.

These last few days (weeks? months?) have been like a bad dream: there was illness, wild and ferocious weather, mud up to the knees which

[1] In fact it is Albany [trans.].

never dried off, and the sort which you would never be able to clean off; a terror at what was disappearing out of reach, or rather that the possibility of shooting the most important scenes was vanishing, and that if we did not shoot them immediately, literally at that very moment – the snow would fall and the actors would fall irrevocably ill, and the team would collapse.

Adomaitis, lightly clothed, lay around for hours on the cold wet stones; Shendrikova walked about with a high temperature in nothing but a shirt and with bare feet; Merzin acted the last sequence with an inflamed middle ear, and I myself, to be honest, could hardly stand upright.

Before our departure I fearfully sat down in our viewing room: great heavens what was awaiting me?

Strange as it may appear, we seemed to have emerged out of all this chaos even if there had been great losses. The fundamentals of the scenes were there and there was the possibility of improving the unsuccessful bits with some additional shooting. But what a lot of work there was still to be done! . . .

We were forced to shoot the long shots of the duel (the last day) in bright sunlight. As often happens in Narva by some miracle the weather suddenly cleared, and instead of the cold and darkness there was a blue sky without a cloud in it. But the scene had already been shot on dark misty days. We had with great difficulty gathered a large crowd together on a Sunday and there was no hope of the weather changing.

Gritsus had got even thinner (and he seemed to have nothing left to lose). He threatened to refuse to shoot, shook his fist at no-one in particular and of course the shooting began – what else was there to be done? One of the shots (the only one) saved the situation a little: the wind changed direction, smoke passed across the location and to think that I nearly shouted 'Cut'! It was this very shot which would allow us to tie the two ends together: the smoke itself (looking down from above) turned out to be indistinguishable, but a shadow from it passed over the ground looking just as if clouds were uncovering and then covering the sun. So long as the editing proved successful.

After each take, Adomaitis, exhausted, paused for breath, and for a long time paced about the location while he tried to regain control of himself. This was the only way to act Edmund's death (or rather the moment of truth before his death).

The passage of the two sisters through the fire, as if through the war, was not bad.

The shots with the crowd – Lear addressing the people 'Howl, howl, howl, howl!' and the carrying of the bodies was only just completed. What Hell it all was! It had been raining all day almost incessantly. Our coats and costumes were soaked through, there wasn't one tiny piece of dry material anywhere to enable us to avoid laying Yarvet down on wet boards. There was no longer anywhere to take shelter (the sets had all been burnt, even the auxiliary huts); the crowd actors were liable to go off at any moment. To crown our sorrows, an inquisitive man climbed up on to the wall of the fortress, slipped and fell down on to the rocks below; he was taken away in an ambulance.

And still we went on shooting.

Of course we should have had the dead Lear and Cordelia for longer in the shot, the soldiers should have walked at a more even pace, and the camera should have moved more rhythmically. There were many things that were wrong. I was in despair while we were shooting: the most difficult scenes had been set up in a hurry, the actors had only just got off the train. It was pouring with rain. And in spite of it all, something had been achieved, we could take the close-ups later, under easier conditions.

Then we shot the Duke of Albany (on Banionis' last day before going to East Germany where he was to play the part of Goya) – shot in one go all the remaining sequences from a number of different scenes. And, finally, on the last two days we did the end.

It was really snowing this time. The snow was piling up just as it does at Christmas. We cleared the location with shovels and it soon got covered over again. Snowflakes were clearly visible in the rays of light. We had to combine several shots by using pans in order not to have to move the apparatus, to avoid losing time in shifting it . . .

From a letter from Peter Brook *October 1969, Paris*

I saw a photograph of your *Lear* in *Sight and Sound* (in the same number that has a still from my film) and I was very glad to hear news of you. We filmed in quite dreadful conditions this winter in Denmark, but marvellous locations in Jutland, splendid local people for the supporting roles, beautiful horses – and of course very good actors!

Our entire work in the shooting was to create a flat coarse two-dimensional image (black and white) with an elimination of as much period detail as possible. We tried to reach a simple picture, not by non-period, which is impossible, but by basing everything on shapes and objects that are dictated by climatic conditions, So we've made a sort of Lapland Eskimo world, which is not historical – in the sense that Eskimos have used the same functional shapes for the last 1,000 years.

Then this form of realism was distorted to encompass the contradictory styles of the writing. The result is both very primitive and mystic (England as a small rural kingdom) – and also medieval.

> Now in the editing, we are searching to interrupt the consistency of style, so that many-levelled contradictions of the play can appear. As a result, we are cutting more and more ruthlessly, eliminating more and more text, so that the film which was 3 hours long, then 2½ hours a few weeks ago, is now shrinking to about 2 hours and a quarter!
>
> I am sure from what I understand of your intentions we are both trying to tell the same story. But with very different means within very different cultures.

It would be an interesting experiment to think of an idea for a film, to study the text, and then to forget about it and, after reading another book, or listening to the radio, or seeing something in a place you have never been to before, suddenly to remember your main idea and to discover in the words you had learnt by heart a different meaning, another action. Or, having grasped only an isolated detail, to reconstruct the links with life around it in such a way that these people seem to be close and you can study them in detail.

I find it interesting to work with an actor, and to try to see through his eyes (does he see in close-up what you mean him to see? or should you set him up on a different combination of circumstances?), trying to understand the nature of his soul, which is by nature different from that of any other actor, to feel the difference in the strings which you must touch in a special way in order to call forth an answering sound.

. . . And when Shostakovich unhurriedly takes off his jacket, drapes it round the back of his chair and walks over to the piano, 'Only you must forgive me,' he says as always, 'I will try and play it with one hand somehow, but it will be played by an orchestra'.

. . . And after a long search for suitable countryside you come to a pile of rocks which seem to you to be unmistakably like Lear's curses.

But the shooting sessions are terrible. Success, if that hour ever strikes, happens when you are busy looking the other way. Success is when the plastic idea is realized in the movement of the camera and the disposition of the characters, and you succeed in catching as you go along the actor's spiritual movement. When shooting, everything begins to slide and loses its shape for a thousand insignificant reasons: the details that work against you and the film are too many to count, and all you can do is to fight them not with inspiration or cunning but only with stubbornness. This is why during the last moments of a day's work you often get a feeling of failure; it did not turn out as it might have done, should have done.

There is a great difference between what is suffered and what is extorted in art. What is suffered ends peacefully, but what is extorted ends with nervous confusion and a mis-shapen form.

Chapter Twenty-four

From a letter to Dmitri Shostakovich December 1969

Dear Dmitry Dmitrievich

While our unwieldy household transfers itself from Estonia to Leningrad, I have had a chance to have a rest and think about what is to come next. The filming of the greatest part of the film has been completed, there remain only a few studio scenes and early in spring some shots on location. The main work is now in the cutting room and the places where there should be music are already clear. I have tried several times to draft out a plan for it on paper, but when you are concerned with *Lear*, there are many things which cannot be explained in words. I will attempt to do this now but ask you to forgive me in advance for a certain vagueness of definition.

General ideas. The place and character of the music are different from the music for *Hamlet*. There should be no stylization of antiquity. It should be the language of contemporary art which you use to express the contemporary world.

Main themes are born with far-away echoes long before they take definite shape. Something is in the air: a humming, anxious breathing, the march of time.

A call runs through the whole tragedy. To start with it is an ordinary sound. The beggars are moving, a tramp blows a horn: a hoarse long-drawn out sound, the most elemental. But then the call sounds again and the main characters answer it. They leave their imaginary, illusory life which they have lived up till now and join the majority of the people, the unhappiness and poverty. This is the call of life.

We also have the call of death (very short, 10–15 seconds). The moment before it sounds, an exceptionally strong premonition must be felt of the impending, irrevocable end. The moment of recognition of life's conclusion.

The longest musical episode is the war. We tried to show madness, chaos and destruction on the screen. But I would like the theme of the music to be associated not with ruin or the raging power of destruction but rather with grief, human suffering, which has no limits. Not some individual complaint but the grief of the whole people. In Shakespearean dimensions it is the lament of the earth itself. A requiem perhaps? Only not with an orchestra but the chorus alone and without words. Grief has no words, there is nothing but weeping: the women, the children and the men all weep.

There is altogether very little music which is directly linked with the action. In the play, when Lear wakes up after his illness Cordelia and the Doctor signal to the musicians. We have substituted the Fool for the musicians; he wandered in the footsteps of his master and turned up in the French camp. Now he is ordered to come closer and to play a tune on his pipe. It can be the same tune as his song.

At the end of the film there is complete destruction of the country which the King had wanted to bring happiness to. The soldiers carry the bodies of the King and his daughter through the ruins; only one person accompanies them – the exhausted Fool, hardly standing on two feet; he howls like a dog; in an attempt to console himself he gets out his pipe from force of habit. Charred remains, corpses, and in the silence the barely audible humming of the most simple and sorrowful song. Do you like the idea of such an ending?

We also have the music with which a small orchestra (a quartet) accompanies the supper at Goneril's house. It should be an elegant salon piece. While the music, which caresses ones ears, is playing, a shocking scene takes place: the daughter shouts at her father that he has turned her castle into a tavern, and the father answers her with curses.

The music does not accompany the shots, but transforms them. In the key episodes it wedges itself between events just as the lyrical digressions wedged themselves between the story line in *Dead Souls*.

The music should be the voice of the author.

The film directors of the twenties were young men. And I was probably the youngest of them all – I was nineteen when we were making *The Adventures of Oktyabrina*. I became accustomed to feeling the same age a lot later; the succeeding generation of directors were in fact older. And then suddenly a man who was even younger than I appeared in our midst.

When Dmitri Shostakovich was invited to come to the film studio in 1928 in order to compose the music for the silent film *The New Babylon* his face was almost childish. He wore clothes that artists never wore in those days: a white silk scarf, and a soft grey hat; he was carrying a large leather brief-case.

His room was simply furnished with books on a shelf, mostly Russian classics. He used ordinary phrases when he spoke, with a slight stutter, often quoting from Chekhov or Gogol and looking very pleased: as if to say, 'how well that sounded, what a good way of putting it'.

In those days music was used to reinforce the emotion of the film and, as they used to say, to illustrate the shots. The composer and I immediately agreed that the music would be linked with the inner meaning rather than external action and would develop contrary to the events, independent of the construction of the scene. Our general programme consisted of not illustrating or accompanying anything.

A can-can would suddenly burst through the score of tragic themes, the German cavalry galloped to Paris to Offenbach's *Belle Hélène*; the themes were intricately interwoven, the intonation changing from farce to pathos.

This music was played only for a few showings.

Not long afterwards I saw a rehearsal for *The Nose* in the Maly Opera Theatre. V. Dmitriyev's sets whirled and spun to rollicking galops and dashing polkas: the Gogolesque fantasmagoria had turned into noise and light. The peculiar mode of expression that characterized the new Russian art – which had links both with the most daring experiments in form and with urban folklore (shop signs and inn signs, old prints, orchestras on cheap bandstands) – all this burst in on the kingdom of *Aida* and *I Trovatori*. Gogolesque grotesque raged: was it farce or was it prophecy?

The orchestration was extraordinary, the lyrics – words which you would never expect to be sung ('And why do your hands stink?' sang Kovalev as the Major; there was even a romance set by Smerdyakov to Gogol's text); the unusual rhythms (crazy accelerandos – the assault of the Nose at the Police Station to the chorus of 'take that! and that! and that!'); the assimilation of everything which used to seem unpoetic, unmusical, vulgar but which in fact took on a lively intonation, a parody representing the fight with conventionality. Literature has long since learnt to value the unliterary word, the sketch, the force of reality.

It was a very lively production.

From a letter from Dmitri Shostakovich December 1970, Kurgan

> . . . I have composed new music for the Fool's pipes. I decided that it was unnecessary for him to sing. The pipes must be very sad . . .

I often heard Shostakovich repeating the same word:

> 'There must be a certain sadness in the songs (of Poor Tom).'

> 'Here is "the meeting between Lear and Cordelia": it will be sad.'
> – I have rewritten the finale (the Fool's pipes) to make it even sadder.'

When he is talking about music, Shostakovich uses simple everyday words; the vocabulary of aesthetics is alien to him. Rhetoric (even a hint of it) makes him frown. Elevated words about art inflict on him almost physical pain; an agonizingly fastidious expression comes over his face as if he has come into contact with something disgusting. Even the slightly unnatural is received by him as something which is insulting and shallow.

I have never succeeded in getting him to make a coherent criticism although I have often asked him. He regarded the film (even before editing) as a whole, trusting to his instincts. He not only did not want to judge separate faults and merits; he evidently found this approach to art unpleasant. If he doesn't like something, he says so in no uncertain terms and then changes the subject. He is infinitely kind-hearted. He speaks carefully and gently about the failures of people whom he likes, but nevertheless speaks.

THE CONTRAST BETWEEN the crowded buildings and endless lands, the weight of the stone outcrops and the movement of the clouds, the poverty-stricken peasants' vegetable plots and the sea – all this creates the landscape of tragedy. Tragedy also has a voice : the whole world of nature is drawn into a dialogue. The clouds pronounce soliloquies, fire and the sword speak to people.

I first heard these voices in the hall where before the revolution there used to be a variety theatre with tables and chairs for the audience. All that remained of the former magnificence were plaster alcoves and mouldings on the walls. The hall was now also used as a cloakroom, coats and hats flung over the chairs. There was a disorderly hubbub : jokes and arguments (as is usual in a film studio) mixed up with the sounds of tuning instruments.

There was a general movement and the talking stopped. Breakfasts and newspapers were put aside. The violin bows tapped in welcome on the music stands.

Shostakovich, looking younger, and having forgotten about his illness, was busy : some mistakes had come to light in the copying of the music, and the music had to be cut – it was longer than it should be. He covered the ground between the chair which he sat on for a moment and the conductor's stand over and over again with rapid steps.

It was the dialogue between Lear and the sky.

'You think I'll weep!'

On the screen Lear raises his eyes to the sky. 'I have full cause of weeping', he continues, not getting any answer, 'but this heart shall break into a hundred thousand flaws or ere I'll weep.'

The black edge of the storm-cloud slowly appears on the shot. Darkness encroaches and with it appears the sound. The sound is barely audible and grows stronger with the movement of the cloud; you cannot distinguish any particular instrument or musical phrase –

only a growing resonance without any material element, increasing together with the darkness, gathering strength until, when the screen is enveloped in total darkness, there is a deafening crash of clashing steel.

And it is all on the single note of 'F'.

ONE MORNING I heard the familiar voice saying on the telephone, 'In *Hamlet* we had Ophelia's tune. Why don't I write a tune for Cordelia?'

But I did not want to have themes for the main characters in *Lear*.

'All right', Shostakovich didn't argue, 'only we must find a place for contrasting music: there are already a lot of gloomy, heavy numbers. In other words we need some quiet music. We already have the voice of evil (the storm); it can be, perhaps . . . the voice of goodness.'

'The voice of truth', I suggest, 'one can continue the thoughts and feelings of Poor Tom (it is better to be a beggar, despised by everyone, than to be forced to lie).'

The voice at the other end immediately and willingly agreed.

Soon we were recording the music.

I couldn't wait to edit the scene. Now it had music it would of course become much more powerful.

E. A. Makhankova, the assistant editor whom I had worked with for many years, laid out on the table the sequences with Poor Tom (against a background of the peasants' fields and the scarecrow), and the sound track on which was written in red pencil: 'No 8. "The Voice of Truth".' We found the place for the beginning of the music and, already feeling pleasure in anticipation, I went into the viewing room.

Nothing knitted together or fitted. You could not hear the monologue over the music; the scene which had seemed to be a success was falling to pieces.

We spent all day trying out different combinations of sound and image. We changed the order of the shots, shortened and lengthened the film, tried making the music start in different places. It was useless. Nothing worked. The images and the sound both contained something sharply individual, intrinsically incompatible one with the other. This had never happened before: Shostakovich possesses an unerring feeling for what is taking place simultaneously on the screen.

What were we to do? To leave out the beautiful music which moreover had caught the distinct intonation of *Lear*? We would have to find some other places and to try new links in the editing. Poor Tom's soliloquy was put to one side. For the sake of experiment we took the first sequence with Cordelia which came to hand. Where should we start the music? Anywhere.

And immediately, in this accidentally found combination the music not only blended with the image but the scene, which I had watched many times, changed character. Something new and significant became apparent in our heroine.

Shostakovich had written down Cordelia's inner light and the whole sequence was transformed. In the same way in Rembrandt's portraits it is not only the eyes and the face which are animated but the material which the clothes are made of, the very air flickers, lives, and this breath of light is the most important thing about it – the triumph over the coarseness of the material: primed canvas, paint, over death (what had become of the merchants, their wives, of the artist himself?), over everything which was flat and restricted. With Cordelia there had now appeared on our screen a breath of goodness, the light of truth. It was something which words cannot grasp, which the most talented actress cannot portray – the very poetry of the image entered into the substance of the shots and transformed them.

But why did this poetry so very decisively not go with the image of Edgar – Poor Tom? Surely the elements of truth and goodness are strong in him as well? What was it that distinguished and separated the music from the character's spiritual life, so that the image and sound could not fuse together? It is of course difficult to provide the exact answer. I think that Shostakovich's 'Voice of Truth' was feminine. When he talked to me over the telephone about this piece he was probably already hearing Cordelia.

Before he dies, Lear remembers the voice of his youngest daughter. There are various ways of translating the word 'low' into Russian; the dictionary has a large number of definitions: tender, soft and so on, but the first one is – 'nizky'.[1] I had looked for an actress whose voice contained low sounds, peacefulness. 'The Voice of Truth' began with the deep, low sounds of stringed instruments.

Ophelia's voice was different altogether. It took a long time to find. The short piece (the dancing lesson, Polonius' daughter's first appearance) was to have been played on the guitar, then Shostakovich suggested that it should be played on the violin and piano. Then, a lute was brought from the museum of musical instruments for a new tape-recording. And then one began to hear Ophelia's frailty, her artificiality, her tenderness, doomed to perish.

Sometimes after a successful recording Shostakovich would talk of

[1] Meaning low in tone [trans.].

composing a symphony out of these numbers. But he never did. Other musicians composed suites out of them with his permission. His feeling for the image was so much an integral part that probably to have separated the music from it would have been very difficult. Only a few motifs were developed in his other compositions (the Fool's pipe).

In 1940 he wrote the music for my stage production of *King Lear*. But he did not use any of it for the film. The same thing happened with the music for *Hamlet*. When they made a television ballet to the music everything went to pieces. The choreographers had made out the different tempi but could not hear the thoughts behind the music.

IN POETRY WORDS only anticipate (or bring to a conclusion) spiritual movement: moments of silence are sometimes more significant than the lines themselves. In Shakespeare you only have to take one step in order to emerge into an expanse without sound. Gordon Craig and Pasternak understood this.

The reading of poetry is an endless sporadic process with hold-ups in order to let the audience take in the signal, the elusive sign: the way beyond the text, to one side, into the core of the poetry – towards the echoing meanings. Traces of life stand out in the white spaces between the lines, and in the margins round the page. One must take a breath and go back to the same place, read the text thoroughly and then put the book down (sometimes for a long time) and suddenly remember only a sign, a feeling, and read it over and over again, to find where before had been only words, a whole multitude of faces, movements and thoughts.

It is one thing to read the book, and another to see the play. On stage you cannot break the rhythm, the flow of the text. With films the process of reading is repeated during the editing. Cinematic action (as opposed to theatrical *mise-en-scène*) consists of incessant hold-ups, the switching from words to silence, from the text to the white spaces between the lines and the margins round the page. It is not the sequence of the story which is lying on the cutting table but the spiritual world of the author. This is why digressions from the text are often more important than the steady succession of events. One must stop them in order to give free rein to thoughts. You can then make events catch up, move them into their new stages in order of editing.

The last act is a mixture of planes: the fate of people and the fate of the thought. The few words Edmund has at the end of the play – who listens to them in the theatre? Lear has already lifted the body of his daughter into his arms in the wings – who has time for the repenting of a villain, for Edmund's desire finally to do one good deed 'against his own nature'?

But here, on the cutting table, we have time for it all. When all the voices are distinctly heard, people will understand what the one voice of the author is talking about.

We brought the role of Edmund to his last lines. Or rather not to the lines but to his spiritual ruin. It was not his plans that fell through: his main idea turned out to be without substance. The cult of will and power reduced him to powerlessness and cowardice.

They must both be left alone together at the end, the man and his burning obsession. The idea turned out to be empty, nothing, a void into which he is about to fall. Then it becomes not a monologue but a dialogue: man and retribution. It is a strange dialogue: eyes and emptiness, man and the gaping hole which he has dug for himself; it is there, suddenly gaping open in front of him.

The gaping hole is revealed to music. We recorded No. 10, 'The Call of Death', lasting for 11 seconds – for a small band of wind instruments. The conductor raised his baton, and the bronze sword struck its blow; the black shutter closed, the sound broke off. Silence. There was hardly time to take a breath. It was over. And for this, cunning plans were devised, lie upon lie and countless numbers of people killed.

We had been preparing for this dialogue from the very first rehearsals (for the moment without the other half) so that at this moment – in the last close-up – the total, the ruin of the inhuman idea, the Shakespearean dialectic of the struggle for power should be played out.

The Duke of Cornwall also heard the call of death in the film. Andrei Vokach played this moment of encroaching paralysis excellently – the feeling of emptiness, of flickering light. I wanted both the elder sisters to hear the same call but there was no room for the close-ups.

The music carried on a dialogue with the characters and changed the expression of their eyes. The area of action was immediately made wider and deeper although on the screen nothing more than a face showed. These shots would have lost their significance without music. We tried to show that the earth on which our actors walked was ordinary earth and that the circumstances of the action were real. But with the music there also appeared over it all the 'gods, disasters, spirits, fates, wings, and tails'. One can put it more simply: the metaphors and hyperboles which we had cut were reintroduced into the texture of the work.

OF COURSE SHOSTAKOVICH would not compose any 'war' music. He asked me to make do with the music that had already been written. We would have to manage by repeating parts of the 'storm', mixing the music and the sound effects when we re-ran the tape or using the sound effects on their own. I convinced myself that the effect would be starker like this. I wanted the sound in the film to be dry and bitter.

The sound producer, E. Vanunts, cooked up a whole kitchenful of witches. The sound operators wove a spell round us with their instruments, some drumming their feet on the floor, others throwing stones at metal sinks, hitting glass and shaking sheets of metal. We played back the noise sound track: the crackle of flames (there were many versions), the howl of the wind, some indefinable object grating, making a shiver go down one's spine, and thundering cannon.

All shooting had ceased in Lenfilm's courtyard for several hours, as such a deafening uproar was coming from the windows of our cutting room.

THE DAY BEFORE he left, Shostakovich unexpectedly said to me, 'I am going to try and compose music for a chorus all the same.'

Next morning he brought me the score for the 'lament'.

In spite of the fact that this number only lasted for four minutes, Shostakovich came up from Moscow once again for the recording.

NOW I UNDERSTOOD why there were so many faces of mourning in *Lear*, why different characters in the tragedy cry so often, even stern men sob, tears pouring down their cheeks, losing self-consciousness in their sympathy for others. And how many different meanings do tears have here? Cordelia wins over the King of France's army with her tears; tears can wage war, have healing powers, they can provoke shame, stir up a conscience; they burn, like drops of molten lead. All this is in the stage directions, in the text which I had covered with dirty marks because I did not know how to set up these scenes or how the actors should play them.

And I still don't know. But now, after hearing the 'lament' which Shostakovich composed, I know that one cannot dry this Shakespearean wetness of grief or you would be left with the single taste of wormwood. I do not agree with Blok's words. It is not only 'dry and bitter'. I remembered Babel's description of the acting of an Italian tragic actor, Di Grasso, who astounded the audience by 'maintaining with every word and movement that there is more justice and hope in the frenzy of noble passion than in the joyless laws of the world'. This is the essence of what he was saying; it is not in rules (of the nineteenth century or the twentieth, of Romanticism or the Theatre of Cruelty) but in justice and hope.

The cry of grief, bursting through the dumbness of the ages, through the deafness of time, must be heard. We made the film with the very purpose that it should be heard.

THE LAMENT WAS written in the form of nine fragments, separated by pauses, each one having its peculiar *timbre* and intonation. Shostakovich gave me the option of changing their sequence, repeating one of the fragments over and over again, or using them singly. This was not film music but cinema itself: its fundamental flesh and blood, what makes the editing, the shots.

Nine new shots were introduced into the film, nine crowd scenes. But this did not make it sound like conventional choral singing. In its ancient meaning the chorus was part of the action and took its rightful place in the tragedy. It was a tribal community raising its voice in lamentation for the dead. And so here in the film, in the very place where the powers of hatred and madness, the demonic element of tragedy had broken free and raged, this voice grew strong; grief brought people together, united them, the community grew and now it was enveloping mankind.

The conventions of the theatre and the structure of the play do not allow the whole fullness of life which the poetry embraces to be shown on the stage: many of the events are spoken of in the past tense, quickly skated over in the stage directions. In the cinema one can hold up the action in order to look closely into people's eyes and at the ever-widening panorama of events.

Editing provides an excellent means of following the poetic structure of the play. The action is fragmented, broken up into parts, into different elements. Each movement can be inspected separately, linked with others, continued or broken off.

Here on the cutting table's surface were the reels of film; here were what are called the parallel themes: Lear and his daughters, Gloucester and his sons. In Act Five the lines merge. But is it really only these stories which are united? How many other fathers and children – refugees, homeless victims of fire, soldiers – have been drawn into the catastrophe, will be killed, ruined, and tormented by their losses? . . .

How is one to show this mass movement in the single unity of the rhythm of editing.

I imagined railway tracks, approaching an enormous centre, the rails, parallel, coming together and moving apart in various directions. Some crazy signalman broke the control panel for the tracks and gave the green light in all the signals. And just as in the old ciné films, the trains come on at full steam, the stokers shovel coal on to the fires, the carriages, full of passengers, rock with speed. But no one changes the points, and the engines head straight for each other, into a headlong crash, are derailed and turned into piles of fragments, twisted metal and disfigured bodies.

In contrast to theatrical *mise-en-scène*, cinematic action can begin at several points simultaneously. Figuratively speaking, the curtain suddenly rises on several scenes all at the same time; the location contains, as in the medieval mystery plays, the earth, hell and purgatory. The action takes place both within the real world and in abstract space.

And it is this changing of perspectives – not only from the camera's point of view but in the meaning of the poetry – which the cinema can uncover. Tragic poetry (but not the play) consists entirely of such changes; and the action on the screen must also be built up around these conflicts.

The last Act contains both complete reality and a parable, both the destruction of the world and the hard times of everyday life. Both the hubbub of life and the complete rejection of it. I wanted to show the difference between the various planes of poetry, but to do it in such a way that the boundaries between them were not noticeable, so that the hems should not be showing. The headlong pace of the action does not allow for a separate scrutiny of the composition, the texture, listening to the sounds – the characters are continually developing, their links constantly changing.

We came to the end of Gloucester's story; we met not simply a peer who had had his eyes put out, and his heir who had become a beggar, but a father and son. Everyone's father and everyone's son. Now they had parted. A mound had appeared on the barren earth. Edgar breaks up a plough and binds the fragments into a cross. And that is the end. Nobody and nothing: Edgar/Poor Tom is also nobody, nothing. A naked man standing on ground on which not even one blade of grass grows.

And then in the dry geometry of the imagination there enters the ringing moist sound: the voice of tears.

I tried combining this shot with the lament: a dramatic scene suddenly burst in on the action. I needed to combine the image and sound so that the chorus entered into a dialogue with Edgar. The chorus asks Edgar, 'Isn't it time you went?'

Edgar hears the voice of the chorus, gets up from his knees and goes.

The angle of vision changes together with the sound (increasing in volume); the barren, empty earth vanishes and life and reality appear: the smoke from the fire on the horizon, the road in the distance, the riders spurring on their horses – the battle is on. Edgar walks along the road, descending into the world: he must live and kill.

And there suddenly is the man he must kill, walking at the head of the army. The villages are in flames: Edmund had given the order for them to be burned.

The wide expanses merge together as the shots progress: Edgar and Edmund go to meet each other. And with them fire and the sword burst into the world occupying an increasingly large proportion of the action. Edmund has behind him the might of the army, the powers of destruction; Edgar – a ruined country, the grief of mankind.

This is a story about two brothers but a counterpoint is introduced – the story of the sisters. Regan is jealous of Edmund's attention to Goneril. And now the two women, maddened with jealousy, track each other's movements through the war.

In editing we developed the motif of fire: burning tar is poured from the walls of the fortress, roofs of thatch burst into flames, barns and cow-sheds are set alight: black bulls like spirits of destruction charge through the flames. Goneril finds Edmund in the town which has just been taken by storm and there is a love scene by the horses' carcasses, against the background of the burning town. There are no longer any houses or people. Nothing but flames rage across the screen.

The blacker the deeds become, the purer sounds the voice of tears. We chose a place in the choral music where only the highest and purest voices were singing: the mothers are weeping. The chorus is asking, 'You murderers, what are you doing?'

Now this sound must be turned up to full volume; the clash of steel is powerless to drown the voice of mankind. The narder the steel tries to overcome it (when we re-recorded the sound-track we included the noise tape with the crackling of fire and the thundering of destruction), the clearer it sounds. And then there is nothing left but the chorus.

There was a particular significance in the conflict of image and sound, the chaos of noise and the structure of the music: by its very nature villainy has to drown and deafen – Cordelia is ordered to be put to death quietly so that no scream should ring out, so that no-one should hear so much as a groan. Why are these two defenceless people, Lear and Cordelia, dangerous? Because they could move the soldiers to pity them, Edmund says. They must not be pitied. Pity is a threat, a danger.

Shostakovich expressed pity like a force. There is such an abundance of feeling contained in the grief of his 'lament' that it gives rise to faith: the evil times will pass, they cannot do otherwise if such a voice is heard.

I HAVE NO problem about film music. I do not take it upon myself to judge what sort of music one should have – whether symphonic, electronic, twelve tone, or whether music has altogether gone out of fashion in the cinema. I really don't know the answer. I have not given it any thought.

Shostakovich's music is another matter. There is no point in my thinking about it. I would not be able to make a Shakespearean film without it just as I would not be able to do without Pasternak's translation. What do I think is the main point about it – the feeling of tragedy? This is an important quality. But not just tragedy . . . philosophy, and a general concept of the whole world? Yes of course, how could you have *Lear* without philosophy? . . .

But all the same it is another feature which is most important. A quality about which it is difficult to write. Goodness, kindness. Mercy.

However it is a special kind of goodness. Russian has an excellent word: fierce.[1] In Russian art goodness does not exist without a fierce hatred of everything which destroys a man. In Shostakovich's music I can hear a ferocious hatred of cruelty, the cult of power and the oppression of justice. This is a special goodness: a fearless goodness which has a threatening quality.

IT IS TIME to end these notes. The background for the credits were brought to me: the thunder clouds. But the storm is certainly not the main point of the film. Someone had another suggestion: marble, letters chiselled on marble.

But it is just this solemnity and outward pomp which I wanted to avoid, a style which we were against all along.

But what about trying something quite different, following a new tack in the opposite direction . . . I asked for an old piece of sacking. There was nothing of good enough quality? Good, then some old

[1] In Russian 'lyuty' [trans.].

sack which was falling to pieces or a remnant from one of the crowd costumes. And I wrote on it in rough letters, without a trace of style, the words 'King Lear'. There was no need for an overture. I wanted the sad home-made pipe to sound like a wail in the silence.

Was this really the end of the production?

1968–1972

CREDITS

First shown in the USSR 1971
Grand Prix, Teheran Film Festival 1972

Scenario and direction	Grigori Kozintsev
Photography	Ionas Gritsus
Design	Yevgeny Yenei [Jenöcek Jenei]
Original music by	Dmitri Shostakovich
Sets	Vsevolod Ulitko
Costumes	Suliko Virsaladze

Cast

King Lear	Yuri Yarvet
Goneril	Elsa Radzin
Regan	Galina Volchek
Cordelia	Valentina Shendrikova
The Fool	Oleg Dal
Gloucester	K. Cebric
Edgar	Lionard Merzin
Edmund	Regimastas Adomaitis
Kent	Vladimir Yemelyanov

INDEX